Big League Teams Stay in Good Hotels.

In San Diego, the Astros stay in a garden hotel, the Town and Country. It has walk-ways and several pools. One day when I was out for a walk a truck that goes around to construction sites pulled up. You know, the kind that brings coffee and sandwiches to the crew. This was a little ways from the hotel. I asked the guy if he had Reese's Peanut Butter Cups. He said no. Then I swear he said, "When we don't have them, nobody wants them." It would be an even better story if he had recognized me and had said something like, "I sound like you." But he didn't. And as you know, I am not one to make something up.

YOGI

It Ain't Over...

YOGI BERRA
with Tom Horton

Harper Paperbacks

Harper & Row, Publishers, New York
Grand Rapids, Philadelphia, St. Louis, San Francisco
London, Singapore, Sydney, Tokyo, Toronto

Harper Paperbacks a division of Harper & Row, Publishers, Inc.
10 East 53rd Street, New York, N.Y. 10022

This book is reprinted by arrangement with McGraw-Hill
Publishing Company.

Cover photography by Herman Estevez

First Harper Paperbacks printing: April, 1990

Printed in the United States of America

HARPER PAPERBACKS and colophon are trademarks of
Harper & Row, Publishers, Inc.

10 9 8 7 6 5 4 3 2 1

To Larry, Timmy, and Dale

Y. B.

To my mother who felt the two most beautiful buildings in the world were St. Peter's in Rome and Yankee Stadium in the Bronx. To my dad who took her to St. Peter's once and Yankee Stadium 57 times.

T. H.

Contents

Acknowledgments

More than thirty years in college textbook publishing taught me one thing about acknowledgments. The only people who read them are family and friends, so thanks to both. Cousin Dale and Cousin Leigh for sure. New friends, Dennis Liborio, Barry Waters and Helen Conklin. Valued friends Milton and Rose Friedman. The public relations people for the Padres, Giants, Indians, White Sox, Red Sox, Dodgers, Pirates, and Yankees were all helpful. Special thanks to Rob Matwick and Chuck Pool of the Astros.

I would truly like to thank both George Steinbrenner and George Thomas Seaver, the great pitcher. Alas they wouldn't speak with me. Their people were most gracious. Thanks to them for their efforts. I guess I should leave it at that.

Ann, you know how much it all meant. To Marcia

Jane, tough but fair, to Karen for a happy face, and to Lee Ann for dignity. To Dick Fenton, who didn't think I could do it and didn't care if I did. And Ed Robson who knew I could and Dave Boelio who showed me how. Three people can be blamed for this book: Yogi for being Yogi. Carmen for not saying no. And me for not hearing it if she did.

The Other Voices in this book created other voices that will always be in my heart and head. Thanks.

Roy, I hope you like it. Tom Quinn, my editor (and I have been waiting for thirty years to say I have one), did wonders. Several people had a lot to do with this book even though they probably don't know it. Jack Taylor, Carl Hector, Don Freuhling, James W. Millar, Paul Bragdon, Ross Sackett, Bill Bryden, Joe Jordan, Sid Metro, Frank Enenbach, Jim O'Grady, John Ruiz, Doug Latimer, R. Lorenzo, Chubb, Joan Armstrong, Nanky, Ed McGuire, Ruth and Darlow Maxwell, Gail and Glenn Matthews, Ruth and Rey Roulston.

1
SAYINGS

Jerry Coleman must have been a pretty baby. He was a handsome infielder for the New York Yankees for nine years. The late John Lindell tagged Coleman "Sweet Lips," and it's obvious the decorated marine pilot is not pleased with the name. It also seems obvious that, if surveyed, 92 percent of American males over the age of 40 would like to look as good and speak as well as Jerry Coleman. It is a mystery how the San Diego Padre TV announcer has escaped being nabbed for the movies. Hollywood is 90 miles away. A little training and watch out Jack Lemmon and Tony Randall.

    "What you have to do when you consider Yogi is think

*about where he started and where he ended," says Coleman.
"I don't mean that he was poor—a lot of us were that. I
mean that all he ever wanted to be was a baseball player,
and almost everyone told him he couldn't be one. He not
only became a ballplayer, he became a great one and one
of the most loved and respected of the last fifty years. Everytime I see him I feel good.*

*"I think he was the smartest player I ever knew. He
was smart enough to know how to play. And even more
important, how to learn. He was able to learn from Bill
Dickey. Yogi got better, and Ralph Houk and Charlie
Silvera just couldn't keep up. Everybody thought they were
smarter than Yogi, but they were wrong. He knew how
to learn, and he also knew that he could not do what Bill
Dickey did. Dickey used to say to me and a lot of other
guys, 'If Yogi would bear down, he could hit .350.' I am
not sure when I figured it out, but Yogi was way ahead
of me. He knew how to pace himself. He was a 'money
player' before they called them that.*

*"It's a shame they didn't keep records like they do now,
because if they did, people would know what baseball people
knew. They knew that in the seventh, eighth or ninth with
men on base he batted way over his life time .285. It seemed
like .400. He could bear down, but he didn't when it didn't
matter.*

*"Yogi had a handicap. He had the keenest baseball
mind I ever saw, but he couldn't teach what he knew to
others. When he was a player he didn't have to. The only
ones he had to teach were Reynolds and Raschi. They were
slow learners, but after a while they knew that when they
pitched the game Yogi called, they won. The pitcher and
catcher almost always have conflict. He knew how to make*

the most of it. He would get on Vic. He called him 'Onion Head.' When he wanted a fast ball, he would say, 'Is that as hard as you can throw it.' It sounds schoolyard, but it worked.

"I happened to talk with Yogi the day after Vic died. It was during the California World Series, L. A. and Oakland. I know Vic's death was a shock to Yogi. It was to all of us.

"I will never forget the first time he got fired. I was walking up Fifth Avenue and I ran into him. I wasn't watching where I was going nor was he, and we bumped. It was October 1964, and I said, 'Yogi, did you get two years?' I was broadcasting the Yankees' games, and we thought he would get a two-year contract after what he had done. He won the pennant, and if Ford had been sound, he might have won the Series. He was coming out of the Yankee office, and I was going in. He said, 'I got fired.' Three words, but he looked like he had just lost his family. I had known him for years and never saw him look that way. You may not remember, but it was a public relations disaster. He was very popular in New York, and for the Yankees to sack him that way, after he won, was hard for the fans to swallow. Good thing for the Yankee brass that they didn't have radio call-in shows in those days.

"I think when they hired him it was to get the spotlight away from Stengel and the Mets, and then to fire him the way they did. Hard to understand, but it made sense to somebody, at least, at the time.

"In that Series with the Cards, he was short of pitchers and had to pitch Stottlemyre with two days' rest. That seldom works. I broadcast for the Yankees that season, and

I thought he did a good job of managing, but I don't think that is why they hired him. He was a character and good with the press. When he was hired, some of the players said, 'Boy, we are going to have fun now.' But Yogi was dead serious. He was not good copy for the papers, and he had a tough year. I think he thought the team wanted to win as badly as he did. He was wrong. Some of them didn't play hard for him. When he knocked that harmonica out of Phil Linz's hand on the team bus in Chicago, the team caught fire. I think Frankie Crosetti put Yogi on that track. I mean Frank heard the 'Mary Had a Little Lamb' coming from the back of the bus before Yogi did and said, 'Are you going to take that?' When you lose three games to the White Sox by one run, you don't play a mouth organ on the bus.

"I don't know if that turned the team around or if they were going to win without that, but they did. After they fired him, they didn't win again for a long, long time. I remember sitting with Red Barber in the booth in 1965 and saying to him, 'We are not going to win.' At that time we always won. I played nine years, and six times we went to the Series. It was unthinkable we would lose. You don't win by putting on pinstripes unless you are good and work at getting better. I managed once, and I think I know what I am talking about.

"On the other hand, the two guys on the Yankees I didn't think would become managers were Berra and Hank Bauer. They both took teams to the World Series.

"I don't read baseball books, but I sure want to read Yogi's. He is one of the most unusual people I have ever known. He has the most unusual shape I ever saw and

a mind to match. If he looked like Robert Redford, no one would know he was alive. He would just be another old ballplayer. He is a classic; he is one of a kind. Nothing even remotely looks or acts like him. Probably never will.

"That's the great charm of being Yogi Berra. I think he knows it, and I also have to think that he is a little defensive about all the kidding about the Berra-isms. I know in my own case I get a bit tired of it and tell people that if they ever make a bust of me, it should have a pointed head. But, I guess it goes with the job. I may be wrong, but I think Yogi is hurt by the things said about him. He is sensitive enough to always know the right thing to do, so it stands to reason he is sensitive enough to be hurt by being called a clown."

Coleman is assured that if Berra minds the gibes, he not only hides it, but he makes a point of telling others that he takes it as a tribute. "They like me or they wouldn't talk about me," is one way Berra puts it.

Coleman goes on to say, "That's wonderful, and just one more example of selling Yogi short. If he is happy with himself, that is all that matters. I don't know anyone in the world I would rather see happy than Yogi. He made a lot of people happy. He still does. You can see it here in San Diego. Sometimes the Astros have him take out the line-up card, and you can hear and see the fans react. Even the Red Sox fans loved him! The fans knew he was different, and we knew he was different. He didn't have a mean bone in his body, and with a body like that he should have.

"The only mistake Yogi made as a manager all of

the modern managers make, and I was one of them. He thought the players wanted to win as much as he did."

"Yogi, now that it is over, would you do it again?" You mean this book? "Yes." Well, now that it is over, I would do it again. That's the way I feel about a lot of things. I think the main reason I wanted to do this book was because it was nice to be asked. The second reason is that I wanted to tell my side of the story. I don't lie awake at night thinking about all the bad things that have been said about me and in some cases done to me. All the same, it is nice to give my side and to have someone be interested. Another reason is that I have six grandchildren and I would like them to know what I did before they were born. They told me that if you do a good book, it pays good, so I guess I should be honest and say I thought about that part, too. I am not going to go into my childhood until later in the book. When I do, I hope you are interested enough to read it. I want to start with what I am asked about the most.

"90 percent of putts that are short don't go in" —did Yogi Berra say that? I don't know if I have said 90 percent of what I am supposed to have said, or even 10 percent. I really don't. I don't think it is possible I will ever know. Carmen would say it is possible that no one cares. The subtitle of this book—"It ain't over until it's over"—is supposed to be the best thing I ever said. I hope not. (And I try to say: "It *isn't* over until it's over.") I said it, but I am amazed to this day that somebody didn't claim that Rocky Bridges said it first. I mean I'm amazed that some reporter didn't look back after I got credit and find out that Rocky or Clint Courtney said it first.

Rocky played for the Dodgers and the Reds and some other teams. He and Courtney, who played one game for the Yankees and a lot more for the Washington Senators, were great talkers. Clint managed in the minors. One time when his team lost by a lot of runs and because of a lot of errors, he told the lone reporter, "We may lose again tomorrow, but not with the same guys." Another time Rocky was in the same spot and said, "If you don't catch the ball, you catch the bus."

The other thing about the "it isn't over . . ." saying is that I said it in 1973. The way the Mets were bouncing around in the standings that year, it was true. We won the National League division by winning 82 games and losing 79. That was a 50.9% average, and it meant it isn't over until it is over, or until the team is in first place after the last game.

Sometimes it is over before it begins—if I fought Joe Louis in his prime, it would be over before it began. But in 1973 what I said made sense. When I think back on that year, I get a little mad, but I will save that until later. Let me just say this much. A lot of writers said it was awful that the Mets won with such a lousy percentage. But when the Yankees later would clinch their division by September 1, those same guys would say, "Break up the Yankees."

You have to give 100 percent in the first half of

the game. If that isn't enough, in the second half, you have to give what is left. The first time I said that is right here.

When I was watching a Steve McQueen movie on TV, I said that he "must have made that before he died." I said the same thing about Jeff Chandler and some other actors, too, I am sure. It seemed to make sense at the time.

When I went to the mayor's mansion in New York City on a hot day, Mayor Lindsay's wife, Mary, said to me, "You look nice and cool, Yogi." I answered, "You don't look so hot yourself." I didn't mean for it to sound that way, and Mrs. Lindsay knew what I meant.

This next one happened when a lot of reporters were asking questions, trying to get me to say something. I almost think this was one I worked at. The question was, "What would you do if you found a million dollars?" I said, "If the guy was poor, I would give it back." I was a manager when I said that. Now it seems like such a dumb thing to have said that maybe I say I worked at it so I'll feel better. Maybe it was the way the question was asked. It made sense at the time, that's all I can say.

Another one I did say, and am sort of proud of, was when some of the guys wanted me to see a dirty movie. I didn't want to go. I really didn't want to go, but I have never been good at saying no. I kept saying, "I want to see *Airport*." (This all happened before I got the movie critic job; now I could say, "I have to see *Airport*.") Anyway, I got tired of saying "No, let's go see *Airport*," so I said, "Okay, who's in it?" People seem to think that response is great, and it may be. I am just happy that they know I don't like going to dirty movies.

"Baseball is 90 percent mental; the other half is physical." I have seen this written as: "Baseball is 50 percent mental and the other 90 percent is physical." Either way, the writer will say something like: "Yogi may think fine, but he can't add." It may be 95 percent or it may be only 80, but anybody who plays golf, tennis, or any other sport knows what I mean.

One day last year, three guys in our dressing room put on conehead caps. I saw them at the other end of the clubhouse and said to Matt Galante, "Those guys make a pair." The funny thing was that Matt went to St. Johns for four years, and he didn't even say anything about it until at least an hour later. Well, maybe it wasn't an hour, but it was almost an hour.

"You can see a lot just by observing" is the way I felt when I said it. I don't know when that was. I think I would say it the same way today. I don't think it is that bad. Like when Ken Boswell, an infielder with the Mets, told me he was hitting up, undercutting the ball, I told him, "Swing down." Do you think that should be in the newspapers? Don't get me *right*, I'm just asking.

"If you come to a fork in the road, take it." I really don't know about that one. The commencement speaker at Arizona State used that in his speech last year. Somebody sent me the student newspaper. The Dartmouth College student newspaper called a big meeting on campus "A Yogi Berra Affair." The reason I thought it was funny is that I didn't finish high school, and now college people use something I said, or maybe never said, to make a point. The Dartmouth story was about a long meeting. That was not a cheap shot, but I don't think it was a good shot. Maybe I should say it this way. If the Dartmouth reporter wants to use my name in the headline of a story about a long meeting, that's fine. I think it is like reaching for a pitch out of the strike zone. But it was sort of fun to see it, and they didn't try to make me look bad.

A writer for the *Wall Street Journal* once said, "Yogi Berra, on the other hand, is a figure of mirth, or—to use the technical term—a dummy." I thought that was a bad and cheap shot. The story had a good headline, "You can hear a lotta Yogi-isms just by listening." I thought that was nice.

I think headline writers are like bullpen catchers; they do very good things, and most people don't give them enough credit. I like a good headline, and the one I would put in a headline writers' Hall of Fame is the one the *New York Daily News* used after a Red Sox–Yankee game: "Sox cop two—Ted poles pair." Even when the Red Sox beat you twice and Ted hits two home runs and your team has lost two, when you see that headline the next morning you just have to smile. Not for long, but you have to admire the guy who wrote that. I never met a guy who wrote headlines.

The college mentions would be enough to make you feel good, but when then-Vice President Bush used "wrong mistake" in a debate and said that I said it, I not only got a thrill (I guess I have to use that word), I also am not going to say I didn't say it. He not only went to college, he went to Yale and is a Phi Beta Kappa. (Maybe I am supposed to say *was* a Phi Beta Kappa?) He is a baseball fan and played first base for Yale. He threw out the first ball at an Astro game when he was making a swing through Texas when he was running for President. The late Herbert Walker, who used to own part of the New York Mets, is related to George Bush. Vice President Bush said, "Mrs. Walker is still living in the same house in Connecticut and watches the Mets on WWOR." The *W* in George W. Bush is for Walker. I think it may have something to do with the Walker Cup in golf. Anyway, he said, "I wish Herbie could see me now." I really felt good for him when he said that. It was the way I felt when I wished my mom could see me do well, and if you run for the President's job, you *are* doing well. It was a nice thing for him to lean over and say that to me, and I hope he doesn't mind my telling it here.

I also have to tell the rest of the story. Vice President Bush was leaving the dugout because the game was about to start, and I said something about good luck. He said, "Yogi, Texas is very, very important." He said it as though I was sitting next to George Will on that Sunday morning TV show. I said, "I know, Texas has a lot of electrical votes." He didn't smile because he knew what I meant. I don't know who told the press, but I will bet it wasn't George Walker Bush.

So many people claim that they have asked me what time it was and I said, "Do you mean now?" that if I listed them all, this would be a very fat book. Not many people ask me what time it is anymore, and if they do, I don't answer. I thought my answer made sense when I said it. I will admit that when the waitress asked if I wanted my pizza cut into four or eight slices and I said, "Four, I don't think I can eat eight," I knew she was going to laugh and write it down. I was with my son, Tim. He knew what I meant, but I know why she didn't.

Twenty questions is a game. If you know it, I don't need to explain it; and if you don't it really isn't worth it. One time when we were playing on a train trip, I asked the question, "Is he living?" Then, without thinking, I asked, "Is he living now?" I got a lot of heat about that one. But one time when I was playing with Del Webb, who was part owner of the Yankees, driving from Minneapolis to Rochester, Minnesota, Webb asked a question way down the list, maybe number 17 or even 18. After we had gone through bread box and all that, he asked, "Is he short and fat?" Nobody laughed or said anything. I guess if you are an owner, you can get away with that. I just said, "Is he alive now," without thinking. I know Webb was thinking when he asked his question because it was the only one he asked. Later on we let Webb win a game so he could be "it." Nobody came close to guessing his secret. It turned out to be the clubhouse man for the Philadelphia Phillies. He was short and fat.

I am not going to say I didn't ask, "What kind of bird is a cyst?" I asked that question of Joe Page when he told me he had been hunting with Enos Slaughter, and Enos had been jumping in and out of the bushes so much looking for quail that he got a cyst on his back. I don't hunt, and I thought it was a good question. People have asked me dumber questions. Lots dumber.

When Carmen and I went to see the opera *Tosca* at La Scala, I really liked it. I told somebody I did and added, "Even the music was nice." That was true, and so was a story I still think is funny—a story about Venetian blinds. We were going to have some of ours repaired, only I didn't know it. I was upstairs when our son Larry called out, "The man is here for the Venetian blinds." I told him to look in my pants pocket and give him five bucks. Numbers are not big with me. That may come as a surprise to some people, but when somebody asked me if I take a nap before a night game, I said, "I usually take a two-hour nap from one to four."

When I said, "He is a big clog in their machine," like Tony Perez with the Reds, or Ted Williams, I meant to say "cog." But it didn't come out right, and they didn't let me forget it. Other times I don't understand as much as I would like. Once I bought a lot of insurance and was getting some heat from a guy in the clubhouse. He was a selfish player and selfish in other ways. He would buy a new car before his wife had a washer. He was the kind of guy who would be happy if he did well but we lost. I got a little hot when he said I was foolish and what good would all that money do me and I said, I will get it when I die. I didn't understand as much as I should, but I understood that a young father should have insurance—some kind of insurance. I am still not sure what the best kind is, but none is bad.

"Contract lens" is easy for anybody to say, and I hope you have, or something like it. One of my friends calls those low-slung German dogs "Datsuns." I can't prove it, but I bet he tells people he got it from me. I know some people say I told them, "When I was young and green behind the ears . . ." and "Never answer an anonymous letter." I didn't, but the anonymous letter idea is a good one.

"Why buy good luggage? You only use it when you travel." I did say that. I thought that made sense when I said it, but I don't think so any more. The good stuff lasts longer and looks better, too.

I didn't say about a sick friend that he was in "Mt. Sinus Hospital," but I could have. I could also have said, "We've had enough trowles and tribulations," if I knew what it meant. I don't, but it has been written that I said it.

I did say "It gets late early out there." I said that when I missed a ball in the sun. I was playing left field in the World Series. It was 1961, against the Reds. What I meant was that because of the shadows in Yankee Stadium at that time of year, it was tough to see the ball even early in the game. Baseball parks are all very different. I played right field, left field, and third base. Once a reporter asked me which field I liked the best. I said, "Chicago." He thought it was funny, but I thought I answered his question. If he had asked me which ballpark I liked best for hitting, I would have said, "Detroit."

In 1973 the Reds beat the Mets in the play-offs. Pete Rose won the game in the twelfth inning with a home run. A reporter asked me if I had been apprehensive. I said, "No, but I was scared." I missed that one.

I don't remember which year GM stopped making the Corvair, but that year I told a friend I was going to miss the car because it had the engine in the rear. It was great in the snow. I said, "They are not going to make them next year, so I am going to buy a Volkswagen or a foreign car."

Another car story that came back to haunt me is one that Frank Scott, an old friend, likes to tell. He can make it last 15 or 20 minutes. Frank came to our house once with a big dog in the back of his car. He said, "What do you think of my daughter's Afghan?" I said, "Looks nice. I am thinking about a Vega." I have seen several versions of that story. The name of the dog is the same in all of them, but the name of the car changes.

I used to work with Yoo-Hoo. It is a soft drink with a chocolate flavor. It used to be good. I haven't had any for a long time, so I don't know anymore. It was not a real big company when I started to work with them, and that is one reason I liked it. One time I was in the office and the phone rang when no one else was around. I always answer a ringing phone, so I did. The woman who was calling asked if Yoo-Hoo was hyphenated. I said, "No, ma'am, it's not even carbonated." I've forgotten what she said. It may have been better than what I said because she was from a library. One of the reasons I liked the product was that I thought it was good and might even be good for you. At least it was better than some of the other stuff people drank.

I hope that I have gotten over this much. I don't mind people making up things I have said. I don't know what is true and what is not, and I don't spend time wondering what is and what is not. I do wonder about this next story—wonder in the way you used to when you watched the TV show, *Twilight Zone*.

Big league teams stay in good hotels. In San Diego, the Astros stay in a garden hotel, the Town and Country. It has walk-ways and several pools. One day when I was out for a walk a truck that goes around to construction sites pulled up. You know, the kind that brings coffee and sandwiches to the crew. This was a little ways from the hotel. I asked the guy if he had Reese's Peanut Butter Cups. He said no. Then I swear he said, "When we don't have them, nobody wants them." It would be an even better story if he had recognized me and had said something like, "I sound like you." But he didn't. And as you know, I am not one to make something up.

Something I have said to a lot of people that I have never seen in print yet is that "If the world were perfect, it wouldn't be." I don't know if that's a good thing to say or a bad thing. But I believe it, and since this is the chapter where I am going to put down all the things I said and didn't say, I wanted to mention it. As I have said, I believe you have to have some ups and downs or you don't know what up is. Also, and I know this has been said better and long ago, I feel that you have to make the best of every day. Life is a train trip and you can't expect to find a rainbow at the end; it's the trip that counts. I thought that fit in here, and I am going to hear a lot of chug-chug-chugging and "the Berra Special is coming" in the Houston clubhouse as soon as this book comes out.

Two people in the Houston clubhouse are Mark Hill and Gene Clines. Mark Hill was a catcher for the Giants and White Sox, and Gene played with the Pirates. I see a lot of them during the season, and we get along well. I get along well with everybody. The reason I mention Clines and Hill is that one day last spring we were driving to a golf course. I was in the back seat, which meant that I couldn't see too well, and all at once it began to rain. I said, "Where is that coming from?" Count 'em—five words. Those two guys couldn't get over what I had said. They tried to find a phone so they could call the networks.

We did play golf, and on the first hole I asked them what they were shooting. Gene said, "Ultra 2," Mark said, "Top Flight 2," and I said, "Then I will use a Molitor 3." They thought that was worth slapping their knees over.

I hope you realize I am not bad-mouthing Hill and Clines. If I can say hello and it makes somebody feel good, fine. I also know that over the years I have said some funny things. Some of them have been said on the golf course. I was playing in a scramble one time, and I really have heard so many versions of this story that I have forgotten who was in the foursome. Let's say it was Mickey Mantle, Whitey Ford, and Billy Martin, although I don't remember ever playing with Billy. I am sure it was Mickey and Whitey, and the fourth one really doesn't matter. I have heard the story at banquets and seen it in books, and the foursome goes from George Jessel and Don Knotts to Dave Winfield and Harry Carey. It doesn't matter.

You know that in a scramble all four players hit, and then you pick the best ball. You all hit that, and again pick the best ball. If the golfers are any good at all they come in 15 or 16 under par. After playing seven or eight holes, a Berra drive had not been used. On the next hole I got off a good one, but the other three said they did not want to use mine—it didn't have a good lie. Mickey's ball had a better angle to the green, or whatever you want to come up with. I got mad and said, "If I was playing alone, I would use my ball." Boy, was that funny!

This may not be funny to the Jiffy Lube people, but when I finished making their commercial, someone asked me where I had been. I said that I had been doing a commercial for Linseed Oil. Funny thing, no one said anything about that at the time. It hit me later. Carmen was in the ad. She had one line. All she had to say was, "And a free cup of coffee." It took her 21 takes. When I was doing movie reviews, she liked to sit in the background and laugh whenever I said "Ducactus." Now she knows what it's like.

The kind of Yogi Berra story I like is one that Robert Merrill, the opera star, likes, too. At least I've heard him tell it four or five times. He always tells it exactly the same way. Maybe that is because he was trained. I didn't think of that before. He had a rabbi friend who was the brightest Harvard graduate of all time. At least that's the way Merrill tells it. He and the rabbi come to the clubhouse, and the rabbi tells me about the way he teaches his Hebrew students the *Ja* sound. Let me stop and say Robert Merrill is an opera star, and when he makes the *Ja* sound, it is low and you can almost start to dance to it. The rabbi, as played by Robert Merrill, goes on: "So, Yogi, I have them learn the *Ja* sound by saying 'Yogi, YOOGI, Ja and YOOGI.'" Merrill goes on with this, and after a time he says, "And Yogi said, 'Rabbi, does it work?'"

I think I listen better than a lot of people. Ira Berkow, a *New York Times* writer, did a column about my first spring with the Astros. It was a nice story and I read all of it. He said that while I was signing autographs, a woman said, "Hey Yogi, do you have a minute?" I said, "For what?" At least that is the way he wrote it, and I am sure it happened. He also said that she blushed and I did, too. I am not sure I blushed, but if I did and he noticed it, I am pleased—pleased that at my age I can still blush. I am glad that when I go to the movies to do my reviews it's dark because some of the new movies could make a donkey blush.

Not listening can make you look bad. One time I came out of the dressing room. I think it was during spring training with the Yankees. During that time you could have forty or fifty or even sixty players in camp. When you have been around as long as I have, you know how important it is to speak to everybody. No matter what is on your mind, you have to look at the other players and speak or nod. You don't want anyone to think you are high hat. Not only because you aren't but it could upset them, and you are a

Yankee and these guys are teammates. It is part of winning. Not a big part, but most of the winning parts are not big. Anyway, I came out into the parking lot and saw this kid. I knew he was on the team and I said, "Who ya waiting for?" He said, "Bo Derek." I said, "I haven't seen him." He was kidding me and I ended up getting kidded.

Another time in spring training I was that young player, and the clubhouse man asked me what size hat I wore. I told him I was not in shape yet.

I said somewhere in this book that I really don't work at trying to say something funny, and I think maybe I should have added that if I do try, it doesn't work. When I was a coach with the Yankees, Joe Altobelli had a birthday. It was number 50. I told him that now he was an "Italian scallion."

When I said that a nickel wasn't worth a dime anymore, it was true. It's not anymore. I didn't say, "It's déjà vu all over again," and I didn't say, "always go to other people's funerals; otherwise, they won't go to yours." But I did get a phone call from William Safire, the *New York Times* columnist, asking if I had. He didn't seem disappointed when I told him no. That made me like him even though we had never met. Carmen got on the upstairs phone and they had a nice chat. She told him some things I had said and maybe some more for all I know. I didn't listen to all of it. I was watching the Giants and the Redskins.

By the time Johnny Bench broke my record, most home runs by a catcher, I had the reputation I have now. They sent him a telegram and said, "Congratulations. I knew the record would stand until it was broken." I don't know who the "they" was, but it was signed Yogi Berra. It was a public relations stunt.

I don't know if you think I have been too critical of sportswriters. I don't think I have. I know they have a job to do. While I am on the subject of what I said and didn't say, I can bring up one writer who thought about the truth. The truth and not another Berra-ism. Murray Chass, a *New York Times* writer, spent part of a column telling what really happened. If I could, I would pretend I was Paul Harvey and say, "And now, the rest of the story." I can't, and the rest of his stories—at least the ones I've heard—are about important things. This isn't.

Chass said a writer thought he heard me say about Craig Biggio, a young Astro catcher, "If we didn't want to bring him up, we might as well have let him stay down." Not bad. Chass said the other writer was not listening closely. We had had to use Biggio every day because our other catchers were hurt. It was hard on him, but it had to be done. What I actually said was, "If we didn't want to use him every day, we might as well have let him stay down."

I have said a lot of times that I don't mind people making up things I said and didn't say. It has helped keep my name in the public. That is not all bad. It is not all good, but it is not all bad. It is nice to see a story like the Chass story and that's why it's here.

Oh, I don't want to forget. George Will—and if you don't know who he is, I didn't either so don't feel bad—said, "Yogi Berra, the syndicated movie critic, confused Glenn Close, the actress, with Glen Cove, a suburb." I don't want to start a fight, but when I was asked if I really did confuse the two, I said, "A little bit." I am not sure that is a good answer, but it is my story and I am sticking with it.

Jack Buck has been broadcasting games in St. Louis for so many years he has become a fixture. He asked me to be a guest on his radio show many years ago, and I said I would. After the show he gave me a check for $25.00 made out to "Bearer." I would have done the show as a favor, and I know that is going to get some comments but it's true. As I walked away, I looked at the check. Then I went right back to Jack and said, "How long have you known me and you still can't spell my name?"

Jack Buck swears that one time he saw me during a World Series, and I asked him what time his plane got in. When he said, "About 1 AM." I asked what time he got to the hotel. "About 2 AM." Then Jack said I asked him, "Was that local time?" If I did, I didn't mean to. I don't think I did. I think he needed some filler for dull games.

Another mix-up in words happened, they said, when I went to see a writer and said, "I went three for four yesterday and your paper said I was two for four." The writer said, "It was a typographical error." "Like hell it was. It was a clean single to right." Nice story. It never happened.

At least once a week someone will yell from the stands, "What time is it?" The answer I am supposed to have given to everyone from Tom Thumb to Tom Seaver is, "Do you mean now?" I did say, "Do you mean now?" but it was when Rube Walker, the Mets' pitching coach, asked me what time it was. We were flying from New York to Los Angeles. We may have been over Kansas or Nebraska, and I said, "Do you mean now?" I didn't know then and I don't know now. At least one flight attendant said the same thing happens to them even when they fly all the time. They get turned around on the time zones. I don't know what time it is in Nebraska right now. I probably should have said so, but if I had, Rube wouldn't have had a good story to tell on me and maybe I wouldn't have gotten a call from Stove Top Stuffing to do a commercial.

Our son Dale played in the Baltimore system last season, and they won the Governor's Cup. They played Tidewater and were getting ready to play Indianapolis. They used to call it the little World Series. I wanted to call him to wish him good luck. I know that your kids can misunderstand a phone call like that, and they can misunderstand a phone call you don't make. I made the call. Dale was pleased, and I am glad I did. The reason I mention it is if your name is Yogi Berra and you make a person-to-person call to your son in the dressing room, the telephone operator may say something like "Are you the real Yogi Berra?" I don't know what to say to that. Then when you are asked to tell a Berra-ism while the clubhouse man looks for your son, you have to say something like "I don't do them on the phone" or "I am fresh out." No matter what you say you know the operator is going to feel short-changed.

I feel the best about having said something that people repeat when someone I like says, "I wouldn't say it that way, but that is good," or "that is a great way to say it." That happened to me with Nolan Ryan just last season. We were talking about the 1969 Mets. We were both on that team, and I said that we were "overwhelming underdogs." Nolan is not only a great pitcher, he is a smart one. He really liked the way I put it. He said that is *exactly* what we were. He said if I had gone to college, they would have made me talk clearer, but not better.

2
EVENTS

know what I am about to write is risky. So was
putting the winning run on when Bucky Harris
did it in the 1947 World Series. It came back to
haunt him. Bucky did it in front of millions of
people. I am doing it in front of a lot of people. At
least I hope I am. I am doing it here, early in the book,
because a lot of people told me that many book readers
don't read the first part of a book like this. You probably already know that I was born in St. Louis, that
I would want to thank my mother and father and Casey
Stengel, that I got my first hit on a change up and my
last hit off a fast ball—stuff like that. What I am going
to say is important, at least to me, so I am mixing up
the normal writing pattern. That was the way I used
to try to call pitches. If Ted Williams ever caught on

to a pattern of pitches, he would hit the next one out. I hope that what worked way back then will work now.

I want to thank three different kinds of readers, maybe more. First are the baseball fans who cheered for me and yelled against me all the years I played. I worked hard to get as good as I could. If they are reading this book to say, "Thanks, Yogi," then I say, "Thank you." Not for making this book necessary, but for reading it.

The second kind of reader I want to thank is the people who have been put down, maybe even by their family, and didn't let it get to them. They might want to see how I did the same thing. I hope it will make them feel better, or even good. I should say right here that I was never put down by anybody in my family. I just mentioned family because sometimes people are not as lucky as I was and don't have older brothers and folks who start you off feeling good about yourself.

The last readers I want to thank are those who are reading this book to see if I am like what the writers said I was like. I hope those readers think I am not, but it is up to them.

I am asked a lot if it hurt to be bashed for all the years. I give different answers, depending on how I feel and how the question is asked. I'm starting to answer those questions with a question. Like, how come when writers were saying the only way I could read is if my lips moved, I was reading without moving my lips? Or how come when I was really being hurt in the press, nobody asked me if it did? I can do that sort of thing now, but I am 63 years old and have done better than anyone thought I would. The serious answer to that question is this. It did hurt, but I think it made me work that much harder. I don't think I needed all the abuse to work hard getting better, but it did motivate me. As soon as they knew I could hit, most of the Yankees kidded me and I kidded them back. I was being treated bad in the press but not at home or in the clubhouse.

For a long time after I first got to the big leagues I wanted to say "Thank you" when someone asked me for an autograph. I never did because I didn't want to get ragged anymore than I was already. Then, as I got more secure, I was out of the habit of wanting to say it. I don't mean I lie awake at night thinking I should have thanked that man and his son in Cleveland. I am just saying when someone wants you to sign something, it means they like you and it would be nice to say thanks. Now that I think about it, maybe the reason I didn't say "Thank you for asking" is that they didn't say "Thank you" after I signed.

Now with autographs being a business, it does not seem right at all. CBS News said the baseball card business is a bigger business than baseball. People in that business call it sports memorabilia. They tell me that my autograph is worth about $8. Pete Rose's sells for more because he does not sign as many autographs as I do. Supply and demand. Well, if someone asks you for yours and you say, "Thank you," and he says, "Don't thank me—I am just doing it so I can sell it for $8," you would feel dumb. As I have said so often, times have changed. I held a door open for a woman in Philadelphia last year and she gave me hell. I didn't understand why, but it is too bad you can't do as you were taught without some lady telling you she is just as good as you. I want to say one thing to Pete Rose, and I hope he reads this. Your autograph is not only worth more than mine, it is a pretty one, too. When I said the people in the collecting business call it memorabilia, I should have added that I don't. I just call it the collecting business—just like I call tin cans tin cans. (My sons tell me to call them aluminum cans. If you can't use the word good, don't say it.)

To get back to what I was trying to say about saying "Thank you for asking for my autograph." As I said, I never did. I am not sorry I didn't. But I would be sorry if I didn't say this: thanks a whole lot for reading my book. That someone wanted to come to Yankee Stadium, or any of the other parks, to see a ball game in the sun with their child or friend and yell for me when they got there, that's fine. That's great. But to make the investment of time, as Milton Friedman calls the reading of any book, that is special, so I wanted the readers to know. You may be surprised to see a Nobel Prize-winning economist's name in a ballplayer's biography. To tell you the truth, I am, too. But after I spent a few hours with him, I find what he told me creeping into a lot of things. The supply and demand thing I just mentioned, for example. Later on I will tell you about a long breakfast we had.

I also want you to know a little bit about the way the other voices sections of this book came about. When the book was first started, they didn't seem to think too much of what I was doing. It was one of the times they said I was not interested enough in myself. "Yogi is less interested in himself than almost anyone I ever knew," was the way one person put it. I thought that was a nice thing to say. Better than saying Berra is stuck on Berra. Or Berra is full of himself; all he can talk about is Yogi. That would be awful. An awful thing to live with.

Some of my Astro teammates heard about what they called the "self thing," and called me an id, or said I had no id. Stuff like that, worse stuff than I ever heard on the Yankees. A lot of the Astros went to college and know about ids and libidos and even quantum physics. To tell you the truth, I have never been out of ammo when someone gets on me. I have been called a lot of things and told I was not good enough to do a lot of things, but I could come back with something. All this bush league head shrinking I was getting bothered me a little. Not a lot, but a little. I guess the publisher was bothered that I wasn't doing what Tommy Lasorda said he does and I should do, "Tell your innermost thoughts."

In baseball the catcher and the pitcher are trying to figure out what kind of a pitch to feed the batter, and the batter is trying to guess what is coming next. At the same time I was wondering why I started this book. I was doing the best I could, and what I was getting was "Let us know more about what makes you tick." While I was doing that, they were thinking of ways to see Berra through other eyes.

They decided to get some of what they called "other voices." You have seen some of them if you flipped through the book. I don't think it was anything original, like Lou Boudreau's Williams Shift. Groucho Marx, Catfish Hunter, and maybe several hundred other people did something like it. I know Catfish will be happy he did because it gives me a chance to mention him in the same sentence with Groucho Marx.

Other Voices
PHIL RIZZUTO

Phil Rizzuto looks as if he would break if you hugged him, and you want to. Hug him or take him home to Mother. He is a favorite uncle, and makes you wonder why you agreed the last time someone said, "I always have trouble with little guys—little CPAs, little plumbers, it doesn't matter."

Phil, unlike many of us, is friendly over the phone, and right away says, "Sure I would like to talk about Yogi. When do you want to come by?" Golf is first on his priority list. Just as he danced around second base on a double play, Phil shuffles through the options and says, "Fine, I will see you at three, and if you are a friend of Yogi's, that means you will be here at 2:45."

The Rizzuto home would be impressive in Anytown, USA, and that's only the outside. The real estate ad would say gracious and spacious, and in this case the ad would be correct.

"I roomed with Yogi long enough to know that your best bet is to make the book up. He is not one to communicate the way the rest of us do. He makes noise. I always understood it, but he would rather listen and observe than talk. When he does, he is like E. F. Hutton. I'll say that

for him, but my advice is to make it up or get a whip, gun, and chair and put him up on a stand with some other lions and snap the whip a lot and say, 'Tell me all about that second no hitter when you dropped the pop-up Ted Williams hit and almost cost Allie Reynolds his chance at two in one year.'"

When Phil is asked about Allie Reynolds, or any other pitcher, calling their own game in Berra's first few years, he says, "I played short, and if it had been going on I would have known. Yogi called the game." Is it possible Stengel called the game from the bench? "Casey Stengel did a lot of strange things, but all before he came to the Yankees, or after the first year when he got the taste of big media. During 1949 he was not funny, not a clown. He really just watched. I think it was his best year as a manager, but I am not objective about Casey. He couldn't wait to see guys like Joe D. and me leave. That may sound hard to believe. It was not all at once that he got the taste for press coverage that he had till the day he died, and wanting to see the old guys leave so he could begin to platoon and get credit for being a genius. He was great at getting his picture and name in the paper. He loved Yogi, and with good reason; but even if you don't love Yogi, you have to like him. Now that you have me talking about him, I am starting to sound like him. Casey may have loved Yogi, but you can bet your house and icebox he didn't call his pitches.

"I don't need to tell you that Yogi was a natural hitter and a quick learner. He used to eat a loaf of bread before a meal, but I would like to say that a lot of people made a bundle of money telling Yogi Berra stories at banquets during the off-season. Most of what they said was

*made up. Most of what they said about Stengel was made
up, too."*

*Don't you feel that Yogi and Stengel did a lot to
generate interest in baseball even though a lot of what was
said was not true but also did not harm anyone? Rizzuto
says quickly, "Sure, without question. They were both good
for baseball. I am just trying to give you some information
that is not in the newspapers."*

◆

Sometimes you get hurt playing and they put in someone for you. He does a great job—gets a bunch of
hits, steals some bases. When that happens, you can
get well—and quick, too. The same thing happened
when they got some good "other voices." I got better.
If I hadn't, Don Zimmer would have had about 75
pages of this book. He wanted to do a chapter on Don
and Yogi at the dog track, pictures and all, including
Don and Yogi at the pay window, Don and Yogi at
dinner, and so on. I can do it in four sentences. Don
lives near a dog track in St. Petersburg and goes a lot.
He took me there a short time after I was elected to
the Hall of Fame, and they didn't charge us for dinner.
He screamed, "I have been coming here for 15 years
and I never got anything for nothing. Money-bags
Berra comes once, and it's on the house."

I said that I got better. Maybe I should have said
that I tried hard to get better. You can judge if I did.

I played baseball with some fine men, and I would
like to tell you about some of them. The press called
Joe DiMaggio the Clipper, the Yankee Clipper, but
he was Joe or Joe D. to us. He was a leader, like Gil

Hodges. He didn't say much. He didn't have to. His 56-game hitting streak in 1941 was a record I don't think will ever be broken. Getting back to the name Joe D. for a minute, I think it is interesting that some people have public names, like John Wayne, and private names, like Duke. Then with the number of press people, the private names come out and are not as good as they were. It may have something to do with the id or the other for all I know.

Ted Williams was an example. He was the Splendid Splinter, the Thumper, and I have forgotten some of the rest. I guess Teddy Ball Game was one. It got so you didn't know what to call him. I called him Ted. One guy on the Yankees who didn't have that problem was Al Downing. He was a left hander from Trenton, New Jersey, who pitched for me in the 1964 World Series. He was called Giggig. I never knew why, and I never heard him called that by anyone except his teammates. Kind of a secret society thing. Several years ago I was driving from San Bernardino to Los Angeles and listening to a sports radio call-in show. The host was really good. I wondered after an hour why he didn't give his name. I still don't know why the host didn't give his name, but I know it was Al Downing. He didn't talk down to the callers, and he didn't let them push him around. I thought he was good, but that he should tell people who he was. Maybe not as often as Larry King does but once in a while.

The one person I have to talk about is Casey Stengel. Ted Williams thought he was a big deal, and I did, too. Talking about Casey will take a little explaining. To start with, I liked him, respected him, and owed a lot to his confidence in me. I could also understand why some people, like Phil Rizzuto and even Joe D., did not feel the same way. You would never hear anybody say Casey was not interested in himself. He was, and he could make you interested in him. He could make the whole room interested in him.

The only one I have ever seen in baseball who comes close to Casey is Tommy Lasorda. They are different, and you don't have to be all different to be very different. If you listen to a tape of Casey, it is pure Casey. Lasorda is just as quick as Stengel; he makes sense quicker than Stengel. In other words, Casey was smart enough and had worked at his act long enough to make you think about what he said. Tommy is not that good, yet. But the real big difference is that Tommy is not the center of the thing. You may think he is but he isn't. The reason you may think he is, is that it can sound like it. But if you listen carefully, Tommy is not talking about Tommy. Lasorda spends a lot of time during the off-season speaking. He spends a lot of time during the season speaking, too, but in the winter he gets paid for it. An organization or company will pay him to give a talk. He is great. One of the reasons is that he has a natural talent. Another is that he has a lot of show business friends and some of that talent rubbed off on him. I may be wrong about the reasons Lasorda is so good at holding your attention, but I am not wrong that he can hold it.

I liked and respected Casey, and he called me his Assistant Manager and other nice things. I was his pet some writers said, and they said it like I was the teacher's pet. You know, not nice. I may have been. Some even said I was kept around to give Casey some laughs. Don't believe it. Let me put it this way. Casey was tough. Billy Martin was his pet, and Casey sent him away when it suited him. It took Billy years to get over it. I am not sure he has yet, even though Billy says he loves Casey.

People paid to see us play. I would have paid to see Casey—not for 154 games, but for a lot of them. If you worked in a factory and felt good when you went to work and saw your foreman, that would be a fringe benefit. I worked in a factory next to my brother, Tony, and that was a fringe benefit, too, but Casey was not like a brother, not like a father. Casey was not like anybody.

Carm and I used to like to see a lot of Broadway shows. We saw *Auntie Mame*. Angela Lansbury played the part. She was terrific—better, I think, than she is in *Murder, She Wrote*. Maybe not better, but she sang in *Auntie Mame*. It was a great show. We took some friends, and one of them said on the way home, "Gee, wouldn't it be great to have an aunt like that?" After seeing the show, you had to say yes. Casey was an Uncle Mame for most of the Yankees. He used to say, "It's easy to get the players. Gettin' 'em to play together, that's the hard part." Being an Uncle Mame helped. But if you can't copy him, don't try to imitate him.

The Yankees were the first team to have Old-Timers' games. One year they brought in Ty Cobb, Bill Terry, and Ted Williams as guests of honor. I don't think they put on uniforms, but I remember they came to a dinner at Toots Shor's. Ty Cobb, Bill Terry, and even Ted gave brief speeches. If my life depended on it, I could not tell you a thing any of them said. It's one reason I don't watch political speeches; you don't remember what they said. I am not saying Cobb, Terry, and Ted were politicians. Cobb never was, for sure. They figured it was a dinner—say a few words and sit down. You could hold my feet in the fire and I could not tell you a thing Casey said, but I know that the people at my table fell off their chairs laughing.

Mickey Mantle, Whitey Ford, and I were seated with some guests who were not ballplayers. One of them asked me as we were walking out, "You see Casey every day. This is my first time, so I can see why I was knocked out, but I was surprised at you and Whitey and Mickey. Several times Whitey fell off his chair or banged on the table like he was a nervous guest on the Carson show. It was hard to believe. I don't think anyone will believe it when I tell them about the re-action. Whitey and Mickey could have been shills." As you see, the guest was impressed. I tried to explain to him. You think Casey is going to stop, you don't think he can say anymore, and then he takes a deep breath and goes on and on. The other thing is that what he says only makes just enough sense, so you have to listen. He talks so loud and then so soft that you can't sleep. If you had tried to sleep, he would have gotten on you the next day, so you didn't.

I am not saying that the guest would have gone to sleep. I am saying Casey's players were part of the act. At least as I look back, we were part of his act. Once you started laughing, he could feel he was on a roll. It was like a train. He was the engineer and you couldn't get off and didn't want to, except when he finally did sit down and you looked at your watch.

This guest said to me, "Mr. Berra, you are remarkable." I remember it because he was almost as old as me. I didn't think he should have said "mister," but I also think he really meant it. What I told him is pretty much what I have just told you. I didn't think it was remarkable. I just thought it was a story about a guy I worked for. The guy just happened to be Casey Stengel. An easy guy to talk about. You could talk a long time just about the way he walked. I wondered what the guest might have said to Casey. If he had said, "Mr. Stengel, you were terrific," Casey would have said, "Young man what is your name?"

I've said a lot of times that much of what you read is wrong. I'm thinking of the story about Mickey Mantle wearing a supporter outside his uniform. It just did not happen. Whoever wrote it didn't do any real harm, but it was too bad someone even thought it was true.

Casey was once asked to testify before a group in the United States Senate. It was about antitrust, I think. They didn't ask me and I was just as glad. I was even glad to learn from Milton Friedman that testifying before Congress "is largely a waste of time." If that is true, I think it is too bad.

Casey Stengel's testifying was not too bad—it was too much. His speech has been reprinted, and if you want to have a good, long laugh, get a copy. I am sure he went on for 12 or 15 minutes. Here is the part I wanted to get to. After Casey finished and was thanked by Senator Kefauver, he rolled back to his seat. Not in a wheelchair—that's the way he walked.

Some other baseball players had been asked to testify. Ted Williams and Mickey Mantle were sitting at the table behind Casey and the TV cameras showed them smiling. Not laughing, but close to it. Senator Kefauver asked Mickey Mantle, "Do you have any observations with reference to the applicability of the antitrust laws to baseball?"

Mickey said, "My views are just about the same as Casey's." Not only did Mickey say it, it is written down in the *Congressional Record*. Mickey did not laugh as hard in Congress as he had at Toots Shor's, but he told me that Casey was even better than he had been at the Old-Timer's dinner.

In 1960, Gordon Bridge, who at that time was sports director for Armed Forces Radio, asked Casey to interview me for a show. He said they were going to send it to all the overseas bases, so we had to do it for him. I am sure glad I did. Here is a sample of part of the tape. It would be impossible for me to make this up.

Casey: I'd have to say, Mister Berra, that you was one of the three outstanding catchers in the American League—there was Bill Dickey and Mickey Cochrane—and in the National League there was Hartnett and Campanella. So that's pretty good company for you. Now, you've talked to so many umpires, and you've conversed with them, the umpires are your friends, and so on and so forth, and I know they haven't fined you so much in the last few years. How do you account for that?

What you just read is exactly what he said when he was told to start. Before I put down exactly what I said, I want to say that, way over 30 years later, I can still feel like I did then. The first thing you know is that he knows this is being recorded. He is not talking to some writers with a pen and note book in his hand. (I know he loved to go on and on just to see them try to get it all down.) He knew the ground rules. He knew that he was supposed to interview his catcher and that I had to say something. I knew it, too. I was like a catcher in a bunt situation. I knew it was going to come, but when? He was going to stop, and then it would be my turn. He stopped.

Yogi: Well, you know a lot of people think I'm always arguing with the umpires when I turn around, but actually I'm not. I'm just talking conversation to them.

As you can see, I knew when to stop, and I wish I had quit one sentence sooner.

We then played bat-the-ball back and forth. It may have been interesting if you were on Guam or somewhere, but it is not worth putting down here. He said things like, "Don't swear at them; it will cost you money."

Then I said something about umpires' missing a play. I really meant this. If they would just say, "I missed it." If a good umpire who didn't miss many said, "Look, Yogi, I missed it; get off my back; you ain't perfect," I would say something more and back off. After I said some things like that, Casey was off and running again.

Casey: That's what they told me for years. They

never missed one from the heart. But they use their eyes. You know, they call them with their eyes. But from the heart they never missed one. Do you think your hitting has held up, Yogi, in the fourteen years you have been playing for the Yankees? Do you think you can use your bat or can you swing as quickly or do you have the same wrist action that you used to have when you first started in baseball? Do you think you've overcome the fact that you don't chase as many bad balls as you used to when you were first in baseball? I thought you were getting over it. But this is one thing that you did this year. You almost hit a one-hopper. Someday you may hit a home run on a pitch like that.

Yogi: I had a bad year last year, and maybe the reason was I tried to hit too many good pitches.

That's what I said in 1960. Later I looked up what I had done in 1959. My batting average was .284, I hit 19 home runs, drove in 69 and scored 64. Not a bad year. Looking back, I think I was playing along with Casey. I almost always did. It was a good thing to do.

I want to give you several more examples of the way he would go on. When you see stars on the *Today Show* plugging their movie and they are going to show a clip from the movie, the host will say, "Do you need to set this up?" Sometimes the celebrity will say no or will tell a little about the scene they are going to show. One time I was playing in a golf tournament and it was hot and I was awful. On one hole I popped up three or four shots, and I said to the caddy, "What club do you think I should try now?" He said, "It don't make any difference."

That's the way it is with Casey's questions, with his answers or his words, just his words. You don't need to set them up. The caddy was right about what club to use, and I am right about Casey. Casey on the rocks or Casey on the beach. A little bit went a long way. I miss him. Billy Martin told me he loved the old man. I didn't, but I miss him.

Casey: "I think you're right. There's nobody playing where they go. They can't be playing for a ball over your head or one that's pitched on the ground. Now, let's get into something else. You used to be a serviceman, Yogi, and I know you got a lot of friends out there among the men in the services, and there's one thing I would like to ask in their behalf. You used to wear a white glove when you were catching, and I wondered why you would wear a white glove like you had just come from a wedding and you forgot to take off the white gloves. Why is it that you used a white glove when you was a catcher?"

He went on and on, and at one point he said he thought that when I put my arm around the late Vic Raschi, we both looked a little effeminate. He really did. Can you imagine what the guys on Guam thought of that.

He ended up by ranting about what he called my mansion and that I had room for all the guys who had been on the Yankee team if they wanted to come and visit. Like a lot of what he said, the ranting was a little true. When we bought the house, I didn't see it until after Carm made the deal. When I went around the house, I said something like, "This is some house, nothing but rooms." That is just the way I felt. When we sold the house after the kids grew up, the guy who bought it felt the same way, only he didn't say it until after we had made the deal. Besides, I am sure that Casey never even saw our house.

I can close my eyes and almost hear Casey talking. Somebody told me that when you talk about the Babe to old-time ballplayers who played with Babe Ruth, they always smile. Even people who knew him smile when they talk about what he did or said—sometimes even when they tell things that were not too good, for example, that he came in late for a game hung over. It's a nice thing to say about somebody. When you think about how long Babe Ruth has been dead and the number of great ballplayers and movie stars since then, it's more than nice. He died August 16, 1948, over forty years ago, and for people to still remember you is one thing; to still make them smile, that's special.

It's nice to think you can hear Casey singing. That's what he was doing in a way. He was singing a song, and the notes made sense or the music did, but not together. I want to add again. The dialog you read earlier was Casey with the spotlight on. When he talked to me and the rest of us, we understood. If you understood what he said in this book and what was entered into the *Congressional Record* on July 9 1958, I am sure he would be disappointed. He would be disappointed even more if you thought it was double talk. You know, the kind some comics do. It wasn't that. It was better than that because he was the only one who could do it. One of the Mayo Clinic doctors who treated Casey told me, "The only patients I ever had that could do that were crazy. He is not, and I never saw him do it in my office. Only when he had a crowd and they had note pads and pens."

Casey Stengel could be serious, but he didn't like to be. I never knew anybody who spent as much time talking about baseball, and that was all serious. You might not think so to listen to him, but it was and he was.

<hr>

Other Voices
BOBBY RICHARDSON

Bobby Richardson pushed the blank contract across the table saying, "The Yankees have treated me well, and I am not interested in filling in the blanks in that contract. My interest is filling in the blanks in my life as a husband and a father. My last game was my last game."

Del Webb, Yankee co-owner from 1947 until the team was sold to CBS in 1964, said it was the "most remarkable contract negotiation we ever had. We gave him a blank contract and he gave it back. Bobby never tried to convince me or any of us we should believe as he did, but we all knew how he felt. After that I knew what he was made of. He was just 30 years old, and we needed him. The team was better with him at second. We were running a business, and he was running his life." Webb spoke these words with great emotion.

Bobby Richardson smiles, as does most everyone when asked to recall his first reactions to Yogi Berra. "I was just 20 years old when I first walked into the Yankee clubhouse.

He was a big name, as were most of the rest, and Yogi and I had nothing in our backgrounds to draw us together except one thing. He knew I was shy and lonely.

"I was living in a hotel by myself while my wife stayed in South Carolina. He had done the same thing when he was called up in 1946. He had not married yet, but he knew what it was like. It is one thing to live in a hotel in Little Rock. It is something else to live in a hotel in New York City. Shortly after I got there he said, "You're coming out to stay at our house this homestand. Be sure to check out so they don't charge you." As we drove into Montclair and up the circular drive to this huge mansion, I asked Yogi, 'How many bedrooms does your house have?' 'I don't know, Carmen takes care of that.' And she did, and everything else as well.

She was a wonderful mother. Anybody who knew Yogi knew how lucky he was to have Carmen as his wife. She had a huge measure of energy and charm. Most of all he knew it. 'How did you ever get Carmen to marry you, Yogi?,' I asked, and he said, 'I just said yes, quick, after she asked me to.' I never knew if he was kidding, but I spent enough time with him on the road to know how much she meant to him.

I was in his home several times and don't think I saw all the rooms, but one I remember and remember well. It was on the third floor and it looked like a sporting goods store. Guns, boots, fishing gear. I had never heard Yogi mention any outdoor sports except golf, football, and watching his son, Dale, play hockey. I said, 'What are you doing with all this stuff?' 'I just got it,' he said. We talked about what he was going to do with it, and when it became clear that we could make a deal we did. I bought the entire inventory. That fall when I got it all back to my home in South Carolina a friend in the sporting goods business figured out I paid slightly more than retail for the whole shebang.

He was a Yankee catcher and a Yankee trader. I often wondered if Ford and Mantle kept track of the interest on the loans he made to them on the road. He was something special. I have been waiting for years to tell that sporting goods story.

And one last chapter. I held on to most of the inventory from the "Berra Sporting Goods Store" (Walk up three flights and save!) until he was elected to the Hall of Fame. We all knew he would be. It was remarkable how many people wanted a fly rod used by Yogi Berra. He did all right on that transaction and I did as well. It was a treat to know him and to play on the same team with him. He was my manager in 1964. I never understood why he got fired, even though a lot of people who didn't know told me why."

◆

Del Webb was the co-owner of the Yankees during most of the time I played for and managed the Yankees. He liked to tell three stories about Stengel. I enjoyed listening to Webb. He pitched at the Triple A level, he was a good golfer, he quit school in the eighth grade, and he liked me. He pitched for the Oakland Oaks. He used to tell me about riding the streetcar in Oakland out to the ballpark.

Webb was a former drinker. He did not want

people who worked for him to drink or smoke. What he wanted and what he got were not always the same. One night he went to a party in Los Angeles and ran into Casey, who was drinking. He did that a lot. Webb left the party early, but not because people were drinking. Probably because he had made a deal or was going to go someplace else to make one.

The next morning before seven he was driving to work, and he spotted, as he said, "this old guy" talking with a bunch of kids in the park. It was in Glendale, California, and it was a little park with a baseball field. He stopped. It was Stengel telling a bunch of kids how to do something or not do something. Webb said, "That's the man I wanted to manage the New York Yankees." The way he put it was, "He was talking baseball to anyone who would listen when I left the party last night and now here he is doing the same thing the next morning."

Webb liked you to be as interested in what you did as he was in what he did. He had a business manager who had a phone in his car, and this was before many people had phones in their cars. This guy had a phone in his car, his home, his girlfriend's home, and in his office. He said that Webb would call no matter what time zone Webb was in and expect the phone to be answered in three rings.

Webb had never liked Bucky Harris because he came to the park late and had an unlisted phone number that he wouldn't even give to the team. To tell you the truth, I found that hard to believe. George Weiss, the Yankee general manager during my playing days, knew everything. He knew who smoked. He knew how many baseballs were in the clubhouse. He knew when they ran out of paper towels in the ladies room in the bleachers. I am not kidding about George M. Weiss. So I found it hard to believe they didn't have Bucky's home number, but Webb told me years later that the team did not have Bucky's home phone.

On the other hand, when they asked for his phone number and he didn't give it, Bucky might have signed his walking papers. You don't always know when you are doing something that starts your walking papers moving, and maybe Bucky didn't know. Maybe they had the wrong guy ask him for his phone number. I don't know for sure, but I can't imagine George Weiss asking for it and not getting it. I don't know much more than I am telling you now, but I will add this. If this sort of thing went on when I was playing, and I guess you would have to bet it did, I didn't know about it. It wasn't in the papers. I would not know it from anyone in the front office because I didn't talk with them. I talked with George Weiss only once or twice a year. He never came in the clubhouse unless it was to see Casey, and then he came in the back door to Casey's office and left the same way. Really, the only time I talked with George, and it took me a long time to call him George, was when we talked contract. He hardly ever looked you in the eye. The only time he looked you in the eye was when he reached for your hand to shake on the deal. The other time I would see him was at the victory party. We had fourteen of them. What I am saying is that you did not see the general manager on the field, in the clubhouse, or in the dugout.

When Casey was hired, the team had a press party at 21. At the time, 21 was the most expensive restaurant in New York. Maybe it still is. Dan Daniel, a writer and as Webb said, "an important one" backed Webb into a corner and asked him a question. Webb told me about it much later, not while I was a player. It was a big deal. At least Webb told it to me like it was really important. Like when you change a pitcher in a big game. Or make an important trade. Webb felt he had to give a good answer. He did not want Dan Daniel to show up the Yankees. The question was, "How can the New York Yankees, the class of baseball, hire a clown as a manager?" Webb said, "It has been my experience since first starting in business that the man who has a sense of humor, the man who can see humor in himself and others and bring it out in comedy, that is a smart man. We want a smart man to manage our team." Webb may have said it better than that or maybe not as good. It has been a long time since he told me, and I wasn't thinking about this book. He did try to save his bacon and Stengel's hide from Dan Daniel. It worked. Webb was afraid that if the press got on Casey, it would be bad. What he got from Dan Daniel was some time. That's what he wanted.

As long as I am on this let me take a minute to talk about New York teams and the press. Today we have football and basketball and a lot of other sports going after your dollar. When Casey was hired, baseball had three teams in New York, and the owners knew how important it was to have good things in the papers. That's why they gave reporters free lunch, a place to park, and a nice place to watch the game.

Webb also gave Casey a watch when he turned 75 years old. Before he got the watch, Casey said, "Most guys my age are dead." I am sure he said thank you after he got the watch because it was engraved with the words: "All things considered, the best manager in baseball." I am not saying I agree with what Del Webb said, I am just saying he said it. I always thought it was funny that Webb would say "all things considered." Sounds like something you would read in an annual report, if you read one.

Casey was serious about baseball, but he thought some sportswriters tried to make baseball too serious. It's on the sports page, not the editorial page, was one way he used to say it. I think he was right. I love baseball, but it is a game. It can be a way to make a living but not for a lot of people. It brings pleasure to many people. Some cities think they must have a major league team to feel good. They may even feel good for a while watching triple A players in big league uniforms. Some of the people in those same cities may wonder why the taxpayers need to cough up the money.

Writers could see life in a bullfight and death in a passed ball. I never saw a bullfight but I had a few passed balls and they were just that, passed balls. It may be that I missed something, or it may be that when you do something for a living you miss something.

I've got to be careful now. When I say I did something for a living I mean both when I played and when I managed. When I played, the game was (at least, most of the time) in front of me as a catcher or an outfielder. If you play second or pitch, the game is around you. During the years when I managed, the game was in front of me and in me. It is always with you. If my eyes were open, I was working. You are always thinking. When you make out the line-up card, you just write down the names. How they get into your brain, that's the problem. I used to wonder why is it that the guys you need are always hurt?

Now I am a coach, and that's why I say I have to be careful. I want Houston to win, but I have to be honest (I am supposed to need lessons to learn how to lie). If we lose, I don't feel, like the manager does, that it's my fault. It's not the manager's fault, but I know he thinks it is. A lot of times when I managed I did, too. I still see baseball from this perch, as Red Barber might say, the same as I have all along.

I don't think the dugout is a hold on a ship. The umpires wear dark blue or black because the colors don't show dirt. The home team wears white because they can wash the uniforms easier at home. They wear gray on the road so they can get more games out of a uniform. It is not a good guys wear white hats or a Moby Dick thing (I never did see all that some people saw in that movie). Baseball is nothing more than a wonderful game. The guy who said the base line should be 90 feet was an Einstein. The next time you see a game, just think what it would be like if the base line were 87 feet or 93 feet. It would be a whole new ball game. But it is a game, not life. Although if you play it for money, you can learn a lot about life.

─────── **Other Voices** ───────
CHARLEY KELLER

Charley Keller (King Kong), with Joe DiMaggio and Tommy Henrich, made up the Yankee outfield for the better part of ten years. The Yankee Clipper, Old Reliable, and King Kong—great names for the baseball fan. All of them in one outfield. Not an All-Star team, just one team, playing 154 games. Charles Keller's voice is soft. Somehow the caller is surprised that the "Maryland Strong Boy," as the New York press dubbed Keller, is not only soft spoken but has a soft voice as well. "Sure I'll talk about Yogi. He won't talk about himself, and you are going to need all the help you can get."

The directions Keller gives to locate his farm are as precise as the throws he used to make from the outfield. The directions are low keyed, like Keller's play for the Yankees. With Joe D. in center, even outstanding players like Keller and Henrich were overshadowed. The shadows in Yankee Stadium during Keller's portion of the glory years fell on the pitcher's mound. Is it any wonder that American League pitchers came down with a case of the vapors when they had to face the Yankees? Three or maybe four of that crop of Yankees would have batted in the cleanup spot for any of the other seven teams in the league. Pitch around Henrich to get to Keller? To get to DiMag? If you got by them, you could pitch to the weak-hitting infield. Start with Joe Gordon.

A brick house that could be the set for a TV series, The Breeders. In this case the breeder is Keller, and the home and barns are surrounded by trotters and pacers. The farm is called Yankee Land and Keller is asked, "Do you have all your horses here?" "Not all of them," explains Keller, "most of them. The best ones are working."

"Come on in out of the rain," Keller says warmly. "I thought you would be here tomorrow. It must have been a bad connection." Not a hint of "come back tomorrow" in his voice. "Let me put another log on the fire and turn off the football game and we can talk about Yogi."

"The first thing I want to set straight is this. The Dynasty book about the Yankees said that I got on Yogi for not running out a ground ball. It never happened. I never recall him not giving his best, even when he was hurt. If you work as hard on his book as he did polishing his baseball skills, it will be one hell of a book.

"One year at the University of Maryland was all I had before I signed with the Yankees. I played over 1000 games in the big leagues and only 200 of them with Berra. I did not know it right away, but I know it for sure now. The world needs more people like Yogi Berra.

"You know, some of us used to wonder if he had a press agent. He had a way of saying things that made you think and smile and then say, 'I would never say it that way, but I know what he means.' Sometimes it seemed to make more sense the way he said it than the regular way, and that may have been part of his charm. I bet people will laugh if they see Yogi and charm in the same sentence. We did not always smile, sometimes we laughed, and as time went by I really think he used to work at saying something. He didn't do it for long, if he did it at all. But if he did, it was a homestand or road trip at most. Then he went back to being natural.

"It was hard to be natural when everything you said was in the paper the next day. He was a natural hitter, so I don't need to talk about that, but he was also natural. I never saw a glimmer of a pretentious side, and with all the hoopla surrounding the Yankees it was not easy to keep your head. It was not easy for anyone, but if after the game four or five guys came by your locker and waited for a line that would be spoken like John Foster Dulles and delivered like Henny Youngman, well, you can imagine. No, I don't think you can imagine. I don't mean you, I mean all the 'yous.'

"Joe D. called his book Lucky To Be a Yankee, and he was right, but it was not all cookies and cream. If you were a character—and Yogi was one and has a ton of it as well—it could be tough. He handled it. He handles most everything. He was the best .285 hitter in the history of baseball.

"Several years ago we played in a Pro Am golf match. The pay-off was good, and even if it had been dimes, it was important to us to win and we really tried. Yogi had a par, birdie, par, par, and I said, 'Yog, you can carry this foursome. We are going to win this thing.' Yogi said, 'Charley, don't count on me. I'm playing way over my mind.' As is often the case, you are so dumbstruck you don't comment. Then think better of it. Why break the spell? I did mention it in the clubhouse at the cocktail party—after we lost." Yogi said, 'Sure Charley, I knew what I was saying. I was just making up a new saying.' "First time I ever saw him lie, the only time," said Keller with no rancor.

"Trying to put your finger on what makes him tick or why he ticks the way he does is not of interest to me. Just savor the time and in my case the memory." Keller is then told a Berra story that long-time clubhouse man Dennis Liborio told. Yogi was gently, very gently lowering himself into the hot whirlpool. He had pitched a little batting practice and said his arm was dead, his legs, too. He kept jumping up and down, saying nothing. Liborio felt responsible for everything that went on in the clubhouse, from the kind of gum the players chewed to the quality of the sanitary socks they wore. He asked Yogi if the water was too hot. Yogi responded, "How hot is it supposed to be?"

Charley Keller sat back in the fine leather chair in his grand old home, and smiled as the fire lit his face. "That is Yogi. I often wondered how hot it was supposed to be but never asked. He is special. The Yankees know that and that's why they put up the plaque in center field for Yogi and Dickey. The Yankees asked me to come back for the day they had for Dickey and Yogi. I just didn't want to, and I was sure Yogi wouldn't show. He didn't, did he?" Keller is told that Berra did not. "Just like him," commented Keller. "I guess I really didn't want to see Bill Dickey in a wheelchair," said Keller. His voice was sad. "I am getting ready to take a bunch of my horses to the auction in Kentucky so I will have to supervise the loading. You can watch if you like, and if you need to get moving go along and call if you need any more help." Keller proved to be a hands-on supervisor, muscling several balky pacers into the horse vans.

"Tell Yogi I think his movie reviews were a lot better when he gave them in his underwear," laughed Keller as he waved good-bye.

◆

It is kind of funny to think about Casey and the way some people feel about baseball. He did a lot to make people think about the game of baseball. When they did and they thought about the way he talked about it, they may have thought they were missing something. I don't think they did. I feel the same way about some of the movies I review. It's a movie, the people who put it out had a reason. You had a reason to go. If you tell your friends to go, the people who invested in the movie are happy. It seems that simple, but if you make movies, you know it is not. It's hard work. If you play baseball, you know it is not that complicated—hit the ball, catch the ball, throw the ball to the right base—but it is not easy to do.

Let me say one more thing about seeing things that I didn't see. Or people who write about things that I didn't see. Let me give an example. I have read this or close to this, "If you have a game and the crowd is small and doesn't really understand the game, you don't have a baseball game." I think that is baloney. Our youngest son Dale signed with the Pirates the same year the Mets fired me. They sent him to Niagra Falls. I had a lot of free time at the end of the summer, and Carm and I watched him play in the low minors. We saw him play before some tiny crowds. Some of the people didn't understand the game. They came out for some fresh air and to cool off or to drink beer. They kept score and the umpire shouted "Play ball!" and they did. The next day it was in the paper. I am not saying it was any different for me because I had been a manager and it was our son. It was just that I don't think you should add something that isn't there.

During the games in Niagra Falls I tried to stay out of sight. You know, pressure from a Little League parent and all that. Sometimes we would watch from a little press box. Anyway, one night after a game I went down to the field. The lights were still on, and I said to Dale, "How do you see the ball with these lights?" He said, "I have 18-year-old eyes." I don't know what is the first thing to go, but eyesight must be high on the list.

I tried to tell you how I see baseball. Watching baseball from a press box (that is where the writers watch from) can be very different than watching from behind the plate, the outfield, or even the bench.

Sure I have seen a few other games from a press box. The Dodgers–Giants playoff and some others like that, but they were so special they didn't count. They didn't count or add up to a long summer of chasing truth or whatever they say we chase. I have seen a few games from an owner's box when I was being considered for a job, but that is not the same. Or at least when I was trying to size up the offer I might get and was being sized up by the owner, I didn't see into the real meaning of the pitcher knocking some guy on his ass. Maybe some day I will watch 40 or 50 games from a press box, if they will let me in after all this, and I will change my mind.

I read most of a review of a book called *Streak*. It is a book about Joe DiMaggio's 56-game hitting streak in 1941. I haven't read all the book either, but I read enough of one review not to want to unless I knew and admired Joe. I did and I will read the whole book. The review talks about expectations and standard deviations and baseball imitating life. As I said,

I may have missed something. One thing I didn't miss and I hope the book mentions it, and it's this. Joe DiMaggio had a 61-game hitting strike in the minors. It was in 1933 when he played for the San Francisco Seals. The Pacific Coast League had some wonderful team names when I was a kid: San Diego Padres (just like today), Los Angeles Angels, Hollywood Stars, Sacramento Solons, Oakland Oaks, Portland Beavers, Seattle Rainers, and the team Joe made famous, the San Francisco Seals. Some kids used to read about big bands and I did some of that, too, but those names out of the past can make my mind dance. Sacramento was a long way from St. Louis, and I still haven't been there and I still don't know what a Solon is or was.

Let me tell you what I didn't miss. Baseball is a great way to spend your life if you are successful and I was. Going to a game with your family is also a great thing to do. It can make you understand your kids, and they can get to know you. All those good things. It is a wonderful thing for you to do in the afternoon, at night, and from April until October. All summer. You can start when the first robin builds a nest and see baseball until the geese fly south, and that is as far as I am going to go. It is also much better to take your family on a long walk and to church.

I think that part of the reason I feel the way I do about baseball is that people try to complicate things. We have done a good job of that in a lot of ways. Agents and incentive contracts, to name two. Something as simple as the shin guards a catcher wears. All the years I caught I had two straps to hold them in place. We all did. Now they have four or maybe more. I never lost a shin guard, even when some wild man like Jim Rivera slid into me.

I know some complicated things are around. All that stuff under the hood of my car, for example. Some of the guys on the Astros and the Yankees used to know not only what went on under the hood but could help make it go. They had cars as kids. When I was a kid, I didn't have a car. My dad didn't have a car. The first car I ever got was given to me on the Day they held for me. Yes, it was the time I said, "Thank you for making this night necessary." It was a Nash. I wish I still had it.

At my age if I have missed it, I probably missed it. I don't mean to sound like it is over, but let's face it, I am not about to learn how to become a shade tree mechanic. And I am not about to see truth and beauty in the visiting team. But that does not mean that I am going to feel bad because you can tell me about the character of the wine and all I can say is it's good.

Milton Friedman, to get back to him again, has a wonderful way of making things clear. An example was when someone said to him, "I think they play too many baseball games." He said, "You are obviously not an owner, nor do you earn a living selling beer and hot dogs during the games." Later on he said something else. I have forgotten the point he was trying to make, so it may not be a good lesson, but I am going to tell it anyway because I like it. He was trying to explain inflation. That is why I can only remember this part. In other words, don't ask me why we have it or how to stop it. Professor Friedman put a string on the table—for all I know he carries one just in case inflation comes up—and he said, "See how easy it is to pull this string?" Then he waited, and it would be a good idea for all of us when we are trying to make a point to wait and look to see how it is going over. Then he said, "Now see how much harder it is to push the string. You see it is really quite impossible."

Ted Williams used to talk about hitting like Casey talked about the game. He used to say, "Don't you know how really hard it is to hit a ball?" He was trying to make a point to other hitters and you do that by getting things over like Friedman. Some of the Red Sox pitchers used to get mad as hell when they saw Ted giving advice to other team's hitters. Sometimes one of them would yell, "That's right, give them help." They would yell it in a sarcastic way, but he never let on they were getting to him. He never gave me any help. He said I was an "awful sight." No kidding. You may think that all the language on the field is bad, but that is just the way he said it—sight. They say he had the best eyesight of anybody who ever played. I talked with guys who hunted with Ted and they would say he would look out of the duck blind and say, "Here they come." The other hunters would look and see nothing. Then after, say, 30 or 40 seconds, they would all see them. If he could do that, just think what he could do with a white ball from 60 feet, 6 inches.

Other Voices
TED WILLIAMS

Theodore Samuel Williams, spring training hitting instructor for the Boston Red Sox and anyone who will listen, pay attention and give an impression of understanding the lecture. This day Professor Williams's platform is a golf cart, and he is explaining location theory to some minor league nonroster outfielders, his son John Henry, and some older sportswriters. The writers are in awe. John Henry, who wears number 18 on his uniform, has heard a lot of this before, but is respectful and the minor league kids seem to have a "will this be in the book," glaze in their eyes. Williams has been known to turn and walk away when his students give evidence of not passing the first course with a sufficient grade.

"Yooogi Berra, so you want to talk about Yooooogi." Williams's resounding voice fills the classroom. "Why don't you guys take a break and give me ten minutes. None of you want to hear any of this." Clearly they did, but they went to the cloak room and John Henry went to talk with a friend from the college he attends in upstate New York.

"When I saw that little SOB come up to the plate, I really thought it was a joke or something. Veeck had that little guy go to bat, the midget in St. Louis. Now don't get me wrong, he was under 4 feet, but Berra was way under 6 and I just thought, well, think about it. Bill Dickey was an impressive looking guy, and here was Yogi. Well, he just didn't look like he should be a Noou Yoork Yankee." Williams is stretching out the words and he is enjoying the process. He is Mr. Security and he is going to tell you just the way he feels.

"I will tell you this, I never saw anyone like him. He looked like hell, but what happened when he attacked the ball was right out of a computer. He could move the runner, and move him late in the game like no one else I ever saw play the game. A lot of people said their shortstop Rizzuto was too small, but, damn, those two guys knew how to beat you. Makes me sick to think about it.

"I had his oldest boy Larry in my baseball camp. I think I even gave him a free ride. He was good, but he didn't have that pop in his wrists like the old man. Not many do, and not many walk and talk the way he did. He would drive you batty. 'Do you like your room? Where are you going for dinner?' Just on and on. Bobby Doerr and a lot of us hated it, but we didn't hate him. You just couldn't. He was a wonderful guy. You could tell it, and you tell him this, 'I would rather read about you than watch you hit.' And let me tell you this: if you don't write a good book about Mr. Yogi Peter Berra, I will have you killed!"

Class dismissed. John Henry reacted to the information that Dale Berra, a nonroster invited player in the Houston Astro spring camp, was assigned uniform number 4. The handsome young Williams indicated no reaction but said without a trace of emotion, "I didn't ask to be his son," his eyes looking toward his dad already deep in the second semester of Hitting 101—Waiting for the Right Pitch. It was an extraordinary moment, full of whatever additions or subtractions the listener wished to make.

"Nice to talk with you," said John Henry. Catching Ted Williams's eye as one left the ballpark is a simple task, as he is constantly looking at his students. Thanks for the time. He said, "Say hello to Yogi and don't forget what I told you."

3
MEDWICK

Sportsman's Park in St. Louis had two major league teams when I was growing up on Dago Hill. The Cardinals and Browns played their home games in Sportsman's Park. Most people in St. Louis thought the Cardinals were, if not the best team, the one they were proud of. The Browns were poor relations. Like they were renters and the Cardinals owned the place. I don't know if they did or not, but the Browns didn't feel like they were the New York Yankees, that's for sure. The use of Dago in front of Hill may shock you, but that is what it was called. Our family never felt like we were poor relations, or renters for that matter, even though we might have been when I was a kid. We own the house now. I am proud we do and I hope it doesn't sound like I am bragging. The Browns left St. Louis to go to Baltimore and they became the Orioles. They left in 1953. I left almost ten years before that and became a sailor and then a Yankee.

I don't know what it cost to get into Sportsman's Park when I was a kid, but it was probably 50 cents for the bleachers, maybe less. We got in free with the knot hole gang. Branch Rickey was the first to promote the idea of a knot hole gang, so Charley Finley wasn't the only one with ideas. Later on I would work out way before the games and stay around afterwards. Both the Browns and the Cards thought I was a prospect. It made me feel 10 feet tall. I know now that a lot of kids are prospects and that most prospects don't play even one game in the big leagues, but I didn't know that then. Maybe that was good.

Watching the Cardinals play was my idea of a day at the beach, even though at the time I had never been to the beach or seen the ocean. I don't think the kind of pure joy I felt then is still possible as an adult. And I don't mean that in a bad way—like I wish I was a kid again. I am just trying to look back and look around and think about all of it. I think it is good for you if you have had the kind of life I have.

A lot of people would say that catching a perfect game in the World Series would be pure joy and it was, but it was not like going to Sportsman's Park. Playing baseball as a kid in St. Louis was pure joy, too. I don't want to downplay Don Larsen's perfect game. When it happened, it was the first time, and it hasn't happened since. Larsen was perfect, and our team made some good but not great plays. In other words, the perfect game wasn't saved by a spectacular play. Mickey hit a home run off Sal Maglie in Yankee Stadium that could have been caught in Ebbets Field, and Larsen never shook me off. It was once in a lifetime, once in two lifetimes. Maybe I can put it this way. When Dale Mitchell struck out and I ran out and one writer said, "Berra, chimp-like jumped up and kneed Larsen in the crotch," for those few moments, that was pure joy. Real fast, though, you get back to thinking about how the kids are doing in school and wondering if Newcombe will pitch tomorrow.

To get back to that writer who called me "chimp-like." The next day I told Whitey Ford, "I am not going to pay attention to that writer. He don't even know where Larsen's crouch is." I showed Whitey the picture in the paper of me jumping up on Larsen. "Look here is my knee, nowhere near his crouch." Whitey laughed and said it's "crotch" not "crouch." That game has been covered in so many different books. As far as I know, all of what I read at least was accurate except for the crotch thing, so I don't plan to do more than go into it a little bit later when I can talk about pitchers.

I think pitchers are different than baseball players and should have their own chapter. Stan Musial was a pitcher before he became a ballplayer, and now they have a statue of him out in front of Busch Stadium in St. Louis. He is hitting. If the statue came to life and he hit a ball, it would probably land on some property he owns. I didn't get that line from Garagiola. I didn't get it from anybody. It seems to me a nice way of saying Stan is loaded. He is, and I am glad he has done well. He was a great player and is still a wonderful man. At one time people thought he would run for office. I am sorry he didn't. Whatever he did, he did well.

Joe Medwick was my idol and my favorite player, too. You could tell by the way he moved he was good. Some guys move well but can't play well, but I never saw a player who looked bad when he moved who played well. An exception might be a pitcher. Some of them can look pretty awful, even from the stands.

It is hard to say this next thing without sounding like I am stuck on myself, so I will just say it and hope for understanding. Several books have been written about me that I didn't know about until someone sent me one. The books were about me and had my name on them. I never got a check with my name on it, and a lot of what was written was wrong. What I am saying is that I didn't get paid for the books. One of them said I sold newspapers and that Joe Medwick was one of my regulars. I didn't have a stand, and I went by the corner the last time I was in St. Louis and they still don't have a stand. It was at the corner of Southwest and Kings Highway. It felt funny to go back and look at it when I was working on this book. Not funny but strange. It is true and it is also true that he gave me a nickel every time he bought a paper, and the paper was 3 cents and he said, "Keep the change." But it is not true that is why he was my idol and my favorite baseball player. You might say if that's the worse thing that happens to you, you are lucky. If you did say that, you would be right. It's not a big deal, but some people think that if they see a book about somebody, the somebody got a check. It's what they call royalties in the book business. I just wanted you to know I didn't.

Sometimes we would wait to see players come out of the Cardinal dressing room. I don't know why really, but we did and it never occurred to me to ask Joe for his autograph or to speak to him. I spoke to him, of course, when he bought the paper, but I mean speak to him the way it is done today. Had I known his autograph would be worth money, I would have asked for his name on something. I didn't ask President Reagan for his autograph either, and I do not think anyone would ask the Pope for his. You could say that I am not an autograph seeker. But I am not like some movie stars I have read about who think asking for an autograph is bad, like pollution or something. It's just something I don't do, but I don't mind signing mine unless I am eating because the food gets cold.

One more thing on the Pope. I still don't understand why anyone laughed when they heard what I said to the Pope. All I said was, "Hello, Pope," and the Pope said, "Hello, Yogi." It did not seem funny then, and it has never been explained to me why it was such a big joke. Not a joke, really, but taken as a joke. Sure I know that some people say nothing, nod or sort of bow, look at him and then down at the floor. Some say Your Holiness, or something like that. To me "Hello, Pope" was natural, and I could tell by his eyes he liked it and I like to think he liked me. It did not bother me that people laughed. I just didn't understand why they did, and I know that saying that will make somebody say, "in a pig's eye," or else why bring it up? The reason is this. If you can't put your thoughts down in a book about your life, it's a sad thing. This book is not sad and my life is not. I don't want to change a thing, not even the few bad things. If you didn't have them, how would you know the good from the bad?

"Yogi would need lessons to learn how to lie," was the way a good friend described me. I am proud of his comment and am happy to repeat it here. Since I have, I guess I better say it did bother me that some people laughed when I first came to the big leagues. I was shy and did not say much of anything, but when I did it came out wrong. Jim Frey, the Cubs general manager, said a few months ago, "Sure I know all the stories about Yogi, but he can make as much sense in as few words as anybody I ever knew." That's nice to hear even if it is not true, but Jim Frey didn't know me when I first came up. I could be pretty bad. What I said was not called a Yogi-ism. What I said didn't have a name. What I said had a reaction. It might be a shake of the head or it might be a wrinkled forehead. It was not a good thing. I really can't think of an example from 1947 or 1948. I think I talk the same way now but people listen different. Here is an example. I was giving directions to Yogi Berra's Hall of Fame Racquetball Club. It is in Fairfield, New Jersey. I said, "It's not too far, it just seems like it is." For some reason that part of the road makes it seem that way. Now, when I give directions to our place that way, the people who follow them come in and say, "Yogi, we know exactly what you mean." I do have to say that more and more buildings are going up on the road and now it is getting to be as far as it seems.

Now even Cagney and Lacey will say things like, "Yogi says . . ." One time Mary Beth was wearing a bulletproof vest and her husband hugged her and said, "Now I know what it is like to hug Yogi Berra." He didn't, but it was nice that they thought of me and not Carleton Fisk.

A show I liked, *The Days and Nights of Molly Dodd*, didn't stay on the air long, but I was told that in one show Blair Brown said, "And thank you, Yogi Berra." My son Tim told me about it. I don't know what she was thanking me for, but again I am glad she did. What I am trying to point out is that in 1950 a TV show would not have said something like that. When I said something that people thought was bad, it was just bad. Some might say you ain't too hot now, Yogi. I bet someone will. I tried to say as little as possible to reporters to avoid being ridiculed in the papers. Later on when I began to hit, I got more confidence and it didn't worry me as much. Casey Stengel used to say good things about me and that helped, too. I knew what I meant and most times others did as well, although sometimes it took them a day or two.

To get back to needing lessons to lie, maybe I should say that sometimes I *didn't* know what I meant. I knew what I was doing on the field and never lacked confidence as a player, but when a reporter stuck something in my face, I know I said some things I would like to have taken back. A few times anyway. I don't want to get too hard on myself just because my friends say I am trustworthy. One more thing. I never lacked confidence in myself as a hitter. Sometimes I did in catching and throwing, but not often.

Other Voices
KEN "HAWK" HARRELSON

"You may get shown up in a business situation or in a social setting and never know it. Or know it's too late to do more than feel the back of your neck get hot. It's best not to show your neck is heating up. In baseball when you strike out and the pitcher does a little dance, or if you hit a home run in a big game and look at him as you round first base and make a gesture, not the bird, just a move of your head to let him know he is there and you are where you are, going around the bases, well, that is showing him up. It is not a good idea. When you can do it and make the guy you show up like it and talk about it 20 years later, your name has got to be Yogi Berra. I played 9 years and have been a general manager and TV broadcaster and let me tell you, Yogi is one of a kind. The mold was broken when they made Yogi.

"Watching the Yankees in all those World Series makes going there to play that much more spine tingling. I really mean it. Coming out of that dugout two hours before a game is something I will never forget. It didn't have anything to do with the fact that I was playing for Kansas City. It was that I was playing in Yankee Stadium. The two or three hours before the ump says 'play ball' goes quickly or slowly. I can't recall, but I do recall my first time at bat. It was an NBC Game of the Week. When I stepped into the batter's box the first time, I thought about

three things. My mother is watching in Savannah, Whitey Ford is pitching, and Yogi Berra is catching. Strike one. Strike two. Mom is watching and I had better bear down. She doesn't want to see Kenneth Smith Harrelson look bad. Whitey set up, and just as he did, I felt something warm on the back of my sanitary sock, you know, the white part of the baseball sock. Strike three! Yogi had spit on my calf just before Whitey delivered. I was dumbfounded. As I turned, my mouth hanging open I am sure, Yogi said, 'Welcome to the big leagues, kid.' "

◆

Now, or as some guys on TV say, at this point in time, I don't worry about that part of my life. I don't for two reasons: one is that I don't, and the other is that it doesn't do any good. When it's over it's over, and nothing I could say here is going to change anything. My comment when they had a night for me in St. Louis was "Thank you for making this night necessary." The press had a field day with that, but I said it then—so why worry about it now? Worry about something you can do. Worry about it until you do it or fail three or four times and then do something else. You can't live in the past and you can't live in the future. As you get older you should be happy just for feeling good.

I don't think I worry about much. My son Tim says I am obsessed about three things. He could say I *worry* about three things, but he says *obsessed*. The first is being on time for appointments. The second is the weather. Since he forgot the third, I don't think it was an obsession.

I do want to be on time. Even as a kid I did. My dad wanted us sitting in the kitchen when he came in from work. We were and we had a pint of beer for him. We stayed in our chairs until he told us to leave. We were all good kids. I can never remember leaving a light on. Maybe when Tim reads this he will recall the third obsession. Most people over 60 turn lights off. Sometimes kids who leave them on talk about the energy problem. Even Reggie Jackson told me he turns off lights and understands a little more about owning something rather than just renting. I don't want to do a chapter on lights, but I do think that the guy who told me that he couldn't wait to have his son grow up and buy a house so he could go visit and leave all the lights on hit a nerve, as they used to say in the dentists' office.

Being on time is polite and I am. I always am. One time my son Dale and I were going to fly to Houston. I called him from our home in Montclair and told him I would pick him up at his home in Glen Ridge, New Jersey, at 7 AM and drive to the airport. He said, "What time do we need to be there?" I said, "8 o'clock." He said, "Dad, the trip is 20 minutes tops, 20 minutes." I remember thinking Phil Rizzuto always says he is 9 minutes from the airport, but I didn't say that to Dale because he would say, "I know, Dad, I know." So what I said was, "So we'll be early!" Dale said, "I'll be ready." He was and we were a little early. It was nice. I would do it the same way again.

A lot of sportswriters have picked me apart. Since it was what they got paid for, I didn't resent it. Dick Schaap, a writer and an ABC announcer, told a friend,

"I was pretty hard on Yogi, too hard as I look back, and do you know he never said a word. He was always gracious to me. Never turned his back. Never made me feel uncomfortable, even though I may have been critical of him in print or even on the air. George M. Steinbrenner, now that's another story—not a nice man. Yogi Berra wears well, George wears thin."

———— Other Voices ————
DICK SCHAAP

"Yogi Berra was mellow when I first knocked him. That may have been way back, in 1973 or 1974 when he first managed the Mets. Over the years I did [knock Yogi] and sometimes, thinking back, rather harshly. I didn't think he did as well as Gil Hodges when he managed the Mets, and I said as much. The remarkable thing about him is that he always treated me the same way. Like I was a gentleman, and of course he was always one. He was all along. I have mellowed as well and it may have been age, but I think being around Yogi played a role. You say something in print or over the air about a guy and he says, 'Hi! How you doing?' the next time you see him and it does something to you. It doesn't make you wish you had pulled your punch, but it does make you think what a remarkable guy you have covered.

"Most people thought my book on George Steinbrenner was balanced. I thought it was. I worked hard at making it come out that way, but he hated it. We have been in the same room several times since the book came out and he has never spoken.

"When I read that Yogi won't go back to Yankee

Stadium as long as George is there, I think to myself how different the two men are. Yogi doesn't need George, but George seems to need Yogi. He gets the rest of those guys to go back and come back and it is a sad thing. Makes Yogi look all that much more special. He looked special from the very first time he put on a uniform, if you know what I mean, but in a very different way. I mean he looked special in the Fifth Avenue sense."

My friends were bugged by what was said and written and that may have made it easier for me. You know, if someone has knocked you in the paper and the next day a friend will say, "Cheap shot, Yog." I am not saying that for sure. I am saying it might have helped. As they say on Seventh Avenue in New York, "It couldn't hurt." I knew the press was important and tried to be nice to the writers, not so much because we were expected to be nice to them but just because I was raised that way.

I thought then and I think today that the writer should cover the game. Not the stuff that Liz Smith does. She is called a gossip columnist. Liz Smith does what she does well. I like seeing her on TV more than reading her column, so I don't read it. Liz Smith is on TV in New York City, so maybe a lot of people don't see her. When I was a kid, we had Hedda Hopper and Louella Parsons. Liz Smith is not like either one of them, but if I had to say, I would say more like Parsons than Hopper. I don't mean to be rude to Liz Smith or anyone else who does what she does for a living, and that may not be the name they like. Gossip columnist, that is. But that's what they used to be called. They used to call it "Dago Hill," too, and now they call it "The Hill."

I was driving into New York several months ago, and I saw a Sears Fashion Distribution Center right near Giants Stadium in New Jersey. It looked like what we used to call a warehouse. The Giants play in New Jersey, and I'm glad. I live in New Jersey and I like the Giants. They took the *NY* off their helmets. Look the next time you see them on TV. The media has a lot to do with what happens, or maybe what happens has a lot to do with the media. Frank Crosetti used to say when asked a question, at least any hard question, "Who's to say?" He would say it at least two times. "Who's to say?" in that high-pitched voice of his. He was right to say that. The phrase "Who's to say?" works in a lot of places.

Getting back to reporters' questions, last fall I heard one of the New York Rangers interviewed on a radio station and the guy said this when he was asked a question, "I don't get paid to comment on them, only to play them." He was not being interviewed like he would be on a Sunday morning TV show with David Brinkley and Sam Donaldson and George Will. Somebody just put a mike in his face and asked a question. He might have said, "No comment." I did once when I was the manager of the Yankees, or it may have been the Mets when I was rushed or maybe even mad. But he didn't, so I give him credit for saying something. At least one person thought it was worth repeating, and I wish now I remembered the guy's name. The New York area gets a lot of coverage, so

I have an excuse. They have the first 24-hour sports radio station, WFAN. I can remember when we didn't have radios, and I can hear my boys saying, "Yeah, Dad, and how far did you walk to school, Dad?" I wonder what would have happened had one of us on the old Yankees said, "We get paid to hit the ball, not talk about it," when George Weiss was the general manager.

Most of the comments about me were not so much what I said but the way I said it. Joe Garagiola said that I don't say funny things, I say things funny. I don't know what that means and I don't think Joe does, but I am sure of this. It was good for him to say all he has said about me over the years, and it has been good for me, too. At least it was not bad. That's the way I would like to say it. It wasn't bad, and the people who thought it was didn't know it all. It was not a put-up thing like Fred Allen and Jack Benny. I don't mean to put the two of us in that league, but it makes my point. We were childhood friends and still are and will always be. Joe is not the only one who used me as a stooge, if that is a good word (I am not sure it is, but I am going to use it anyway). He was the most well known. A writer friend suggested I use "foil" in place of "stooge." It didn't work for me.

Jimmy Piersall, one of the best center fielders I ever saw, told me, "Yogi, I built an addition on my house in Chicago on the money I made on the banquet circuit telling stories about you." Then he'd tell me one or two, or more if he was wound up, but he never asked me to come over to see the addition or stay in it and he never sent me a check. Funny thing about

Jimmy Piersall. When he is trying to needle me, he tries to sound like me. A lot of people do—even some women—but when Piersall tries to get his high-pitched Boston accent to sound like me, it sounds like hell.

The best story Jimmy tells is this one: "Yogi and I are both Roman Catholic, and one time we went to this huge church in Cleveland. It was even air conditioned. We were told there was supposed to be a 'silent collection.' Pretty soon eight guys came down the aisle and we put some folding money in the collection plate; coins rattle in the collection plate. A little bit later twelve guys came down and we did it again. After a while Yogi turned to me and said, 'How long is this going to go on?' I didn't know and told him so. 'I am going to get something to eat,' said Yogi and I went out with him. As we got back toward the rear of church a man walked up to us, and Yogi turned to me and says, 'Whadya think, Jimmy? They gonna search us?' " I seldom miss going to church on a Sunday, and I have been to church in Cleveland many times, but it was never air conditioned and I never went with Piersall.

One story he likes to tell did happen and you can see how. He had asked me to appear at a fundraiser in Waterbury, Connecticut. It is a long story and a bad mike and a large crowd helped get the laugh. I was supposed to answer questions and I did my best, but the mike was weak and I couldn't hear. Repeating the questions was getting all of us ready to call it quits. Somebody asked if my sons went to public school. I said at that time they did. Somebody else asked a long question about how long it had taken me to drive up from New Jersey. Somebody else said I had gotten lost. I did not get lost and was early for the dinner. Somebody yelled, "We ought to give Yogi an encyclopedia." He meant an atlas. Some other guy said, "We ought to give Yogi's sons an encyclopedia so they can use it in school." I said, "They can walk like I did." Larry bet me that I was going to have to say "You had to be there" at least once. Maybe when he sees this he will say, "You were better off not saying it, Pop. You would have been better off forgetting you were ever in Waterbury."

The commercials I've done have been fun and they pay well. They put you up in a nice hotel and you eat well. You learn something by doing them. One thing you learn is how long it takes and how many people are working to make it good. I knew the reason they wanted me was because I was well known. I knew that, and they knew that. If I was still catching for the Newark Bears or the Norfolk Tars, they wouldn't have wanted me. If Joe and some others didn't talk about me, it might not have happened either. I know that, too, and I guess I would have to say that I was a little different. It was not that I was like that "Where's the Beef" lady. She was great. I wonder if she sold hamburgers or people just talked about her? I don't know, but somebody does. Somebody also knew that maybe I was not as smooth as Ricardo's "rich Corinthian leather" but that I was someone people trusted. They did some market research on that, and I am proud it came out that way.

I was asked what was the worse thing about commercials and I said, "They keep you there." Then the same writer asked me what was the best commercial I ever made and I said, "The one I did with my three sons because we got to spend all day together." This guy knew I was doing this book and said, "Be sure you put that in, Yogi, because it tells a lot about you." Maybe I should have told him that the kids were so young they didn't get paid.

Playing for the Yankees for a long time and playing in a lot of World Series games gave me what they call marketability. I played in 75 games. During those years the baseball season was 154 games, so I played almost half a regular season. Hard for me to believe. Frank Crosetti, who played for the Yankees, was in 29 World Series games and then coached in a lot of others. The Elias Sports Bureau or someone keeps track of everything. Frankie is supposed to have been involved in 23 World Series, as player and coach—I think all with the Yankees. In other words, he has cashed 23 World Series checks. I don't know the amount of those checks because each team decides how they will cut the pie before the Series. That is when they have a meeting and say we will cut the pie X number of ways and include some players who spent a month or so with the team and got hurt, or were traded, or whatever. The team votes, and since they are voting shares of money, it is serious. The trainer, the clubhouse man, and even bat boys can get a share. It all depends on how the team sees it.

As a player, manager, and a coach I have been in 21 World Series. Every time I see Frank we talk and when we say good-bye, he yells after me, "You will never catch me." It's hard right now for me to believe it. Frank doesn't mean the number of checks or the amount or that Frank would try to get my goat—that I can look up and I know Frank—but that I was involved in 21 World Series. Making myself think about the number of good days I have had has been quite special. Some people say I have a great memory. I do remember every pitch to certain hitters, in some games, just like I know every shot I take on a golf course, but I cannot separate each of the games. Some guys who only got into one World Series recall every pitch of every game. Must be nice, but I will take my blurred memory, all 75 games.

─────────── **Other Voices** ───────────
RALPH HOUK

Ralph Houk was called "The Major" because he was a decorated Major in World War II. He was also a major league manager for three teams, the Yankees, Tigers, and Red Sox. He is now a vice president of the Minnesota Twins.

"*I was called the Major and I played in the major leagues, but I was never that kind of hitter. I was catching and I couldn't blame Bucky Harris, the manager in 1947 and 1948, for sitting me down and bringing Yogi in from right field. He was hitting like mad and I wasn't. He was not a good catcher at that time, but you had to have his bat in the line-up. As I recall, and if you have ever watched a big league team over 164 games, you will understand that you tinker and tinker and then try to let the thing work, Bucky put Tommy Henrich in right field, Joe D. of*

*course in center, and Johnny Lindell in left. That gave
him a great outfield. Yogi got better, and that put me out
of business in a hurry.*

*"I used to think sometimes about that tinkering they
did and I did when I managed. You know, I wasn't a
bad catcher, hitter, just not a bad ballplayer or I wouldn't
have been in the big leagues. Sometimes you do something
and the manager sees it and says to himself, this is going
to work. Then you get to play more and people expect you
to do well and you do. Yogi seemed to rise to the times that
tinkering was in order, and once he got in you couldn't
get him out. I played 91 games in eight years and I think
he played in more World Series games than that."* Houk
is told Yogi played in 75 World Series games. He smiles
and says, *"Close."*

Houk is asked if he ever remembers pitchers calling
their own game for the inexperienced Berra. *"I can never
recall that happening, and you can be sure I was watching
every move he made because in those days, let's face it, I
wanted his job. But no, that didn't ever happen."* Whitey
Ford overhears enough of this conversation to say with a
laugh, *"Yogi called the game, and if I shook him off too
much, I would hear about it from him, Stengel, or the
outfielders who had to chase the line drives. Mantle was
the worst. Always telling me, 'Listen to Yogi.' "*

Houk with obvious respect, *"Yogi learned how to work
the pitchers, he knew the hitters, he worked on his throwing,
and nobody needed to help him with his hitting except not
to do it like he did, and he became a great, great catcher.
He just kept on getting better, and he is one of my favorites.
He is hard not to like. It was hard for the Yankee fans to*

know how good a left fielder he was because I don't think they liked to see him out there. They brought their youngsters to see the Yankees, and that meant Yogi was behind the plate and Stengel was in the dugout. The only thing was, this was 1961 and Yogi was getting older. Casey was old and Yogi was doing what he always did, what was best for the team. Stengel was not only old, he was gone. I was the manager and Yogi played a lot of left field for me. I can tell you this, in a very big game with the Detroit Tigers, Yogi saved the game when he doubled up Kaline at second. Kaline still doesn't believe it. It was the game for us and no one ever mentioned it. It was lost in some other play or hit but it was the key play. He knew how to make sure you won. And not just in baseball. You ask Al Kaline about that game with the Tigers in 1961. It was a one-run game, and Yogi went out and backhanded the ball and cut him down at second. Kaline was astounded. He still is. You know how Nettles turned back the Dodgers with those great plays in the World Series? Well, Yogi did that in the most important game of the 1961 season to get us into the Series. If I had been in the Series, it would have been a big deal, but he doesn't need anymore of them, does he? The one thing about him I like the most—he is the same kind of guy now that he was then."

◆

I managed in two World Series, and those memories are different than playing memories. I was lucky enough to go seven games both times. If you want to, you could second-guess almost every move. Even the good ones. The good ones are the ones that work.

They all make sense before you flash the sign to the third base coach.

Another clear memory is the best thing I ever said. I said it to Carmen Short and it was, "Hi, I am Yogi Berra." After I said that, I tried to get her to go out with me. She was willing to go out with a ball-player but not with a married one, and she thought I was Terry Moore. Terry was a great St. Louis Cardinal centerfielder. Carmen was not a baseball fan. A fan would not have thought I looked like Terry Moore. But a fan might not know if Terry was married. Carmen knew, and she let me know that she wasn't interested in going out with me. She didn't say, "I don't date married men." All that came out later, but I knew she brushed me off.

I don't remember the first thing I said that got in the papers, but I think it may have been a comment I made about a restaurant in St. Louis. "It's too crowded. Nobody goes there any more." The place was Rugerio's, and I was a headwaiter there one winter. I liked the job. That was good because in those days most baseball players had to work during the off-season. They thought having a major league ballplayer greeting people would be good for business. The waiters didn't seem to mind. The only thing they did mind was the size of the party I took to their table. "Don't send me no deuce, Yogi," they would say. Not only did they hate a deuce, they seemed to know a good tipper from a stiff. I used to ask them how they knew, and they would say with an umpire or banker look, "You just know." I didn't. I don't to this day, but it does make eating out more fun. Since I eat out a lot, I am glad I had the experience. I think as a headwaiter I was more eager to please than some of the guys I see doing it now. Most of them look better than I did, but that isn't the reason.

Getting back to the waiters in Rugerio's. I knew that none of them could hit a fast ball even though two of them said they could when they were younger, so we got along. They knew I wasn't the best headwaiter in the world, and I didn't pretend to be. I didn't pretend to be anything, and I don't think I ever have. As I said, two of them had played baseball, but I am sure they were average, if that good. You could tell by the way they moved. Some guys move well and still couldn't play at any level, but if you didn't walk good, you sure were not going to make it to the big time. When I say walk good, I mean with some control. The same way you don't have to see a golfer hit the ball to know if he is good. You just need to see the swing.

I was blessed with good coordination. If you have it, you have it; if you don't, you don't. I don't think you can teach it. When the Yankees signed me, and I am not being modest, I was not a major league catcher but I was a major league hitter. They brought Bill Dickey back in 1948 to "learn me all his experience." He worked me way past fatigue many days, and I used to wonder if the after-the-game sessions would dull me for the next day's game. I never questioned Bill Dickey, my first manager Bucky Harris, or Casey Stengel for sure. Joe D.'s book title was *Lucky To Be a*

Yankee. I was happy to be a Yankee and I was in the go along, get along school. I have always been that way.

I want to go back to the thing I said about not being a big league catcher when I first started. It was true and right today I have seen prospects with big league hitting ability who had old men's softball speed and the attitude of someone going on a cruise ship. Guys like that don't make it.

Carmen says that too much has been written about my childhood on Dago Hill in St. Louis. Just about all I have seen written about that time is true. I played every game I could, and Joe Garagiola said that if they made up a game, in a week I would be the best on the block. I guess he was right. I was quick, to use today's term. If we called it anything, and I do not think we did, we might have said fast or good. Today they say quick, or the scouts will say "he is a player." That means you are really good. Years later I learned from an M.D. who examined me at the Mayo Clinic in Minnesota that I had the fastest eye-hand coordination of any baseball player he ever saw. At that time he had seen Lou Gehrig, Babe Ruth, and Mickey Mantle.

Another ballplayer he examined was Johnny Rucker. He played for the New York Giants and they say he was really fast. I never saw him. I saw Mickey break in. He was the fastest guy going down to first I ever saw. I used to think he could drag bunt his way on at least once a game, but he wasn't paid to do that. I was never fast in that sense. I was Brooks Robinson fast. What I mean is that if you had a hundred-yard dash but only counted the first three feet, Brooks would win. I guess that is why I hit so many pitches that would have been called balls. I was quick. If I could see it and get the bat on it, I did. I hit pitches over my head and below my knees. Ted Williams used to tell me I gave hitting a bad name. I think he may have been kidding, and as I have said, I took a lot of it. I know for sure that he could not hit the way I did and I could not hit the way he did.

Playing sports gave me a happy childhood. At least I think it was happy, but I sure did not like school. I could not wait to quit and I did after the eighth grade. Am I sorry? No. I wanted my sons to stay in school. I am not saying what was good for me is good for anyone else. I did not like school, did not do well, and got out the first chance I had. I don't pine about what didn't happen.

From what my three sons have told me around the dinner table, college might have been different. I think I might have liked some college work. I am not talking about music appreciation because I could always appreciate music. Especially the Dorsey Brothers. Archeology and some of the psychology courses interested me.

I wonder if a Psychology of Motivation course might have helped me when I managed? I took the 1964 Yankees to the seventh game of the World Series and did the same with the 1973 Mets. We lost to the Cards in 1964 and the Oakland A's in 1973. Maybe a Psychology of Motivation course would have turned those two games around. Somehow I doubt it. Maybe that is why I don't lie awake thinking about it. I know it is not over till it's over, but as Bobby Feller said, "When it is over, it is over." Next time I manage I am going to take a Psychology of Motivation course. But I would need to take the course to want the job again, so I don't think that will ever happen.

American League hitters said I was always trying to "psych" them. Bobby Doerr said that I would talk to him so he would lose concentration, but that it did not work because it backfired and really helped him relax. If Bobby was right, I was wrong. I do know that I used to make a lot of hitters think. Some of them were good at thinking. Al Rosen for one. He played third base for the Cleveland Indians. I used to go out and talk to Allie Reynolds, our pitcher. Allie had been a Cleveland Indian before he became a Yankee, and he was part American Indian. He was a great pitcher. He knew it, and that helped him be even better. When I would come back from talking to Allie, I would say something to the umpire, like, "Thanks for not coming out and listening to what we were talking about. It was private." And then I would say to Flip (Rosen's nickname), "The Chief (Allie's nickname) wants to throw you a fast ball. I'm going to call for a curve. Be looking for a breaking ball." If it made him think, it made our job easier. So I did it. What worked for one guy may not work for the next. You have to keep your head in the game and try to keep his out. If talking to the hitter relaxed him, you should figure that out and shut up. I think Bobby Doerr was one of a handful that I messed up. I knew that when the hitter said, "Yogi, shut up," I was going good.

─────────── **Other Voices** ───────────
ALLIE REYNOLDS

Allie Reynolds spent thirteen years in the big leagues. He was 28 years old when he pitched his first game in the majors. Putting a template over his record and that of Lefty Gomez and some other pitchers in the Hall of Fame could make one wonder at the wisdom of the baseball writers. The writers select the players inducted. Broadly speaking, it may also be a comment on the overall quality of the Yankee teams, and a tacit understanding among the writers, "We have enough Yankees."

If Reynolds has thoughts about the Hall of Fame, they are his thoughts and not a topic for discussion. His ranch home, not far off I-40 in Oklahoma City, is in a well-maintained subdivision. Reynolds is almost courtly as he makes one welcome in his comfortable den. Indian pottery and other expensive-looking Indian artifacts do not give the room a museum feel, but it is not what you would expect in your neighbor's home. Open on the table next to Allie is a book on political theory, and the guests are made aware, and quickly, that the reader is a college graduate.

"The Yankees were different. I had been in the major leagues five seasons, but when I was traded to the Yankees it was like going from a church supper to the Stork Club. We were not only better players than most of the other teams, we had better people. Bobby Brown went to Tulane and then became an M.D. Notre Dame, Oklahoma football, and the Yankees, all pups from the same litter.

"My first year with the Yankees in 1947 was really Yogi's first year as well," Reynolds starts. "He caught some in 1946, and caught a lot of my games in 1947 and 1948, *and most all of them after that. Stengel decided who would play, and when I read that Steve Carlton would not pitch to anybody but Tim McCarver I have to shake my head. It did not do anyone any good to let that happen. Not McCarver, not the manager, and not the other players. Not even Carlton, because he began to depend on someone else. You only depend on one person. Just bad baseball, well, no, just bad management. It was one thing for his Yankees teammates to treat Joe DiMaggio with deferential respect, or even reverence, but it was not up to management to do so, and not wise, not smart, not at all smart. Doing so was not only bad for the team, but it also gave Joe the information that he needed to get more money. The Yankees had built a barricade around Lou Gehrig's $39,000 salary, and it was going to take an army to break it down. In 1951 I was 17 and 6 and they tried to cut me. But enough. Yogi is what you want to talk about, and just like I knew when I pitched that people came to see Ted Williams hit, not to see Allie Reynolds pitch, I know Yogi is worth a book, maybe two.*

"Yogi was not a real good catcher the first few years. He never called the game the way I wanted." Why didn't you just shake him off? "That question shows you have never pitched, or at least never for a living, over a 154-game season. It is just not good to shake off your catcher too many times. It makes the infielders lose the spring in their legs and the outfielders lose the confidence in the two of you, their pitcher and catcher. A lot of baseball and life is confidence, and shaking off is not what you want to foster. Stengel knew all about this, and it was not that I went in to see him, nor did Raschi go behind Yogi's back to Casey. He just knew. He tried to call some pitches from

the dugout, but Yogi wouldn't look at him, and it didn't work."

You talked about management. Wasn't it management's job to see that this happened? "In baseball and other sports, and in business as well, a lot of things happen because of implied authority. You are the catcher; you call the game. You are the pitcher; you pitch. Every now and then you shake him off. Sometimes you do it just to get the hitter thinking, but most of the time the catcher calls the game. Most of the time the loan officer approves the loan, and the plumber fixes the sink. See what I mean? That was just the way it worked. We won a lot of games. I won 182 and lost 107 during the time I played for the Yankees.

"I do not believe that the guy who said that winning is the most important thing was right, at least not in baseball, but winning covers up a great number of problems. My problems with Berra, the catcher, were minor, considering his value to the team. I might get mad as hell at him in the third inning, but with men on in the eighth I was glad he was on our side. I know you are doing a book about him, but I also had a father who read the Good Book for a living (Reynolds' father was a minister). You would like me to say Yogi was the most feared hitter and the guy I wanted to see come up to win the game, but the guy I wanted to see up with the game on the line was Mickey Mantle. Physical ability, he had a ton of it. Even if he didn't hit a home run, if he got on, he was a threat to steal. Yogi was a good base runner, but only for a catcher.

"We Indians have a saying, or at least the ones I know do: 'White Eyes monitor time; the Indian enjoys time.' In that sense Yogi was an Indian. He enjoyed putting on the uniform. I never saw him up, or at least too *far up, and never down. He had the perfect disposition for a player or a friend, but not for a manager. He never should have been put in that position. He was not able to be mean, and the players, at least during his first time with the Yankees (1964), did not put out for him. He did not have enough meetings and did not know how to motivate. I went back for the Old-Timers' game and it was obvious to me what the problem was. I remember thinking that when I retired after hurting my arm on a team bus crash in Philadelphia George Weiss said, 'You're a college man and should stay in the front office.' We did not want to raise our kids in the East, so I turned him down. If I had taken the job, I might have been the general manager in 1964, and if that had been the case, I don't think Yogi would have been the manager. I don't know that for sure because Del Webb and Topping owned the team. If they had said, 'Yogi will be your field manager,' he would have been. I would have tried to work with him and I bet he would still say, 'How come you shook me off so much, Chief?' and 'How come you second-guess me now?' I would like to think that if I had gotten the job and he had the job on the field, we would have worked it out. We worked everything out the first time.*

"No, I never minded Yogi calling me Chief. I called him Dago. After the season I said I was going back to the reservation, and I told him to go back to Dago Hill in St. Louis. I always meant to stop in to see him on my way back to Oklahoma but never did. My wife could always beat him at golf; we might have made some money. I am happy that I made more money out of baseball and if you write a book about, well, say, pick a great catcher on today's Dodgers or Yankees and see if one of his pitchers can say

that when he is 74 years old. That may sound bitter, but let me explain it to you and I bet Yogi already knows. If you retire at age 39, which I did, and your earning power until they put you in the pine box is never as great as it was the last year, well, that's sad. Think about it.

"I was the first pitcher to pitch two no hitters in the same year, but you know that age robs you of a chance to do that again. To say at 39 you will never cash a paycheck as large again, boy, that would be tough. And you know it's going to happen to a lot of guys playing today."

◆

So many people said that I said you can't hit while you're thinking or you can't think and hit at the same time. I honestly don't know if I said it or not. I think it's true; I am just not sure I said it. I do know that when Bill Dickey used to tell me to bear down all the time, he was wrong. "Bear down, Yogi, and you can bat 300," Dickey used to say. I did not believe him then and I still don't. Baseball is every day for six months. That makes it a different game. I talked to Charley Connerly and Doak Walker about this one time at a Boys' Club Dinner in New York. They understood. Baseball every day is not like football. Football is an event game. You can get yourself charged up once a week. When you are down seven runs in the ninth inning, you are probably going to lose, so relax. It might help. Try a new batting stance, you might get lucky. What I am saying is that in baseball if you are like I am or was, you have to learn to pace yourself. I am not saying Bill Dickey was wrong for him—only wrong for me. I also want to make sure you know how much he helped me. I always thank him when I see him. Even though it was his job to help me, I still thank him. He bore down when he helped me, and George Weiss said it worked. To get back to bearing down and baseball. A close game and you are up to bat in the seventh, eighth, or ninth inning with men on base, that's a different story. When that happened, I would say, "This is why I love to play the game." If I ever have to go under the knife, I hope the surgeon feels the same way.

Ted Williams and Bill Dickey were two of a kind when it came to bearing down. I think Ted looked at each time at bat as some kind of a piano concert, and he was on stage with a tux and a spotlight on him. A regular Sarah Bernhardt. For him to swing at a bad pitch would be like the Divine Sarah forgetting a line. I have seen him take a pitch he could have hit, and the hit would have won the game. I never took a pitch I could reach, unless Casey flashed the take sign. The take sign meant I had to take the pitch. I didn't get it often. The pitchers got to know this and it helped us win some games. Ted did it his way; I did it mine.

Some people feel he should have bunted when they started the Williams Shift. The Shift was when the other American League teams would leave the left side of the field unprotected. When our team shifted on him, and we did on a sign from Stengel, I never mentioned it. I would ask him where he planned to go fishing that fall. I wouldn't kid around with him; for example, by asking, "Are you going to send me a tie for Christmas." He never wore a tie and that would have been a joke, but I didn't do that. Since he loved to fish, just saying the word "fish" was enough to get his attention. I did not want him wondering what Phil Rizzuto was doing playing second base. I was sure he knew we shifted the infield, but he didn't hear it from me. What he heard from me was, "Are you a better bone fisherman or a flycaster?" I wouldn't have known one from the other. Still don't.

A lot of writers ask me if I thought Ted should have bunted down the third base line when we shifted. I have had to say I don't know, and I really don't. If someone put a gun on me I would say, maybe once he should have. Without a gun or anything, I will say this, if you had a baseball team, would you want a guy that hit .400 on it?

I like and respect Ted Williams, and as I said, I owe a lot to Bill Dickey. They may have been critical of my slashing at pitches over my head or in the dirt, but to me the object is to score more runs. If you hit the ball, it is better than a walk. The guy who catches the ball might throw it away. If you walk, you walk, and that is that. You don't even get charged with a time at bat, but I will take a hit, or rather, I would rather hit the ball any day. Darrell Royal, the former University of Texas football coach, used to say only three things can happen when you throw a forward pass and two of them are bad. When you walk (in Pete Rose's case, run) down to first base, you might feel good about your eyes. I have good ones. But if you hit the ball, some guy in the field might have bad hands.

Ted Williams and Bill Dickey were two examples of a way of doing something, or as Joe Friday used to say on *Dragnet*, an "M.O." Baseball makes it possible to operate as an individual, more so than some other team sports. Think about it. If the coach or quarterback calls a play and, as a lineman, you say "I think I will block left this time" and the play is right, you are in the soup and will not play long. Baseball is an associational game. I heard this the first time in a sermon by a priest, believe it or not. You associate with eight other guys. One of the team, the catcher, is not even technically on the playing field. You try to beat nine other guys, one of whom, the batter, is closer to the playing field than the catcher. If the batter stays in the batter's box, he is on the playing field. One at a time, until three of them make out, the other nine guys come up to the plate and the pitcher and catcher play catch and some guys never get in the game at all. They never block. In football you block on every play or there is no play. If you are the shortstop, you can catch the ball your way and throw it your way. The hitter can kick his foot off the ground like Mel Ott, the great New York Giant, used to before he hit. Or you could swing if you could swing with the grace of Joe D. Or you could swing like Punch and Judy (Nellie Fox). It was all okay. Especially if you won. In fact, if you won, most everything was fine. The more you won, the more you could be an individual. You were a team, but you were an individual and you cared about the team. That is how it worked.

Since I mentioned the late Nellie Fox, I want to say that in all the years I played, he was the only one who got me mad enough to push him. First you push, then you fight. We just didn't see eye to eye about where the batter's box was. He would try to creep up or back, and we had some words that seemed to last. I mean they lasted over the season and into the next season. We never did push or shove, and I don't think anybody on our team or the White Sox knew that we got close a few times. I mention it here only because it couldn't happen today. The TV would see it or somehow it would have come out. I am not saying it is good or bad. I am saying it is different. I don't think the players today have as much fun as we had, but I will bet when today's players are over 60 they will say the same thing. I hope people are still playing baseball when today's players are over 60. I hope people play baseball when today's players are in the pine box, but it is not going to happen just because I hope so. Hope is good, but it didn't make me a big-league ballplayer.

4

MEMORIES

What was your biggest thrill, Yogi? "Getting into the Hall of Fame was my biggest thrill. Second? I guess the perfect game." Do you mean that being voted MVP three times was not in second place? For Don Larsen the perfect game is his biggest thrill, for sure, but I am surprised it is in second place for you. "Maybe you are right. Maybe the three Most Valuable Player Awards were bigger. I've had so many thrills it's hard to keep them straight. It's better to have too many than none."

It's hard for me to write about all the good things that have happened to me. We were brought up to let our deeds speak, not our words, and saying that gives people a chance to take a shot at me. I mean that I didn't talk good, so I had to hit good. While I am on hitting, I think one of the reasons I was called so many unkind names is that I was not a picture-book hitter. Don't get me wrong; I could have looked like Bob Allison and still been called awful things. Bob Allison played for the Washington Senators and the Minnesota Twins. I thought he looked good at the plate, and he hit good, too. He looked like a textbook hitter. When I say picture book, I don't mean as much the way I looked at the plate as what I did when I got there.

Let me give you an example. Roger Craig, the manager of the San Francisco Giants, still gives me a bad time about a hit I got off him years ago. It is not all a joke. I mean it is not the good-natured kidding you hear at Old-Timers' games or a fish story about the one that got away. It is not the sort of story that makes all the people hearing it feel good.

In other words, I think Roger Craig is still a little mad. To tell the truth, I had forgotten it, and I am not saying that to make him madder if he reads this or somebody tells him Berra forgot the hit. I am saying it because it's true. It was in a World Series, 1955 or 1956, I am not sure which one. He got two strikes on me and was wasting a pitch when I hit it to right field. Then Enos Slaughter got a hit and drove in some runs and Craig lost. He says that if I hadn't hit the waste pitch, it would have bounced. That was how bad it was. That is why they call them waste pitches.

I don't know if the pitch would have bounced. I will take Roger's word for it. I know that I hit a lot of bad pitches, but as I said, they weren't bad to me.

People don't mind if you do what the Yankee catcher John Blanchard did one time. The other team was going to put him on base. In other words, the pitcher was told to throw four balls outside the plate to intentionally walk him. Blanchard stood by, as the batter always does, but when the fourth ball came over he stepped into it and hit it out. It was a big deal. I think it may have been against the Milwaukee Brewers. I only saw it happen that once. It doesn't happen a lot, and that is the reason I am bringing it up here. If somebody swings at ball four of an intentional pass, it makes news.

I hit bad balls, or at least I swung at bad balls, every game. Bobby Brown said my strike zone was from my shoe laces to three feet over my head. He may have been right. Or maybe it was two feet over my head. It was not a normal strike zone. I liked to hit. If I saw the ball and could hit it, I did. Ted Williams, to name a great hitter, liked to hit just as much as I did, but he wanted the pitch to be a strike. I didn't care. That meant that I not only looked less like a ballplayer than some other guys on the field, I didn't swing like I should have. I didn't fit in, even though I played because I had what they now call production. I could hit, and hit better with men on base. As I said, they now call it production. We just said that the guy would get you some RBIs. Baseball players look the same. If they don't, they get nicknames. The names can be cruel. Like No-Neck Williams. I am sure glad

I didn't get that name. I do have a short neck. If you
are a catcher, that can be good. You see a lot of catchers
today who wear that flap that hangs down from their
mask? Well, even if I caught today, I wouldn't need
one.

To get back to fitting in, look at a bowling team.
Look at mailmen, or the next time you are in an airport
look at airline pilots. Most of them look alike, and I
don't just mean that they dress alike. Like a fraternity
on a college campus, they fit together. If you look
different, talk different, and swing different, you had
better hit good. People talk a lot about this country
being a melting pot, and it always made me think we
are melting together. I was different, and not just to
be different.

I said before that I was not a hot dog, but I wanted
to count. If you do, you're noticed. When you are
noticed in New York City, they turn up the lights. If
your hits come off pitches that the pitcher calls
"waste," it makes some people uncomfortable—like a
golfer who laughs and talks to the gallery. The older
I get, the more I understand. When I was 21, I just
wanted to put the fat part of the bat on the ball. Once
I made contact I wanted to hit the ball as hard and
far as I could. The late Mel Ott, a great New York
Giant outfielder, had a strange batting style. Just as
the pitcher threw the ball he would kick his foot up.
Most people said he would never last, but the Giants
management said he would and that he should never
be sent down to the minors. If you are a Giants fan
you may be saying it wasn't management, it was John
McGraw. I have heard it was the field manager,

McGraw, and also heard it was the owner. It was before my time, and I don't know who it was. That's why I said management. They felt that if he were sent down, someone would try to change him and would mess him up. He never did play in the minors. He had a funny swing, as did Stan Musial, but they hit strikes. I hit the ball.

My first year, Rud Rennie, a reporter from the *New York Herald Tribune*, asked Bucky Harris, the Yankee manager, "You're not really thinking about keeping Berra, are you? He doesn't even look like a Yankee." When you are 22, that hurts. When you are over 60, it still does. People often say that nothing is as good as it used to be. Maybe, but I don't think a writer covering a major league team would ask that question today. They might ask it but not in the same way. They might question the makeup of the team by asking, "Do you need five catchers?" Something like that. Or if you make a trade for a hot head, they might say, "Do you think he will fit in here?" But I don't think they would say it the way Rud did.

The best way to say this next thing is to spell it out. I am proud that I worked hard to make myself a better baseball player. I am not proud of the physical gifts I was given to make it possible for me to play in the big leagues, but I am thankful for them. The doctor at Mayo Brothers Clinic in Minnesota who took care of me had notes—"histories" he called them—on a lot of big league players. Babe Ruth, Lou Gehrig, Billy Jurges, Johnny Rucker, a lot of the Yankees of my day. Mickey, Whitey, Bobby Richardson, and Bill Skowron, to name a few. He said that I had the fastest eye-hand coordination of any of them. I was not surprised about Bill Skowron, but I was about the rest. Mickey for sure. You may have forgotten Johnny Rucker. He was what they call a speed merchant, and he was a big prospect in the 1940s. Cover of *Life* and all that. He was a fast Clint Hartung.

The reason I hit so many bad pitches was my quick eye-hand coordination. It was that simple, and it was not that I was some ape who didn't know what he was doing. When I was hitting I knew what I was doing. I knew what worked for me, and I knew what didn't work for me. I saw the ball and tried to swing the fat part of the bat at the ball as hard as I could. I waited longer to pull the trigger than some other hitter because I could. I had fast hands and feet and strong wrists. Next time you watch a game, watch the infielders. The good ones get up on their toes on every pitch, or at least rise up on every pitch. A lot of outfielders get set to move in the same way as the pitcher throws. I never thought about this before, but when they did that when I was hitting and I waited a fraction of a second longer to swing at the ball, I may have thrown them off. It doesn't take much, you know. If most of the hitters were in one mold and I didn't fit the mold, it might have helped me. Swinging late may have helped. It didn't hurt.

Now that I am writing about hitting I can say I was never happy being told I was a bad ball hitter. I wasn't too happy about some other things I was told, but I knew I was no Tyrone Power. I didn't think I was a bad ball hitter. They looked good to me. That's why I hit them. If that made it harder for the American

League pitchers to pitch to me, that was good for me. By the time I hit in the National League, the eye-hand coordination was gone. It went little by little. I am talking about the few games I played for the Mets. After I got fired by the Yankees in 1964, my reputation for hitting pitches out of the strike zone stayed with me. Once you get a reputation, it is hard to shake. That is why I am spending some time explaining. I may even have learned something I didn't know.

I started this chapter by writing about my biggest thrill. Writers often ask who was the best pitcher or the best umpire (worst one, too). I try to duck those questions because on one day the best pitcher couldn't get me out and the next day the worst one could. So it seemed foolish to ask questions like that. I know I have asked some foolish questions, so I am only saying how I feel as a player. I don't think it's foolish to write about some of my biggest thrills. To tell you the truth, I was looking forward to this part.

As I said, making the Hall of Fame is number one. The reason I started off with the Larsen perfect game is that it was the first time in a World Series and it has not happened since. The questions about my biggest thrill went something like this, and you can see from my answers why the Larsen game didn't get an A.

Question: Would you have put the Larsen game second if you had been playing shortstop?

Yogi: Yes.

Question: Then it was not the fact that you and Larsen were the battery?

Yogi: No.

Question: In other words, it was your participation in the event?

Yogi: Yes.

Question: Put another way, did you feel that you, as Don Larsen's catcher, called a perfect game?

Yogi: He never shook me off.

Question: Can you recall every pitch in that game?

Yogi: No.

Question: Well, Yogi, I am still amazed. The perfect game might be called by some serious baseball students a fluke. Well, not a fluke really but sort of like an eclipse. But being voted the Most Valuable Player in the American League, and don't forget the guys who voted were writers, and they were never that kind to you, would be number two to me.

Yogi: Well, why not make being voted MVP three times number one and the Perfect game number two?

Question: You were not only MVP, you should have been voted MAP, Most Accommodating Player. All I am trying to do is to find out how you sorted out all your thrills and you changed the order of the first two.

Yogi: I tried to get along, and I still try to get along. The questions made me think. I don't sit around and think about how to rate my thrills. I would rather play golf and get some new ones.

I tried to say a while back that you shouldn't be proud of something you didn't do—something that just happened. But you should be happy about it. Don't take credit for it, but don't forget to add it to the "good things" list. Here is something from that list. My childhood hero, Joe Medwick, was picked up by the Yankees after he had been released by the Dodgers. He did not stay with the Yankees long, but he did help me a lot in spring training. He was not an outfielder like Terry Moore. He was more like me, so he could help me, and Bucky Harris made it his job. I would like to say that my boyhood hero and newspaper customer and I became buddies. I can't, and I think it was because he was with the Yankees only a short while. It was not the best time for him. It never is in the last days of a baseball career. Baseball players get old twice. He stayed around for one more year, playing 20 games for the Cards in 1948. He was elected to the Baseball Hall of Fame in 1968. I felt good for him. He was a great ballplayer—and a good tipper.

I don't know if Joe Medwick was proud that he wore the Yankee pinstripes, proud that he wore them even for a short time. I am not sure I was, either, when I was first given a uniform. My number was 47. I am proud now. In some ways wearing a Yankee uniform for 25 years was the biggest thrill I ever had. When I really think about it, like I have to for this book, going to Yankee Stadium and putting on the pinstripes was the best thing that ever happened to me. What I am trying to say is that you can hit the first pinch-hit home run in a World Series, play in more World Series games than anybody so far, all that great stuff, but if you love baseball, played with the best in the world, and for 25 years put on a uniform worn by Babe Ruth, Lou Gehrig, and Joe D., that is the biggest thrill of all because it is so long lasting. Somebody said I was what all men hope to be, a famous and gifted athlete. The guy who said that to me was a good friend, and what I said to him I am not going to put in here. But I am going to say that being a Yankee was all it was cracked up to be and then some.

Let me explain in another way because I want you to understand. A friend left Montclair and moved to New Mexico. I asked him if he missed the Jersey Shore, the New York Giants, things like that. The answer I got was he really didn't miss those things because at most he spent a week at the shore and went to six or seven Giants games. What he missed was the *New York Times*. He missed it every day. I am not saying he wanted to leave the little town in New Mexico, but sometimes everyday pleasures can be better than having fun once a week.

I used to go to Yankee Stadium 75 or 80 times a year, most years a few more times in October. I had a place to park—not an assigned spot, but I parked in the same place. I got there early, in the middle of the day, so I didn't get caught in traffic. When I got to what would be my desk if I were going to an office, Pete Sheehy had clean socks and a sweatshirt all laid out. Not just for me, for all of us. My uniform was clean and hanging up, and if you wanted coffee, gum, or a candy bar, it was all right there. I would get dressed and maybe shave, or maybe I would take a shower and get in the whirlpool for a few minutes and get a rub on a sore arm. We would go out into the stadium and it would be almost empty. That was nice. No smoke. On some days with a big crowd, the smoke haze really hung in the ballpark. I would take batting practice, take infield, go back to the clubhouse, and go over the hitters. It made me feel good to know that I was good at that. Then I would go back out and play a game I loved.

Other Voices
AL ROSEN

Al Rosen, the general manager of the San Francisco Giants, spent his playing days with the American League's Cleveland Indians. Rosen is on the 1950's All-Decade vintage team for the American League. He is at third base. Berra is behind the plate. Mickey Vernon is at first base and Nellie Fox is at second. The SS is Chico Carrasquel. The outfield is Williams, Mantle, and Kaline. The pitchers are Ford, Wynn, and Mossi. The utility man is McDougald. Rosen would also be on the best-dressed baseball executives list if one exists. Rosen knows how to dress well. It may spring from his days as an executive in the gaming industry in Atlantic City.

His voice is soft like Sydney Greenstreet's in The Maltese Falcon. *It generates affection and respect, rather than evil. You would hope to find him teaching math. If you had trouble with fractions or Comparative Religion at Yale. If you were trying to find yourself.*

"I will be happy to talk about Yogi Berra but on one condition," *Rosen says.* "You will have to convince me you will not try to hold him up to ridicule. That's been done and I want no part of it." *Rosen listens to the rationale, then excuses himself for an instant. He wanted to comment to Bob Kennedy, Giants' farm director. Taking the mo-*

ment away from the questions about Berra was not to give Rosen time to think. He did not need time for that. He seized the moment for the objective of his job: Win the National League West.

Rosen has spotted what he perceives as a flaw in the pitching motion of a minor league prospect he is watching along with other Giant brass. Rosen does so without the drama associated with a General Curtis Lemay, but the results are the same: action. Al Rosen is an executive.

Convinced that Berra is not in harm's way, Rosen warms to his task. "They said he didn't look like a Yankee. During the ten years I spent playing for the Indians he looked like Mr. Yankee to me. He did to all of us. They say he couldn't throw, couldn't catch, couldn't run, didn't know where the strike zone was. All they said was he couldn't or didn't, and he did. And he did it when it hurt you. I used to wonder if he bore down as hard the first two times he got up, just what he would have done. On the other hand, he knew how to pace himself. I guess if I were Yogi Berra, I wouldn't change a thing. He knew what he was doing when a lot of others didn't. He knew how to make a living doing something he loved and would have done for nothing. He has a wonderful wife and three boys who are good looking. I will bet he is the happiest man I know, and he should be. He has done his best to be good to everyone he ever met, from the White House to the clubhouse.

"After they said he couldn't and didn't all those years, you would think it would stop when somebody was smart enough to make him the manager. You know that story. I also know this story. When the National League teams

come out on the field and see him hitting fungos, they all
wish they had a Yogi Berra. Too bad there aren't enough
to go around."

Maybe I would get a hit and help the team. Or maybe
I would make a good play. I can say that I always tried
to give my best, so even if I made an error and cost
us the game, I didn't mope about it. At least not for
long. The mope was gone before I got to the George
Washington Bridge. If it wasn't, Carmen wouldn't let
me in the house. I am only kidding about that, but
she helped keep things in balance. Can you beat it? I
don't think so. But I really don't miss playing. I think
if you do miss it, at least all the time, you ought to
get some help. You know when you start that it can't
last. You know it, so you shouldn't be surprised when
it stops. I know some guys miss playing and miss it
so much it hurts. That is sad. As I said, they ought to
get some help. Life has to go on.

I played on a team with players who liked each
other. That was true. It was also important. When you
were sent up to pinch-hit or were told to start at second
base, or whatever else you were told to do, you knew
that at least twenty guys were pulling for you. Maybe
even more. That made you feel good, like you belonged. If your car broke down, you could call one of
them and they would come and get you. I never had
to. Maybe if I had called Whitey, he would have said,
"Call a wrecker. I'm mowing the lawn." But you felt
like you could call him. You felt like you could call

most of them, and that they could call you. I don't know how it could happen again that same way. I really don't. Life is so different now, how can baseball be the same?

Several weeks ago I bought a *New York Times* from a vending machine. Stamped on the front page in red ink was this message: IF YOU BOUGHT THIS FROM A NEWS STAND OR IT WAS DELIVERED TO YOUR HOME IT WAS STOLEN. FOR A REWARD CALL, and then they gave a phone number. I don't know what that red stamp tells you, but it tells me that times have changed. The *New York Times* costs 35 cents. I think that is a bargain and also a sad thing that people steal a 35-cent newspaper. I sold newspapers and it was not in the best part of town, but if I had to go to the bathroom, I could leave my stack of papers on the ground. I never lost one that way.

Other Voices
ANGIE DICKINSON

"The Lyon's Den," a gossip column written by Leonard Lyons, never matched Walter Winchell's circulation, but one item in a Lyons' column of the middle 1950s did generate interest in unusual quarters: the Harvard Economics Department and the New York Yankees clubhouse.

"Angie Dickinson is probably the only Hollywood star to have dinner at 21 on Monday with Yogi Berra of the New York Yankees and on Tuesday with John Kenneth Galbraith of Harvard University." Angie Dickinson, Kulm, North Dakota's gift to TV and the movies, remem-

bers the dinners. This is not surprising since she considers herself a friend of the Berra family.

Describing Berra in the husky voice that has become a trademark, Angie says, "His easy-going way is of course very appealing. He is a full fledged Taurus. That is one reason he is so specific. He is basic. His attitude is earth-bound. He is like a quiet stream—placid, tranquil. A stream—one that is easy to sit by. You don't feel as though you have to talk when you are with him, but in order to describe him you have to pretend you are with him. He is not easy to sum up, but he is an easy man and so at ease with himself. The thing that shocks my friends who have not met him but have only seen him play or read about him is his sensual aura. 'Angie,' they will say, 'Yogi Berra sexy? Come on, that makes me laugh.'

"Sensual and sexy are not the same but are connected, and he may be both. He is not reaching out to impress you, and where I live that makes you different for starters. I think what made him a great hitter and a great catcher is that he was and is so centered. Things don't bother him. Maybe it is better to say he will not let things bother him.

"I know he can lose his composure because I have seen him flap with an umpire more than once. I will also never forget one time I took him and Whitey Ford to dinner. They thought I was at least a little bit nifty. They said they did anyway. They did, that is, until Marilyn Monroe sat down at a table about fourteen feet away. Both of them came unraveled. You know, the nice part about Yogi is that he did it with such style. Not that Whitey didn't, but you know Whitey is a city kid. They are very different. Maybe that is one reason they got along so well.

"At any rate, Whitey was ga-ga and Yogi couldn't eat. He just kept saying 'MaDone.' Marilyn had rendered him speechless."

◆

I loved playing, and I was good because I worked hard and had some ability. I also had what is called today a good attitude. Some writers have tried to get me to bad mouth Ted Williams because he would take a pitch and maybe walk when a hit might have won the game. He would walk, and I might have swung and gotten a hit or made an out. Or maybe I missed and moved the count say from 2 balls and 1 strike to 2 and 2. The pitcher may be thinking, "That was a waste pitch! What's going on?" My point is that Ted made a decision, and I did, too. It worked for him. The pitcher knew he would not swing at a bad pitch. That put some pressure on the pitcher. In my case you might say the pitcher was saying to himself, "Berra wouldn't know a good pitch if he saw one." I don't think you should say that. I don't think you should for two reasons. One is that I knew a good pitch. In other words, I knew the strike zone. The second is that counting World Series games I got over 2000 hits—okay, 2221. Some of them, a lot of them, came off pitches in the strike zone.

When people try to get me to second-guess what Ted did, I say, "If you were a manager, would you want him on your side?" Nobody says, "No." I said that one time to a reporter who had been a baseball player. He said, "No," and then added, "You know,

Yogi, from all I have heard about you, I would like a team full of guys like you." I am serious; it was one of my big thrills.

To get back to the 9-to-5 part of the job, I was paid well and people asked me out to dinner and picked up the tab. If I did well, I was cheered. I was never booed at home, and when I was booed on the road I was proud. I must be good or they wouldn't be booing me. I don't know if you can tell one boo from another, but I think I can. I was never booed as a player when I thought it was really a mean boo. I know that I lay myself open now by saying mean and boo, but what the heck. So, wouldn't you say I had a good job? It sure beat the other jobs I was offered.

When you stop to think about it, just being lucky enough to be born in this country is something to be thankful for. Just that alone. Think about the number of people who want to live here. For me to have the dream of playing in the big leagues, and to do it and to do it for so many years, well it was great. To look back and try to describe how it all felt is really hard. They said I had to, so I tried.

I don't want to be accused of being so dull-witted that I walked around with a dumb smile on my face for nineteen years. I also do not believe that big league baseball is played by little boys who never grow up. You can bet that was written by a writer. I suppose I could come up with a better way of saying that, but that is what I mean so that is the way I am going to say it.

Baseball can be a cruel game. When you don't hit and you make errors, it can be a long afternoon. It is also true that even the best of times have down periods. Even when it is good it can seem bad part of the time. I've been told I was good about not taking the game home with me, and the people who said that knew me. They also knew other ballplayers and were comparing me with them. Like you compare two pitchers. So I would think they were right. Even if they were wrong it made me feel good.

Trying to explain this in a different way, I suppose you could say I was happy. I knew it, and I knew that if I worked hard and kept myself in good shape it could go on. Sometimes Carm and I used to say, "Wouldn't it be great just to freeze everything." You couldn't of course, and the only reason I am saying it is to show you I knew how good things were going for us. A lot of people want to get through something. I was enjoying the ride. During a lot of my life if some genie had asked me, "What can I do for you, Yogi?" I would have said, "Hold everything, Genie, just the way it is." It was nice to be a young father. Getting older has some nice things, too. Maybe you just have to look harder for them. Art Linkletter has a book out about how to get old and be happy, but I have been so busy I haven't had time to read it. They say that it is good.

Since I mentioned being well paid, I guess I should talk about how much I earned. Let me start with what I thought about what I made and what some of my teammates thought about my salary, even thirty years later. Gil McDougald, the Yankee from San Francisco who could play short, second, and third, used to say this. In fact, he still says it. "If Yogi had been more aggressive in his dealings with George Weiss and gotten more money, we all could have gotten more money." I want to say a few things about Gil McDougald, but if I do that right now what I have to say might get lost. Some people might think money is more important than what I want to say. If you don't have any, it might be.

I admired Gil when he first joined the team. I do now and did all the time he was with the Yankees. He was class. You may have forgotten, but it was Gil's hitting a ball back through the box that cost Herb Score his career. Some doctors said it almost cost him his life. Herb Score was a great pitcher for Cleveland, and he was never the same again. Gil looked the same afterward. He played a few more years, but I know he really thought about quitting when the ball hit Score. It was not something for the press. He really thought it through. That is only one of the reasons I know he is a class guy. He was also a good father and husband. He was good at all the important things.

Money is important, but if Gil thought that what they paid me had anything to do with what the others were paid, he is wrong. Anybody on the team who thought that what I made was some sort of a gas gauge was wrong. Unless his name was George Weiss. He wasn't really on the team, although he had a lot to say about who was. I am kidding about George Weiss, and that is something not many people did. Even now.

I can explain how I felt about the money I earned and the money other players on the team earned, but first let me tell you how I feel now. Some of this I feel because working on this book brought a lot of it back.

As I've said, some of the Yankees seemed to think that I was kind of a gauge, and that if Weiss had paid me more, they might have been paid more. To anyone on the team who felt that way, I want to say again, "You're wrong." I also want to say that if you felt that way, it makes me feel awfully good to know it. It says something. It makes me feel better than money can make you feel.

George Weiss kept only two contracts, Joe D.'s and mine. Well, that's the way I feel when I hear that people thought I was a gauge or a barometer. Even though I wasn't one, it's nice your teammates thought you were. They called me some awful names, and now it's nice to have a new name, Berra the Barometer. Casey Stengel would love to hear that name. He almost always called me Mr. Berra. Sometimes he called me his catcher. The best thing he ever called me was, "Outside of DiMaggio, the greatest player I ever had to manage." Everybody was outside of Joe D. I think even Casey knew Joe was outside of Casey's influence. When Casey started in 1949, Joe was on the way out. Joe played over 1700 games but only 300 under Casey, so Casey didn't manage him as much as he saw him play. Some people on the team thought Casey was happy to see Joe go so that Casey could have more of the limelight. Maybe they were right, but I doubt it. You would have to be crazy not to want a DiMaggio on your team. Casey was not crazy.

As long as I am talking about Casey, here is one more story about him that may not be as funny as some but it sticks in my mind. Maybe that means it says something about him. A GI stationed at Fort Dix in New Jersey wrote Casey a long letter about a game. The soldier thought that Stengel stayed with Allie Reynolds too long. It was a good letter. By that I mean it made Casey think, and I have to admit I thought a little about it at the time. Not enough to signal to the bench, but I was thinking. When Casey finished the letter, he didn't say anything for a while and that alone sticks in my mind. A little later, Jackie Ferrell, who worked in the public relations office for the Yankees, came through the clubhouse. Casey said in that gruff voice, "Jackie, send this here soldier boy a letter and ask him if he is so damn smart, let's see him get out of the Army."

Getting back to money, and it seems like we do a lot. Guess that is the way it is, or has been lately, anyway. Unlike today, how much you made was not in the papers. Guesses, sure, but not down to the penny, and even the guesses were called guesses. We were told not to talk about what we made. Most of us didn't. I didn't, and no one else ever told me what he made. I am talking about most of my time as a player. Things changed, but not all at once.

Even if George Weiss had doubled my salary after I was voted MVP for the third time, I would not tell anybody. So, what I made didn't matter to anybody else. Gil might know something about a payroll. I don't. He runs a successful business, so he might, but I doubt it.

My first real year with the Yankees was 1947. I made $5000. Then I made $5830 for seven games in October—the winner's share of the World Series. The way I played, I didn't feel like a winner, but let me get to that in a minute. I don't know how that five grand seems to you now. I am told that when you do a book like this, some of the readers don't know who Tom Mix was, or Arthur Godfrey, or Hopalong Cassidy. And the guy writing it doesn't know who Earth, Wind, and Fire are, or Sean Penn, and a whole lot of other people as well. Milton Friedman told me that one good way to understand the value of money is to compare. I think he said he used to teach about two and a half days to buy a suit. He said that's pretty much true today. Inflation is the general way he describes it, and I want to get out of this just as soon as I can. I also want to say this. When I was making $5000 in 1947, I was paying $3.50 a day to stay at the Edison Hotel. It was on West 47th Street just off Broadway. It was not the best hotel in New York City, but it was a good hotel and a room like that today would be way over $100. Maybe even $150. So you can see that $5000 was not bad, and I got more than twice that if you count the World Series.

Other Voices
SPUD CHANDLER

Eighty-two-year-old Spud Chandler put on a clean shirt for the interview. The full-color picture of Spurgeon Ferdinand Chandler in Yankee pinstripes dominated the living room in St. Petersburg, Florida. Chandler, along with Lefty Gomez and Red Ruffing, was a dominant Yankee pitcher. Vin Scully would describe him as a stylish righty and refer to his ERA as sparkling. He won 109 and lost 43 during his 11-year career. His .717 winning percentage is the highest in baseball history among pitchers with 100 or more career victories. The huge living room photograph is in sharp contrast to the frail figure in the chair remembering the first time he pitched to Yogi Berra. It was Berra's first major league game. Yogi's subsequent success made Chandler's memory even more vivid. Chandler was eager to talk about Berra. His exploits surfaced through questions about his relationship with "his" catcher. He thought of Berra that way. At age 82 he still thinks of himself as Berra's pitcher. "Bill Dickey caught me, but I pitched to Yogi," smiled Chandler.

"I had no idea I was pitching to a 'National Treasure,' but Dr. Bobby Brown, and he is president of the American League you know, told me that, so it must be right," said Spud with obvious joy.

"Do you remember Carmen Berra, Yogi's wife?" Spud was asked. Spud takes a moment and says, "Why, yes. She was a lot better looking than Yogi." The questioner went on, "She told me that she did not remember much about you except that when she met you, she was in awe." "She was in what?" asked Chandler. "In awe, in awe," the questioner replied. "What?" was the repeated answer. Three In awes and three Whats?.

A painful moment, as the guests in Chandler's modest home think surely "awe" was a term Spud would have encountered during his four years at the University of Georgia. Spud spun the dial on his hearing aid, and like a man tamping his pipe, gave the threesome a momentary time out.

Billy Jurges squirmed. He was a fine Cub and New York Giant shortstop and manager of the Red Sox in 1960–61, and a long-time Chandler friend. He had ar-

ranged the session. Jurges would be 80 in a few days, but he quickly moved in as he might have charged a topped ground ball. "She admired you quite a bit . . . she thought you were . . . she thought you were something."

Spud's face brightened, and with slow-cooked Georgia relish said, "She were right." Jurges and his companion laughed, still chagrined at the selection of the term "awe." Perhaps more than the rejoinder merited. Spud warmed to the moment, possibly thinking, the guy may write okay, but he doesn't talk good. "She were right . . . I won't argue with her. I was terrific. They called me Mr. Terrific."

Chandler went on to say, "Joe McCarthy, the Yankees' manager, told me I would be pitching to this young rookie. It was 1946, late in the season. I understand Yogi feels that since we were out of the pennant race he was given a chance, but I doubt it. We all knew he was special, and he was going to get a chance race or no race, I am sure of that.

"McCarthy said, 'Just carry him along.' He knew I would because I had good control and did what I was told—at least most of the time. The only time I didn't was sometimes in the sixth or seventh inning when I wasn't pitching. I would get tired of yelling at the opposition. McCarthy thought that was part of our job. Ragging the other pitcher and players within earshot was, as he saw it, like showing up at the park on time and ready to play. McCarthy would look down the bench and yell, 'Get on 'em, get on 'em.' I cranked up my patter of insults as did the rest of us, but I didn't like it. I also didn't think it did any good except to tire us out, sometimes make the other team mad, and most of all showed us who was boss. And he was the boss. The managers all were in those days.

"Sometimes it was good to get on one player. For example, Zeke Bonura played first base for the White Sox and the Washington Senators. If he booted one (and he could hit a lot better than he could field), we would all yell at him, hoping he would press and boot another one. Most of us knew who had rabbit ears and when to yell and when to shut up. I never heard anyone yell at Joe D. But just yelling like a barker in front of a Wild West Show had no pay-off. I'm told they don't do that so much now, and that is one change I like.

"McCarthy was smart about a lot of the game. He knew that I would not have Yogi jumping in and out and up and down. Joe knew I had good control and even more important, I knew I had good control. That was important if Yogi was to gain confidence. The scouting reports on him was that he was a boxer. That is, he jumped around a lot. So if the pitcher was also a boxer, you would have two jitterbugs. Yogi could hit, but he couldn't catch. But anyone could catch me that year. I was 20 and 8.

"I will never forget that first game. Yogi was so self-conscious that he did not know how to give the signs. He gave them way out on his leg, almost at the knee. I called time and told him, 'Berra, they are going to pick your teeth (steal the signs) if you don't get the signs down in your crotch. Don't let the signs hang out that way, they will steal us blind.' He tried but when he hid the signs, it was still hard for me to see his stubby fingers and I crossed him up a couple of times. He would call for a curve ball and I saw the fast ball sign, so I hummed him up a fast ball. The second time I did he called time and came out. He said in a plaintive voice, 'You crossed me up!' I

*countered, 'The hell I did—I didn't cross you up, you
crossed yourself up.'*

"When the inning was over and we went into the
dugout, I told him to go through his signs. He did and it
was painful. His fingers were short and he moved them so
fast that it was hard to pick them up even a few feet away.
Sixty feet, six inches was really a problem. This next part
may sound like bragging, but I am trying to tell you what
Yogi had to deal with. My control was good, but I also
threw five pitches. It was the end of the line for me, and
over the years I had come up with the five. Fast ball, curve,
slider, screw ball, and (I hope some of the San Francisco
Giants see this) a fork ball. Yogi had to give five signs to
a guy 20 years his senior, and he did so quickly because he
was nervous and on top of that he had small fingers. All
this just meant we would get crossed up, and we did.

"The first inning it bothered him when I told him to
move the signs. He was nervous. I told him to slow the
signs down and spread his fingers so I could tell how many
were down. I worked with him and later in the game the
trainer put white tape on his fingers and it worked out.
He was special and we all knew it, and it was not just
that he hit a home run that first game—a lot of guys have
done that and never mattered. He was the kind of guy
you wanted to do well. You pulled for him, and that was
not always the case, even with some very fine players. Some
of them just got run off. They could play but they couldn't
fit in. He was not only special, he was so self-conscious it
bothered me. You know some guys came to the Yankees
and tried to act like it didn't matter even though it did.
I guess they say 'cool' today. Well, it did matter to Yogi.

We knew it and he didn't know how to act as if it didn't. He was a natural. A natural hitter, and when he became a good and then great catcher, he stopped being self-conscious. Funny thing, now that he is in the Hall of Fame and rich and famous, he still isn't self-conscious. Maybe if he were good looking and rich and famous he would be.

"I have never talked this much or this long about Yogi. I am pleased you knew I was the first to pitch to him in the big leagues," said Chandler.

Spud shows no shake-off sign, so the question is asked. "You say he was not a good catcher. Is that because you were used to Bill Dickey? Berra caught in Triple A at Newark and in a fast league in the Navy."

Chandler takes a Georgia moment and says, "He was in tough shape for two reasons. One, he was worried about his catching. And two, he had good reason—he was not a good catcher.

"The thing that sticks in my mind is how much better he got the second year. It was hard for me to believe how good he got and how quickly he did so. He went from being a boxer who fought the ball to being a fine catcher, then after I left, to being a great one. Bill Dickey got a lot of credit as did George Weiss for bringing Bill back to work with Yogi. But looking back, Yogi must have practiced at home at night to get that good that fast.

"He was very quickly loved by most of us, although I would not have used that term about another man in 1949. Perhaps the kids taught us something. But he could not do two things. Play golf or play poker. He had that pop in his wrist, but it did not carry over to golf. Allie Reynolds could beat him at golf and so could Mrs. Reynolds.

He used to go home mad from the Ridgewood (N.J.) Country Club every time she beat him, which I believe was every time they played.

"*It was a joy to see him break in and to follow his growth. I wish it could have been longer. I wish I had played for Stengel. Yogi and Chandler would have had some fun. Joe McCarthy was too serious.*

"*This is a tonic for me," says Chandler. "Any more questions?"*

"*Yes," was the reply. "Allie Reynolds said that with a fast runner on first base, Yogi called too many high fast balls, making the catcher's job of throwing the runner out that much easier but putting the pitcher in a hole."*

"*Well, I can't recall that," smiled Chandler, "but I never did like to see them get too far off first base. I had them marry the old bag, so I did not have that problem. I know all about the conflict between the catcher and the pitcher.*

"*Sure I have some regrets. In some ways I wish I had taken the coaching job at the University of Georgia. It would have meant a longer career. I hated to quit and I miss it every day, but you have to quit any job some day. Playing for the New York Yankees was the best thing that ever happened to me, and I bet Yogi feels the same. I saw him on the way up and I was on the way down. I wish he had seen me get his buddy, Stan Musial, to hit into a game-ending double play in the 1942 World Series. But I am sure he didn't have money for a ticket in those days. Now he could own a baseball team. If I had his money, I would throw mine away."*

Also, Jurges said as we were leaving, "Tommy is sorry he used the word 'awe' when we first started talking with you." Chandler replied, "Oh, well, that's okay. I didn't always select the right pitch, but I did most of the time. He got by with it."

◆

Playing in my first World Series. Pinch yourself. Just think of all the ways to describe how good you can feel and then add inflation. I didn't grow up wanting to play baseball for the Yankees. I wanted to play baseball. I would have been happy playing baseball for the Cards or the Browns or the Tigers or the Phillies. Baseball is one thing, the World Series is something else. I knew what it meant to play in the World Series. I knew what it meant to be on a World Series team. I even knew what it meant to see a World Series game. I had seen Joey Garagiola in the Cards—Red Sox games the year before. The games in St. Louis. Joey did better in Boston, where he didn't have the home-town pressure. He played well and for each of us to get into a Series so early was very lucky. As I have said, some guys never get into one. Buddy Bell, who played for the Astros last year, has played in over 1700 games and not one has been in the October classic.

The 1947 World Series seems to fit in the memory chapter, so even though some of the memory is painful, let me tell you about it. I had done pretty well playing the $5000 part of the season. I hit .280, had 11 home runs, caught 51 games, and played 24 games in the outfield. I scored 41 runs and had 54 RBIs. What I had done—and I know this now more than I did then—was not important to manager Bucky Harris.

This is a little complicated. The regular season is long. Bucky was now trying to win four straight games. He was trying to win them not from one of the other seven teams in the American League, but from the best team in the National League, the Brooklyn Dodgers. If you were a lumberjack, you might use one saw to cut a tree down and another one to cut the tree up. Bucky faced a different problem in the Series. As I said, I know a lot more about that now than I did then. Mayo Smith, the manager of the Detroit Tigers in 1968, knew all about Bucky's problem. During the 1968 season, Oyler, Matchick, and Tracewski played shortstop. Their combined batting average was around .200. Mickey Stanley played most of the year in center field. I won't go into the reasons why because I don't know them, but Mayo Smith moved Stanley to shortstop. Tracewski and Oyler did not get an at-bat during the seven-game Series. Matchick had three at-bats and hit .000. All three of them cashed winner's checks. The Tigers won the Series mostly because of another Mickey, Mickey Lolich. I still feel it is an example of what a manager has to do.

I was pleased that after I wrote about Mayo Smith and Mickey Stanley, *Sports Illustrated* did a story on that move. The writer, Donald Hall, knew a lot more than I did about why Smith did what he did. It's a long story and a good one. I guess it is okay to say it was in the October 17, 1988, issue. Well, back to Mayo Smith or any manager in his spot. What is that old saying, "You should take home the girl who asked you to the dance"? Something like that. Well, in baseball you don't dance unless you win, and you may need a new partner for the Series if you are going to dance by the Harvest Moon. If you are wondering where I got that line, I got it from Nick Pirore. He has been in the Yankee clubhouse for almost thirty years and he knows a lot. He really is good with words. If he would ever talk with reporters, you could get a good book but, just like Pete Sheehy, he won't. He loved Joe D. He told me once that when Joe D. came into a room, the lights flickered. Not just the clubhouse, any room.

Bucky Harris might have set me down and not let me play at all in that first Series. Maybe some people think he should have. He didn't keep me on the bench, but he had to think about playing somebody else. At least, I think he had to. One thing in favor of my playing was that Bucky had seen me play the year before for Newark. He managed Buffalo and had seen me in 15 or 16 games. What I am saying is that he had seen me more than just that season. You should always think when a manager makes a move—any move, pinch hitter, pinch runner, new pitcher—that he knows something. I mean you should think this when watching any game. A lot of people do. People don't boo if they haven't been thinking. But sometimes managers wish they would think a little more before booing. Every move has a reason, if only to get the game over quickly so we can play tomorrow or to see how someone can pitch when he is seven runs behind.

Bucky Harris didn't say anything to me about what he was thinking. I didn't expect him to, and I am just putting it down here because today the manager might be expected to talk to me and my agent if we were in the same situation. I said "*might*."

Bucky had me catch the first two games. The first game I was 0 for 4, and both Jackie Robinson and Pee Wee Reese stole on me. You know, sometimes the TV announcers say the runner "stole on the pitcher." They didn't say it this time. I am not going to blame World Series jitters. I am not going to do more than say I was not good. We won both games, and Bucky had Sherman Lollar, who had spent most of that season with Newark, catch the third game. It was played in Ebbets Field. Maybe Bucky felt playing me in that tiny park full of wild Dodger fans would shake me more than I already was. In that park the fans were right on top of you, and they could really let you have it. Later on I didn't mind. I don't know what was in Bucky's mind. It would never cross my mind to ask. Maybe he was told by the owners to take me out, but I doubt it.

We lost the third game, 9 to 8. It was a wild game. They got 13 hits and we got 13. The game took over three hours, a long game for 1947. Joe D. hit a home run, and I hit the first pinch-hit home run in World Series history. I felt better. If Hugh Casey, the great Dodger bullpen ace, had been sick, we might have won. He wasn't. After I pinch-hit the home run off Ralph Branca, they brought him in, and as Casey Stengel used to say, "That was that." I see Ralph Branca during the winter. We talk about that home run. He likes to say that I bring it up. I don't, but I thought I should here. It was the first one. The first pinch-hit home run in a World Series, and I am only sorry it didn't win the game.

The fourth game was also in Brooklyn. This is the sort of memory you would like to block out when you are feeding pigeons in the park. I was a pigeon in the ballpark that Frank Sinatra used to sing about, Ebbets Field. I don't remember all the words to the song Sinatra sang, but one of the lines was: "And there used to be a ballpark right here." It was a sad song about the Dodgers leaving Brooklyn.

Here is what happened. The game started with the Yankees leading the Series 2 games to 1. Our pitcher was Bill Bevens. That year he was 7 and 13, so you can see why Bucky didn't start him in the first game. I am not trying to be nasty. Bevens was a fine pitcher or he would not have been on the team—even on the World Series team. Sometimes they add guys late in the year just for the Series when they think they are going to win. Sometimes they drop guys, too. Guys who may have helped win the season don't play in the Series. The manager doesn't feel he fits in. But anybody who is in a World Series is good. Let me get a little bit ahead of myself and say this. It used to make me mad as hell to have writers say Don Newcombe, the Dodger pitcher, "choked." You don't choke and win 19 games. He lost some big games. Somebody's got to. One of the reasons I like Jerry Coleman is that he feels the same way about the word "choke." Newcombe helped get the Dodgers to the World Series by winning big games.

To get back to the fourth game, and maybe I am talking about how great Don Newcombe was so I can take some time before I have to mention the fourth game. In that game Bevens was a great pitcher. I had not caught over 2000 games at that time, but I have now and he was great. Like Larsen or Allie Reynolds when they pitched no-hitters. In a trance. Throwing the ball just where they wanted and every time. Bevens had a no-hitter going. Even though he was throwing a no-hitter, they got a run in the fifth inning. He was throwing a no-hitter and his catcher was throwing the ball into center field. I know he walked two in that inning and eight in the game, but he didn't throw the ball into center when Pee Wee Reese stole second. I did. The late Dick Young, a New York writer who could be nasty sometimes, described one steal in that Series as "number seven on the weak-winged Yankee backstop corps." It was a clever way to describe Sherm Lollar, Lawrence Peter Berra, and Aaron Robinson, but I was not weak-winged. I threw the ball clear into center field.

So here is the picture. Last of the ninth. We are the visiting team in a ballpark as small or smaller than Wrigley Field. Bill Bevens is three outs away from the first no-hitter in World Series history. The no-hitter may seem big now, but it was the win we all wanted. Bevens was one of the "all." Can't you just hear Vin Scully? I sure can. I can sure remember how I felt. I had been made to feel welcome by my teammates. I am talking about the whole year. Remember, this is really my first year and first World Series. But I had been written about a lot, and most of it was not good. When I went out for the ninth inning I was sweating, and I could feel the back of my neck getting hot.

Last of the ninth. Bruce Edwards was the first hitter. He was the Dodger catcher, I think he came up when he was almost 30 years old—another way baseball is different; now only the younger guys are brought up. Bruce lined out to the late Johnny Lindell in right. Bevens walked Carl Furillo. One out, man on first. Burt Shotton, the Dodger manager, put in Al Gionfriddo to run for Furillo—a move I second-guessed, so you see we do it, too, like the GI at Fort Dix. Al had come to the Dodgers in May of that year in a $100,000 trade that involved five players going from Brooklyn to Pittsburgh and Little Al, as he was called, coming to the Dodgers. Kirby Higbe, Hank Behrman, Cal McLish, my buddy Gene Mauch, and Dixie Howell went to the Pirates. Some things in base-ball haven't changed all that much. General managers and owners think they can trade for the pennant, and sometimes they can. I am sure they thought this was one of the times.

Johnny Jorgensen, they called him Spider, fouled out to George McQuinn. We had two out, we were ahead by one run, and Bill Bevens from Oregon was one out from the Oregon Hall of Fame, if they have one.

Burt Shotton used a pinch-hitter for Hugh Casey. He had to, and no one could second-guess that move. He brought in Peter Reiser. Pistol Pete, and since I made that reference to Tom Mix and others, you may not know much about Pete. He was like few players, ever. He would try to run through a wall to catch a ball, and he did and paid the price. You could write a chapter on him in a sports medicine book or a sports psychology book. You could, I couldn't, but I can tell you he played like the game was life or death. One year the Dodgers played an exhibition game in Springfield, Missouri. As they got off the bus a TV reporter interviewed a lot of them. He asked them where they thought they would finish, and he meant in the standings. When he asked Pete he said, "In the hospital."

As I said, he was banged up a lot, and this was no exception. His ankle was bad. I was told later that he had broken it the day before but wouldn't let the doctor put a cast on it because the Dodgers would say he was a "problem" when they talked contract the next spring. Strike one. Two more and we win. Bevens is a hero. Ball one. The next pitch was low, and Gionfriddo, who had gotten a real good jump, took off for second. I said before the announcers will say, "He stole that on the pitcher." I don't know what they said this time, but I do know my throw was high, and by the time Phil Rizzuto jumped up, caught the ball, and put it on another Italian, Gionfriddo, he was safe.

Two little guys at second, Phil standing next to the bag and Al on it. Bucky Harris gave me the sign to put Peter Reiser on. In other words, to finish the job and walk him. This was the sort of move that would bring out the second-guessers, and I guess it should. Most baseball people feel you should never put on the winning run. The winning runner might get on, but you don't walk him, even if his name is Babe Ruth. Announcers always seem to think a man should score from second on a single, but sometimes he doesn't. So if Pete hit one to, say, short right, maybe Henrich could hold the runner at third. As I said, if the winning run gets on, it should be because the other team makes a hit or you make an error. You don't walk the winning run. That is an error. I guess you would say it is error, Manager. The other team must get on base themselves. You don't give it to them. That's what the baseball book is supposed to say. Bucky went against the book. I am not second-guessing him. I mean that. I am just setting him up for you. But remember, soon you will have 20/20 vision. Bucky didn't, and he had maybe 90 seconds to make the move. If he asked one or two of his coaches for advice, maybe he only had 30 seconds.

Harris thought the next hitter would be Eddie Stanky, who was not a threat to hit a long ball. The Dodgers had already used Arky Vaughan, a left-handed batter. I bet that most people thought Shotton would go with Stanky, hoping to keep the inning going with a walk or hit or an error on the Yankees. But he sent in Eddie Miksis to run for Reiser and Cookie Lavagetto to hit for Stanky. I knew Cookie. He told me later he thought he was going in to run for Reiser. I don't know how many other Dodgers thought that was going to be Shotton's move, but I will bet Cookie was not alone. Cookie was all alone now. If it had been several years later, I would have asked him what he was going to do if he struck out. Or do you still like a fast ball away? Or are you still afraid of the ball inside? When I had been playing for a few years, I talked to every hitter. Like I would say to Al Kaline, "Hear they are going to trade you to the White Sox. Think you will like Chicago?" I said nothing to Cookie and nothing to Bevens, but I gave the sign.

Cookie dug in. Strike one. The next pitch was a ball. It was a ball for most people, and Cookie was a part-time player and it was a ball for him. He whipped the bat around and creamed that high pitch on a line to right field. Ballplayers call a hit like that a frozen rope. It gave us the shivers. It hit the wall on the fly. Not close to going over, but Tommy Henrich never had a chance. The ball seemed to hit the wall as Tommy moved. It hit a shaving cream sign. By the time I got it back, we had egg on our face and Bevens had lost both his no-hitter and the game. Final score, Brooklyn 3, New York 2. Series tied at two each. Back to the House that Ruth Built—Yankee Stadium. One writer said it was the House that Ruth Built, furnished by Mantle. He said this much later. Mickey was working in a mine in Oklahoma at the time of the 1947 World Series.

The trip in this case was only a few miles, not like the Dodger–Yankee Series from L.A. to New York, but it seemed like a long way to me. All the time I was thinking that if I had thrown Gionfriddo out, the game would have been over. Cookie would have been in the shower, and we would have been up three games to one.

We won the next game. I did not play. To tell the truth, I was just as happy. When Lindell got hurt, I got into the sixth game and played right field. I had two hits, and we almost won. A ball that Joe DiMaggio hit back, way back—way back, as they say on radio and TV, and then "Wow! What a catch!" —was caught. Al Gionfriddo came out of nowhere to get it. He really did come out of nowhere. It was the only time I ever saw Joe show emotion on the field.

As Gionfriddo made an outstanding catch deep in left center, Joe D. was rounding second. When Joe saw the umpire signal the out, he kicked the ground. It was the only time I ever saw him do something like that. It was on TV, so you may have seen it. They replay it a lot around World Series time. Joe usually did not show emotion. I sometimes wonder, if he came up today, how he would handle the high fives after a run-scoring single. That may seem a little nasty, but I am trying to make the point that baseball has changed and so have a lot of other things. When I was growing up, you didn't hear about people living together. I was telling somebody in our clubhouse a few months ago, "When I was your age you couldn't hardly get a girl to do that." He thought it was funny, but I meant it in a serious way.

As long as I have said so much about my first World Series, I will go on to the last game. I am sure you can understand why I was happy not to catch in that one.

I started but didn't finish the game. I was a proud spear-carrier, and the heroes were Joe Page, Bobby Brown (who had three pinch-hits in the series), and Phil Rizzuto. It was the eleventh time the Yankees were World Champs. It was my first World Series ring, and I felt like I had been put through a wringer. I knew I had played in a World Series, and I knew that

Joe Garagiola had played in one, too. He hit .316 in his, batted in four runs, and didn't make an error. I batted .158 and had two RBIs. I am not going to talk anymore about my throws to second base. You can go back and read it again if you like, but it's over.

Sometimes a memory, even a good one, can be better for someone else. I will let you judge the next two. Playing baseball for a living means you are one of, say, a thousand guys paid to play in the big leagues that year. I don't know how many players have played baseball since 1846, but let's say a lot of them.

According to a poll taken in 1969, the one who was the best of all was Babe Ruth. Frank Crosetti thinks that every major league team should retire number three. That was Babe's number, and a lot of people think he saved baseball after the Black Sox scandal of 1919. Frank does, and he gets stars in his eyes when he tells you. I don't know if Frank is right, but he is old and smart and rich, so maybe he is. I do know this, a big thrill of mine was to be a player the day the Yankees held a day for Babe Ruth.

It was April 27, 1947. The Babe had not been out of the hospital very long, and they had to help him up the steps of the dugout. Cardinal Spellman offered the invocation, and Ruth took a deep breath and walked out to the microphone without help. The crowd stood and clapped, but not like the clapping for some old Yankee who came back for an Old-Timers' game. And it wasn't the kind of clapping and cheering Mickey got when he hit a home run off Barney Schultz to win a Series game for us in 1964. It was different. I don't want to get emotional, but I can tell you it was different. I think you can imagine why it was better.

Maybe you've seen the pictures of Ruth on that day. He was wearing a camel's-hair coat. He looked bad and sounded worse. He gave a short speech and said something about baseball being the only real game in the world. You knew he was not going to get any arguments on that. Not that day anyway. He thanked everybody and said he was glad he could do that. I mean he was glad he could thank people. That really stuck with me. Then he started back to the dugout. I don't remember who it was, but someone said, "He needs help." Someone spoke but no one moved. When he got to the dugout, Cardinal Spellman told him that if he would like Communion, he, the Cardinal, would come to his house. That really impressed me. Babe said, "Thanks, Cardinal Spellman, but I'll come down to your place." *Your place*. Only Babe Ruth would say, "Your place." He called everyone kid. He really did. Not the Cardinal, though.

Within a year he was dead. His body lay in state inside the main gate at Yankee Stadium. You know, I really don't know if I passed the casket or not. I somehow think I didn't, but I will never forget seeing him in the stadium, hearing his speech and his talk with Cardinal Spellman.

The second story also happened in a dugout. When Gil Hodges died, I was named manager of the New York Mets. At that time I had managed one year. We had won the pennant, but I don't need to go through that again. I was happy as a coach. I was very happy working for Hodges. When Casey Stengel and George Weiss left the Mets, Gil could have told me good-bye. A lot of guys would have said, "So long, Yogi." He didn't. I went in to see him to tell him I would leave. I told him I wanted to be where I was wanted. I didn't want a job because I was Yogi Berra. I thought I could help, but it was up to him. I really respected him. He treated everybody the same. Fairly. He would tell the bus driver, the driver who took the team to the park from the hotel, "If the bus is supposed to leave at 2, leave at 2, even if I am not on it. I don't care if it is empty, leave." One time the bus left Eddie Yost, Rube Walker, and Ralph Kiner (two coaches and the Mets broadcaster).

When he died both Carmen and I were afraid to say that we were crushed. People might say we were phonies because I got his job. When I say we were afraid to say how we felt, I mean to the press. Our friends knew how we felt about Gil. Even some of our good friends were surprised we liked a Dodger first baseman. All that is part of what I am going to tell you.

Opening day after Hodges died was special. The crowd was large, it was cold, the wind was blowing, and I was in the dugout next to a writer for *Big Red News*. The Mets had arranged for a young black kid from a military school (he was too young to be from the real military) to play taps. He started out of the dugout to play before the game and Carl Nestfield, the writer from *Big Red News*, said to me, "The kid's nervous." I said, "Yeah, me too." He thought it was nice.

Years earlier I saw Jimmy Cannon, the sportswriter, in the lobby of the Edison Hotel. You remember—$3.50 a day. He stayed in the hotel, too, and he got a special rate because he was full time. When I said "years earlier" even I was surprised when I figured out that it must have been 1949, so it was forty years ago. A lot of people never heard of Jimmy Cannon, so let me tell you he was a popular writer. While I was known for what they called "butchering" words, he was known for one-liners. He was the Henny Youngman of the sports page. A lot of his columns started with, "Nobody asked me," and then he would say, "Bet me the next guy you see drinking beer before noon needs a shave," or "A bald-headed man with a sun tan is the healthiest looking of the human species." That's the sort of thing he wrote, and he was popular, as I said. One I remember, "It's almost impossible for a dame to be ugly riding in a red roadster with the top down." I still haven't seen a woman driving any kind of red car with the top down. Anyway, when I saw him in the lobby he said, "Well, what are you going to do tonight, Yogi?" I said, "Nothing much," then I added, "What's there to do in this town, anyway?" He wrote a column about it the next day. What I meant to say was that I would know what to do in St. Louis on the Hill. I would just go outside. You know what I mean. I think he did, too. Well, maybe he did. Anyway he got a column out of it.

Carl Nestfield didn't do a column. At least I never saw one, but, come to think of it, I never saw *Big Red News*.

5

RED SOX

Do you think it is possible for someone to write a book about the last two games the Yankees played in 1949? Several seconds pass. If you remember, the Red Sox were one game ahead with two games to play. "Yeah I know the games you mean," Yogi said with a trace of anger in his voice. Berra then took 9 more seconds and said, "Not unless the guy writing the book knows a helluva lot more about them than I do." Jack Benny never used a pause better.

One of the things that Milton Friedman says a lot is, "The way you ask the question can tell what kind of an answer you get." He may say it in a different way, but that's what he means. I said what you read in the first paragraph of this chapter: "Not unless the guy knows a helluva lot more about them than I do." And I remember exactly where I said it. I was in Dodger Stadium in a storage room behind the visitor's locker room. A young kid named Paul who works in the visitor's clubhouse had just called the Cincinnati Reds in their dressing room in San Diego so he could change the cards they put over the lockers. The visitor's clubhouse man puts new cards over the lockers for each team. At home they are plastic. On the road they are what you would expect for a Boy Scout meeting. Each card has a player's name. The Reds were going to be here the next day, and four players on the Reds who had made the last trip here were gone. Paul or somebody always had to call the team that was coming in next, whoever they were, to check out the roster. It's a routine. Like the homeplate umpire dusting off the plate. All the visitor's clubhouse guys do it. I would hate to see their phone bill.

Paul was singing but not well, a song he said Carol King wrote. One line in it is, "Doesn't anybody stay in one place anymore?" He sings it over and over and it doesn't get any better. His voice, I mean. I think he knew I was doing some work on this book. I also think he thought I knew who Carol King was. What I should have said to that Red Sox–Yankee book question is that it may be possible, but why would anyone want to? That's a much better answer. I think Milton Friedman would think so, too. I am not sure of this, but I think people are more impressed that I met Milton Friedman than they are that I met Ernest Hemingway. It was a long time ago, maybe thirty years. I only met

Friedman last year. I was impressed that Friedman didn't seem impressed with Ernest Hemingway. Friedman didn't think Hemingway was very happy and he didn't write as many good books as people thought he did. I think he said he wrote two or three good ones. One would be fine by me. Friedman is very happy and I am told writes good books, but the one he gave me had a lot of math and the math didn't include ERAs. He said he had one that had no curved lines. That's the way he put it. He said that he was fresh out but would send me one. Carmen read the first one and thought it was "wonderful." Her word. She said it made her think more about the job the President of the country has than anything she has read—and I think she added "for a long time." Anyway she thought it was good. The book is called *Tyranny of the Status Quo*.

I don't know why anyone would want to spend time writing about two games with Boston, or why a publishing company would want to spend the money to print the book. Our oldest son Larry has a bookcase full of books on the Civil War. The Civil War is one thing and two baseball games with the Red Sox is a short series.

A lot of baseball players are interested in the Civil War. Keith Hernandez with the Mets is one. Someone told me they asked Keith why the South lost the Civil War and he said, "They had a bad bench," but I'll bet it isn't true. I mean it's not true that he said that. Larry told me they had a good bench but a weak farm system. Now you know that our son Larry is a Civil War buff and thinks he is funny and that his dad will say so in a book. I will say he is a Civil War buff, but anyone can see he isn't funny.

I am not a great reader, or maybe it would be better to say I don't spend a lot of time browsing in book stores. I am a great reader, but it's sports that interest me. I can't do anything about a lot that goes on, but I can keep up on what's going on in baseball and all other sports. I do keep up because it is part of my job, and I like it. Charlie Silvera was with the Yankees for the first ten years that I was with the team. He used to tell people that I knew not only who won the Roller Derby but the names of all the teams, where the teams stayed on the road, and he could go on and on. He was wrong, but he liked to tell people how much I knew. I did, but not as much as he said.

———— Other Voices ————
CHARLIE SILVERA

Charlie Silvera says it like he has said it many times. He doesn't open with it, but you get the impression he would like to. The line is, "Yankee Stadium may be the house that Ruth built, but my house in San Mateo is the house Yogi built." San Mateo is a few suburbs south of San Francisco, Charlie's birthplace. Silvera's proud reference brings to the baseball fan the countless feature stories on Berra's caddy, Charlie Silvera. "The man who plays in the shadow," was the likely title of at least one. The speculation in all of them was about the total amount of the World Series checks cashed by the San Francisco–born catcher. The total amount is still a speculation. The number of checks is not. It is seven. He appeared in seven World Series.

The seven Series were comprised of 41 games. On only one occasion did his name appear in the World Series box score. One game, at bat twice, no hits, .000 BA. He did not fare that much better during the regular season. In the years he was Berra's backup, he appeared in 227 games. Silvera played behind Berra for ten years, and Charlie is quick to point out that Ralph Houk played behind him. Until recently a Yankees scout, Charlie feels strongly about his time as Berra's caddy.

"It didn't take me long, not a week, but by the second year I knew that I was not going to get what the basketball players call floor time. My friends called it a chance, and I knew I had mine when the Yankees thought I was good enough to back him up. I really mean that. I would rather have been in Yankee Stadium as Yogi's caddy than playing first string a lot of other places. By the time the Yankees sold me to the Cubs, I was first string but by that time my skills were gone, rusted on the bench. But my feeling for being on that team and a part of it all was not gone. Look, very early you have to decide. Am I going to go along with the way the team is being played, I mean who plays and who sits? Then you have to make peace. Go along with it. He is a Hall of Famer and I am proud to have been backing him up. I am probably as well known as any second-string catcher in the game. You know Yankee Stadium may be the house that Ruth built, but my house is the one Yogi built, and I tell him that every time he comes over for dinner. The last time he said he thought we should do something with the kitchen. I'll bet my wife put him up to it."

One more question, Charlie. Did you play behind him with the Newark Bears? "Oh gosh, no. I played for *the Yankee farm team in Kansas City. Lucky for me that he wasn't on that roster. I may never have made it to the big leagues."*

Silvera reacts to a story and tells another. Both help complete the post World War II Yankee picture. Silvera says with obvious glee, "Tell Yogi what Bobby Brown said about Spud Chandler." "I heard it before," says Berra gruffly. "Well, tell it again anyway," commands Silvera. He may have been Yogi's caddy, but he wants the story told.

Networking is supposed to be for Yuppies, not worn-out ballplayers. The story is begun in a vain attempt to become part of the fraternity. "Just tell the damn story," Berra growls and his boredom is apparent. He may have a reputation as a comic book reader and character as well, but he doesn't want to be bored. He would rather stare off in the distance than have a story complicated.

Dr. Brown's interest in Spud seemed to be medical, the story begins. I thought his questions were about his health, not his well-being. When Dr. Brown was told that Spud did not seem contented, happy with himself, his response was, "That's nothing new, that's the way he was. Spud Chandler was weaned on a pickle."

Silvera with relish, "Yogi, you didn't come up until the end of the season in 1946, so let me tell you about spring training. They didn't use the nets in front of the batting practice pitchers in those days, and they didn't have batting practice pitchers for that matter. You know somebody should make a list of things that are different. In '46, '56, '66, '76, '86, and then in '96 when we are all dead." "You're going to be dead before you finish the story," Berra says, looking right through Silvera. "Okay Hall of

Famer, here is the story. Spud was pitching batting practice." "We knew that," chides Berra. "I happened to hit one back through the middle," says Silvera. "Spud had to duck and the next pitch knocked me down. I said, 'Goodness gracious, this is my teammate.' After I got up and looked around for help, and of course no one made eye contact, Spud said, 'Hit em here,' and he pointed to third base, 'or here,' and he pointed to third base and beyond, but not through here, he said, pointing to his feet."

Early in January 1989 Silvera was relieved of his scouting duties by the Yankees.

◆

Charlie lives in San Francisco and I see him every time the Astros play the Giants. Even some baseball people are surprised that we are close. Some scout will come by while we are talking and say, "Charlie, Yogi kept you on the bench for years, why don't you set his pants on fire," or something like that. We were and are good friends. He didn't get to play much, but he was a New York Yankee and he is proud of it. If he resented me, I never knew it. If he did, the resentment is worn out, gone. We had to see each other when we were on the same team, but no more. The Astros play in eleven different cities. When I coached and managed the Yankees, I spent time in the thirteen American League cities. A lot of major league cities have players I played with or against. I don't always see them. I am sure it is that way in most businesses. Just because you work in the same office doesn't mean you go out and fish and hunt and bowl together.

I guess the reason I am going on about Silvera

and me being friends is that so many people don't believe we are. One time a writer in San Francisco looking for an angle asked me, "During the time you and Silvera shared the catching duties for the Yankees he got to bat 429 times and you got to bat over 5000 times, and you tell me you are friends?" The answer was and is yes. I hope I would be the same way if he kept me on the bench. I would have been proud to be a Yankee playing behind Silvera. I would have said he had a great arm, and he did. One more thing on friends. Bobby Brown and I would be called an odd couple. An M.D. and an eighth-grade dropout, or "force-out." But we were good friends and still are. It's a little harder now because he is president of the American League, but he knows and I know we are friends. Maybe I will call him the next time my car breaks down.

As I pointed out, I am not one to hang around the library but as long as I am on reading and books, I want to bring up two other stories. I don't know if the first story is true, but it has been told so often that it might be. Bobby Brown, my roommate, used to study and study for hours. It made me think that doctors were different from other people, and I guess they are. I know that if anybody told me that you couldn't go to medical school and hold down a full-time job, I would say you are wrong. Bobby did it. He did most of his reading at night. I didn't like having a roommate, any roommate. Just as soon as the rules changed and you could room alone, I did. It was not that I was antisocial, I just wanted a quiet room. In the old days I would ask for an inside room, and in the old days you could get one. Now you can't, but I ask for a quiet, dark room, and I turn off the air-conditioning just as soon as I go in the room. I put the "DO NOT DISTURB" sign on the door right away and leave it on when I go out. Even for breakfast. That way when I come back from the park—and the players and coaches kid me about how many hours I spend at the ballpark—I will find the room the same way I left it. Since I left it neat, that's the way it will be.

I am not sure why anybody would be interested in what my habits are on the road. I think it was because I have been in baseball for 40 years and have been on the road for half that time. I guess someone thought that in 20 years I had learned some secrets. As you can see, I have not. At least I don't think that what I do on the road would work for everyone else. They said the same was true of my hitting. Baseball travel can spoil you. It is nice not to have to carry your bag, buy gas for the car, read road signs, get lost, and sometimes miss the plane. Most of the time we take charter flights. So you can see it is quite nice, although while it is going on, most of the players probably don't know it. I am not sure I did when I was playing. What I mean is that later on they will look back and see how nice it was to have so many things done for them. I saw in the paper that former President Reagan said that one of the things he will miss most is the ease of travel. The Houston Astros and the other 25 major league teams are a long way from Air Force One and helicopter flights to Camp David, but we are also a long way from Interstate 40, Motel Six, and McDonalds. We go from San Diego to Los Angeles by bus, and I guess the rest of the National League teams do the same. When I look out of the bus I try to tell myself how nice this all is. It is, but it's not like the train from Cleveland to New York. I am not even sure if they run trains from Cleveland to New York anymore.

Getting back to Bobby Brown. He was reading one of his medical books. He called it studying. I was reading, and the way the story is told it was a comic book, but it may have been the sports page. I am not saying I didn't read comic books. Even if I didn't, people put them in my locker all the time so people thought I did. They thought that's all I read or could read. When I finished reading whatever it was, I waited for him to turn off the light and when he did, I said, "How did yours come out?" I don't know if he told a writer or if I did, and it's not important. It really isn't. It was a long time ago and it is over. I may have said it or maybe I said something else, like "Did you like yours?" I don't know. But I do know the way I felt with Bobby Brown, Phil Rizzuto, Billy Martin or any other roommate, and I had a lot of roommates. So many I can't even begin to remember all of them.

Here is how I felt then, and how I would feel now if we had to have male roommates. Uncomfortable. Now don't get me right. I am not trying to say "male" to be funny. I am just trying to tell you that if I were a businessman and went on a trip and shared a room with another man, I would be uncomfortable. The most uncomfortable would be just before going to sleep. One bathroom is not the problem. At the park forty of us share one. But lights out was a problem to me. What do two guys say, when the lights are out,

It looks like I got a long ball this time up.

This is the only picture I could find of when I was in the Navy. This was taken in New London after I got back from overseas.

The best day of my life, when Carmen and I were married.
Joe Garagiola and his wife Audrey are in the picture with us.

I went after a low pitch this time. It was in a game with the Red Sox. *The New York Times*

Here I am touching home plate.

This is the Grand Concourse Hotel where we stayed in the early Yankee years. It was home to many Yankees such as Babe Ruth and Joe DiMaggio. *Lee Ann Milar*

We had this view of Yankee Stadium from the Grand Concourse Hotel. *Lee Ann Milar*

The Yankee Clipper, Joe DiMaggio. The best player I've ever seen.

This is me in spring training.

Joe D. and the Scooter, Phil Rizzuto, autographing baseballs with me. The tape over my eye is from being hit by a
pitch. *James Kavallines*

This is Casey Stengel visiting with me in 1961, when he was no longer the Yankee manager. *The New York Times*

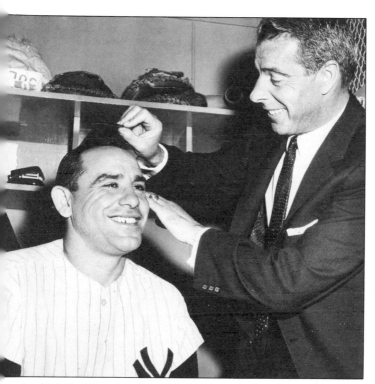

Joe D. is helping me get ready for Yogi Berra day at Yankee
Stadium in 1959. He was honorary chairman.
The New York Times

Here I am thanking the fans and my teammates. I was nervous.
The New York Times

Even my pop, Pietro Berra, came for Yogi Berra day. That's him on the left with me and Carm and two of our sons, Larry with his arm around me and Timmy in front of Carmen.
The New York Times

This is the day in 1963 when I signed to manage the Yankees. Ralph Houk, the general manager, is at my right and Dan Topping, the co-owner, is standing behind us.
The New York Times

This looks like fun with the kids, ours and the neighbors, at our house in New Jersey. *Life Magazine*

This picture was taken at the stadium just before I started managing for the first time in 1964. *Life Magazine*

I'm thinking about changing pitchers. *Sports Illustrated*

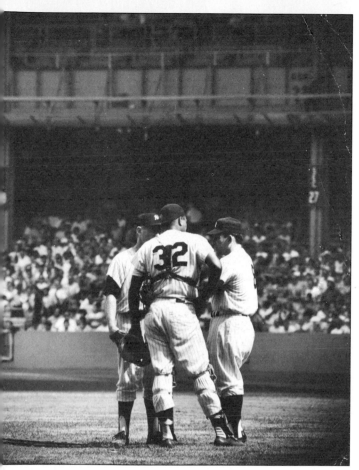
A big conference at the mound in 1964 with Whitey Ford and the late Ellie Howard. *Sports Illustrated*

Here is my plaque out in centerfield in Yankee Stadium.
Lee Ann Milar

LAWRENCE PETER "YOGI" BERRA
1946 - 1963
YANKEE MANAGER 1964, 1984-1985
ELECTED TO THE HALL OF FAME IN 1972
"IT AIN'T OVER 'TIL IT'S OVER"
THREE TIME MVP 1951-54-55
SELECTED TO THE A.L. ALL-STAR TEAM
15 CONSECUTIVE YEARS
HIT MOST HOME RUNS
BY A YANKEE CATCHER
OUTSTANDING CLUTCH HITTER
AND WORLD SERIES PERFORMER
LED YANKEES TO 14 PENNANTS
AND 10 WORLD CHAMPIONSHIPS
A LEGENDARY YANKEE

ERECTED BY
NEW YORK YANKEES
AUGUST 21, 1988

Here is our family in 1964. From the left, Larry, Carmen, Dale, and Timmy. *Life Magazine*

before going to sleep? I didn't know then and I don't know now, and that's one of the reasons I might have said whatever I am supposed to have said to Bobby Brown. I am not trying to get out of what I may have said that was funny. I know that I do say funny things sometimes, and now that other people get paid to tell stories about me I should keep it up.

Even my wife Carmen is going to be surprised when she reads this. I never felt comfortable just after the lights went out. Good night Billy, sweet dreams? Think about the home-run pitch you threw to Ted Williams, Whitey? Next time don't shake me off? I didn't say any of those things. We are all different, and sleeping in a room with another man was something I never got used to. One hundred and fifty sailors, stacked six high in the hold of a ship, that was okay. Well, not really okay because too many of them were seasick and I was one of them, but okay that when the lights went out you didn't worry. I also don't really mean worry. I said uncomfortable and I was.

———————— **Other Voices** ————————
BOBBY BROWN

"Dr. Bobby Brown," that is the caption under his picture in the American League Red Book. *The* Red Book *is an official publication of the league. Since Brown is president, the "Bobby" must have his blessing. His visitor selects for Dr. Brown a more comfortable salutation, "Thanks, Dr. Brown, for agreeing to talk about your Newark Bears and New York Yankees roommate, and I promise not to ask about* Gray's Anatomy.

President Brown did not seem willing to talk at first, and Carmen Berra's word came floating back, "Bobby is not like the rest; he is a different kind of person."

Dr. Brown was drawn to the subject through Billy Jurges, the Cub and Giant shortstop. Jurges had arranged an interview with Spud Chandler and had been a patient of Brown's. After several minutes the arms-length posture relaxed, and Bobby Brown said with passion, "Yogi is one of the most unpretentious men I have ever known. We came up together and so I have known him for over thirty years. I have practiced medicine, played major league base-ball, and am now the president of the American League. Yogi Berra is a national treasure, he has never changed, and the world needs more just like him. Carmen is a spectacular woman; the two of them together are a joy to me and always have been.

"When we first came up, none of us made much money and I wanted to deliver their first child as a gift. I think Yogi wanted me to do so, and not so much that I would do the job without charge but because he knew I would do a good job. You may not believe that because so much has been written about his being so close with a dollar. He is not tight, rather generous in his own way, and I know he was pleased I wanted to deliver Larry, Jr. I did not, as it happened, deliver Larry, Jr., but I know they were both grateful for my offer. Every time I see them I feel a little better about the human race."

◆

One of Babe Ruth's roommates was Ping Bodie. Ping was also an outfielder for the Yankees. He had a great baseball name and an even better one for a golfer.

People said Babe Ruth didn't spend much time in his room, and so when Ping was asked what it was like to room with Babe Ruth, he said, "I don't know. I room with his bags." I bet it didn't happen, but it makes a funny story. One of the things that sportswriters get paid to do is to write funny stories. I am not saying that's bad. I am saying sometimes the stories are not true. At least not all true.

This book story happened last year. Carmen and I were talking with Tom Horton about this book. He said, "Bobby Knight hates John Feinstein." Carmen said, "Who is Bobby Knight?" and I said, "Who is John Feinstein?" When Horton explained to us that Bobby Knight was the University of Indiana basketball coach and that John Feinstein wrote a book about him, Carmen said, "See! If you and Yogi do a book, Yogi will hate you." I knew who Bobby Knight was. Carmen didn't know either one of them and that is just what she said. When we started this book, she was going to be a part of it. It was going to be a book about the Berras. I don't know how that changed. I mean I only know her side of it. Carmen said she wasn't too interested in being in it, but anybody who knows me knows how important she is to most everything that has happened to me, and so I want you to know what she is like.

"See! If you and Yogi do a book, Yogi will hate you," is just what Carmen said and just the way she said it. She said it right out. Carm does most everything right out. Just because she was not interested in being in this book doesn't mean that I can't tell you what she is like while trying to tell you what makes me tick. I didn't think I would use the word "tick" in this book if it came out in three volumes. So let me tell you how the word "tick" ended up in this book and at the same time tell one more story about Carmen.

One time a good friend borrowed our car. We were in Florida, and when he brought it back he was a little late. He said he was caught when they raised a drawbridge. While he was sitting waiting, he thought not only how nice it was that we let him use our car, but he also thought about me. This is what he said. "You know Yogi, I have known you a long time. But I really don't know what makes you tick." Carmen said, "If I don't, why should you?"

Getting back to those two games with Boston. I played in 2120 big-league games. When I look at that number and know that Lou Gehrig played in 2130 consecutive games, I have a hard time believing it. That Lou Gehrig played in that many in a row is almost impossible to imagine, and for me 2130 is hard to believe. It is like I know that Nolan Ryan has pitched for over twenty years and has struck out over 4700 batters, but I find that hard to believe as well. Hard to believe even though I saw Nolie during the years he was with the Mets and with the Astros. The reason I say it is hard to believe the numbers is that so many great players last eight or nine years. Al Rosen played only ten years. Lots of great players played half as many games as I was able to play. They say catchers wear out quicker, so that is another reason I am—well, I guess I will just say it—impressed.

David Halberstam, the writer doing the book on

those two games, as I understand it, thinks that the games were important not only in 1949 but that they were turning points in the life of baseball and the country. The whole country. I know they were important games in 1949. The Red Sox came to Yankee Stadium one game ahead of us. If they won one of two games, they won the pennant. I think they were important games, but they were not more than that. If they were, I missed it.

I love my wife Carmen not only because I love her but because she thinks I am smart. Even Carm would not say I was that smart. Smart enough to know something like Walter Cronkite. I use Walter Cronkite because he saw things other people missed—the big picture, my business friends call it. In baseball I was interested in the little picture. Ninety feet and sixty feet six inches. Let me put it this way. On the days she thinks I am the cat's pajamas, she would not say I am good at saying what we just saw or did was a turning point or benchmark. If we had driven by the first shopping center (I am told it was in Kansas City), I would be the last person to say, "You will see a lot of these some day." Maybe the inventor of shopping centers, if there was one, didn't even say that. I am not trying to put myself down. Enough people do that for me. What I am saying is that I think I am good at some things. Looking into a crystal ball is not one of them.

So if 1949 was a watershed or turning point, Berra has a passed ball. I am doing the best job I can of pointing out the changes I have seen in baseball,

and I know the camel got his nose in the tent somewhere along the line, but I don't know when he did.
I sure did not think it was 1949, so I hope Halberstam's book will tell me. He did a book on the Portland
Trailblazers and somebody sent it to me, so I'd better
get around to reading it first.

Now let me get to the games (as you can see, I
was in no big hurry). The first thing I want to say is
that I was ready to play in both games. Nobody had
to tell me to forget about my thumb. At least one
writer said that I was jaking it. Maybe he heard it from
a teammate or maybe even a doctor, but they were all
wrong. Just in case you don't use the word "jake" I'll
explain. It is a good word, like "bush," and it has been
around a long time. Jake means you are not sick when
you say you are sick, or that you're a little hurt but
think you are really hurt and don't play. The modern
term is "play with pain" and I did. That is a simple
thing to say. Yogi says he played with pain, but what
may be pain to you may not be pain to me. For example, I had some bad cuts in baseball and even some
at home, and it never bothered me to see mine. Mine
was okay, but a much smaller cut on someone, and
not just one of my boys, would drive me nuts. Make
me sick. So what could be a sprain to one guy might
mean traction and a portable whirlpool for somebody
else.

Joe Garagiola and I were talking to some writers
before a "Game of the Week" one time, and both
of us put our right and left hands on one writer's
face, on his cheeks. We did it one at a time like we
were some French Generals getting ready to pin a

medal, and thinking back I wonder what some people thought. Some people in the stands. I know what Lasorda thought. We were playing the Dodgers and he told me.

The reason we put our hands on the guy's face was to show that even on a warm summer night in Los Angeles our right hands were colder than our left. I don't know if my left hand was colder than Joe's because I caught more balls than he did, but I know the writer was impressed. I wonder if Rick Dempsey (the Dodger catcher) or Alan Ashby (our catcher) will have the same problem considering the gloves they wear compared to the much smaller ones we used. I hope they will read this and let me know in ten years or so. Ashby, Dempsey, and all the rest of the catchers of the world should probably resent anybody saying they jaked it just because they were catchers. Now that I think about it, a catcher probably has more pain every game than anybody else except the pitcher.

If one of my hands is a few degrees colder than the other all these years later, I hope you understand that before the two games with the Red Sox I was not jaking it. One time I was catching the second game of a double header and it was hot and muggy and we were way behind or way ahead, and I got on the home-plate umpire real good. I think it may have been Cal Hubbard. I was trying to get thrown out of the game so I could take a shower. He said, "Go on, Yogi, go on, but you're going to stay out here with me. I am not going to chase you." And he didn't, and what I did was not called jaking. I am not sure what it was called, but I did it and I might even do it again. I didn't jake and I tried not to be bush even when I was in the minor leagues. That's where the term came from. The minor leagues were out in the bushes. Calling someone bush is not a good thing to do unless you know him well or are bigger. I don't think I ever used the word in that way. If someone was bush, I might call him a dandy, but then I sometimes used that word with people I liked.

A lot of this book came out of several hundred hours of tape recording. In one session I was talking about George Weiss, the Yankee general manager. I said that he never looked at you, even when you were in his office, and some other stuff like that. Some time later Horton said, "I couldn't understand one word when you were talking about George Weiss. Here listen. Are you saying dandy or are you saying bandit?" We both laughed when I said he was a dandy bandit. I liked him a lot, and Hazel and George Weiss were good friends of ours. George was a businessman, and he knew a lot about contracts. It doesn't rank with the Hall of Fame, but I will say this, I am very proud of the fact that after all the contracts he signed, George Weiss kept only two of them. When he left the Yankees, he took just two contracts. He kept them in his desk in Greenwich, Connecticut. One was Joe Di-Maggio's and one was mine. It meant a lot to me that he did that, and I think I made him understand that it did. But I would like to have had a chance to make sure. He died before I could. I am not real good at showing emotion.

Let me say some more about playing in pain. The only one who knows what it means is the guy in pain. If you are getting paid to play, and that means win, then it is even more important. If you are in pain and can't give 90 or 95 percent, maybe you shouldn't be out there. You can hurt the team if you are hurting. I am talking about real pain. One of the doctors I saw at the Mayo Clinic told me one time, "If you are not sick when you think you are sick, you are very sick indeed." I don't mean that at all. I mean a pulled hamstring or something so you can't run hard without doing bad things not only to your leg but to the team. That's like faking doing your exercise. You are only kidding yourself. Knowing when you can play, knowing when you shouldn't play because you might hurt your team, are all hard things to figure, but you have to try. You can't just say you want to be out there because it is a big game.

I hope some kids are reading this book. Think about playing when you are hurt. You might hurt the team and yourself. Just think about it. I knew guys who tried to impress someone. Before they were warmed up, they started to throw hard and hurt their arm. That's just as bad as trying to come back too soon. I know sometimes in football they patch people up, give them a shot, and send them back. That's another reason I like baseball, although I don't think baseball is better than football or even boxing. I mean baseball is not above it. It just doesn't work in baseball. Not in the same way. You might foul a ball off your foot and have the trainer freeze it, but you can't deaden the pain in a pitcher's arm or the other team will hit him hard. So if you are in pain and not 100 percent, think about it. It is a fork in the road. Somebody said that I said, "If you come to a fork in the road, take it," but if I did, I don't remember it.

Other Voices
JOHNNY NEUN

"My goal is to be drawing a paycheck when I am 90," said Johnny Neun. At age 88 he is well on his way. Neun, one of the three Yankee managers in 1946, was on the bench when Berra arrived. Joe McCarthy and Bill Dickey were the other two.

Neun reports on the American League teams for the O's of Baltimore. "I can see all I want in four or five innings. I can tell the base runners from the base stealers. When I scouted the National League for the Yankees for 19 years I would make a report just before the World Series. Yogi Berra was the smartest catcher I ever knew. He asked the best questions about the other team of anybody in the room. He wanted to know what you knew and he knew how to find out.

"Used to make me laugh when people said he was slow witted. Casey was the smartest manager I ever saw even when he had bad teams, and when he had good ones, look out. He and Berra were like Ike and Omar Bradley. You had to know what was going on in order to track along with them. I spent all my life watching and trying to learn baseball. They never lost me but they lost a lot of people. Stengel knew enough to let Yogi alone once the game started. He called his own game and he did it the way

Leonard Bernstein directed the Philharmonic. He was a genius at that."

To set the stage again for that first game, Boston had to win one to win the pennant. We had to win both. Casey Stengel started Allie Reynolds, but he was wild, so Casey brought in Joe Page early in the game. It may have been the fourth inning. If it happened today, the TV announcer would say, "Page is not the Yankee 'Long Man,' but Casey knows if they don't win today, there is no tomorrow." Tomorrow was Sunday and we would have played even if we lost, but that is the sort of thing they say now and even then, for all I know, because saying "there is no tomorrow" started someplace, just like that shopping center.

Page did a good job, as he almost always did, and so did Allie Reynolds. I am glad I didn't have to make the decision about taking Reynolds out. Sometimes when one of the pitchers was losing his stuff, I gave a sign to Casey to let him know. I knew before the pitcher did. It was a little sign. I would turn my leg out and put my hand down on the outside of the leg and sort of whirl the first finger around. Like you were trying to put some foam back on the head of a beer, if you were bush enough to do something like that. I never did, but I saw a TV technician do it. The beer they were using in the commercial had gone flat. So had some of the guys in the commercial, to tell the truth. Anyway, this TV guy (and I remember he was a Mets fan) put his finger in the beer and it had a head in nothing flat. I gave that sign to Stengel every now and then. He always saw it, and I don't ever remember him not doing something. Coming out to see both me and the pitcher, or getting someone throwing in the bull pen. Sometimes both.

I didn't signal Casey in this game, and to this day I don't know if I had been the manager if I would have taken Allie out. Casey did. Page held them. The late Johnny Lindell hit a home run, and we won 5 to 4. Lindell hit only six all that year and played in only 78 games, so he may have been playing for someone who was hurt and hurt in a way that he would have hurt us had he played. I have forgotten.

You can't forget Joe DiMaggio. He was hurting in that game. He had been hurting for weeks. He had pneumonia, or at least he had had it and was getting over it. He had lost a lot of weight and didn't look good. He played. I don't remember his doing anything great, but he didn't have to. I know this sounds sappy, but all he had to do was show up to make the Yankee clubhouse, the Yankee dugout, and the Yankee Stadium a better place. He was the Yankee Clipper, and as I have said, the best player I ever saw.

I have forgotten the year, but it was in the late sixties or early seventies. The New York Knicks were playing the Lakers for the championship. Willis Reed had been hurt, and he came back for the last game and didn't do much except limp on the floor. Madison Square Garden went nuts. The Knicks didn't go nuts, but you could tell. Willis Reed limping lifted the team. They won. I know exactly how they felt. It sounds so phony to say it, but Joe didn't have to do well. He just had to show up. I think everyone who saw him knew that, but I am sure a lot of people that didn't will not understand. I can't point to a team in baseball and say Joe is like so and so. We had the only Clipper.

So we won the first game. Some of the other players may have felt it was all over but the shouting, but I wasn't one of them. I thought the Red Sox were a good team. They had Ted Williams, and that made them a great team.

───────── **Other Voices** ─────────
JOE DIMAGGIO

It would be hard to say something about Joe DiMaggio that hasn't been said, or sung. "Where have you gone Joe DiMaggio?" "I went to the doctor feeling pretty good," said DiMaggio. The first thing a visitor is struck with is the voice. It is refined, not a David Niven, drawing room refined, but refined just the same. "It doesn't seem right that you go to see one feeling okay and then you end up with a lot of pain. My leg hurts and I was thinking, if you were doing a book on anybody else in baseball, I would tell you to go to the library. That should tell you how I feel about Yogi. If it doesn't, get to be my age, have some physical problems, and have someone want to talk with you about a guy you worked with forty years ago. The guy doesn't want for anything, fame or fortune. The only thing he needs you can't give him, and see what you will do.

"The first time I saw him? Contrary to what I have seen written, I did not see him in the clubhouse. It is traditional, as you know, to greet new players. At least in my day." DiMaggio expresses pleasure that the two new players from Tucson the Astros had brought up the day of

this interview were greeted by every player and by the broadcasting team as well. Everyone except the writers. It is a ritual, almost choreographed he is told. "Well, that's nice to know. Pete Sheehy would be surprised to hear anyone describe anything that happened in his clubhouse as choreographed, but that's a good way to describe the way it is done. For some reason I didn't meet Yogi that way. I can't recall why, maybe I was late or Johnny Neun, the manager at the time, wanted to see me. I don't remember. It is just as well. It makes a better story now. For some reason I didn't even hear about him.

"I want to make sure you understand this. It was normal for someone to bring a new kid around to shake hands. I just didn't connect with Yogi. In my own way, I did with all the rest." Joe D. does not seem surprised that Yogi has a different memory. When told that Berra remembers meeting him in the clubhouse and even had a response to the question, "Do you think that Joe greeted you any more warmly because you were both Italian?", Joseph Paul DiMaggio sounds like kindly Judge Hardy. "Yogi or any rookie kid brought into that clubhouse would not have a clear memory. If you were a baseball player you were going into Valhalla. Ruth, Gehrig, the 27 Yankees. Not surprising in the least that he forgot. We didn't meet in the normal way. If you have been told that I kept to myself in the clubhouse, you were told the way it was. I am the same way now when I play golf. The first time I saw him was a day or two after he came up and Johnny Neun, the third Yankee manager in 1946, had him catch the first game of a double header. Joe McCarthy started the season and was replaced by Bill Dickey, and Neun finished the season. We finished in third place.

Larry Berra, and that's what we called him then, looked like a fire hydrant walking up to the plate. I really didn't know what I thought, except that he looked like a showoff but he didn't have anything to show off. Make sure you make this clear. I am talking about 1946 and this is 1989. I know Yogi. You have to like him. That's the backdrop. When I say showoff, I don't mean he swaggered like some of these guys do now. Some pitchers do for sure. That guy who used to pitch for St. Louis, Hrabosky, Al, I think. Not like that at all. When I say showoff, I mean he was swinging three bats. Most of us used two. He had all three going, and then he flipped two of them away and you had to watch. Bang, bang, he had two strikes. Then he took two pitches, and I will never forget this, he hit a pitch, a ball so far out of the strike zone I would never swing the bat. A good hitter would say 'ball' the instant it left the pitcher's hand. Not only was it a ball, I really don't think I could have hit it. I mean hit it, not out of the park like he did, I mean just put the bat on the ball. Yogi is five seven and I am six two.

"Funny thing about that game that I just learned. I played in Don Drysdale's Hall of Fame Golf Tournament in January of 1989, and Whitey Ford told me he watched the game from the center-field bleachers. He was just a kid and typical of a pitcher who has forgotten Yogi's home run but not the pitcher. It was Phil Marchildon who pitched for the Philadelphia A's. Yogi remembers the pitcher and the pitch. He said, 'It was a high fast ball.' All three of us had a good laugh. Berra had a gift, and I will bet that if some hitting instructor had a kid like him today, he would never make it to the big leagues. I mean the kid. They wouldn't give him a second look. Yogi was born to play baseball, and I am glad I had the chance to watch him.

"I played with two good ones, Bill Dickey and Yogi. I can't tell you if you wrote fifty books how different the two of them were. If I had to pick which one was better, I would do what Yogi would do." What would Yogi say? "You don't know what he says when he is asked to answer a hard question?" asks the man voted the greatest living baseball player. After a pause, DiMaggio laughs and says he is surprised. "Yogi would say, 'I couldn't say for sure.'"

The Jolter, Joltin' Joe DiMaggio is right. Why isn't the refined voice, the courtly manner, his understanding of the personality of his teammates and their abilities been featured in stories on the Yankee Clipper? Much of what has been written about DiMaggio relates to his raw talent as a player and a leader, his easy grace as an outfielder. Yogi and dozens of other Yankees confirm that Joe D. never left his feet. He never made a diving catch because he knew where the ball was going to drop and he was there first.

DiMaggio seems to be hiding other abilities. Maybe he wants it that way. DiMaggio is pleased with the direct hit. "That's one of the many reasons Yogi is so durable, why he wears so well. I couldn't say for sure. Perfect comment. Now Frankie Crosetti—and come to think of it, Cro may have been Yogi's teacher—Frankie would squeak out his answer to a hard question with a 'Who's to say.' Who's to say. That's Cro.

"I missed Yogi at a baseball card show in St. Louis because he didn't show up until he had to. He hit the same way—when he had to. It is interesting how some people never change. Yogi always knew what was going on around *him and what was expected. Even the fuss about players signing autographs for money at baseball card shows is clear to Yogi," says DiMaggio. "As far as Yogi is concerned, they wouldn't have them if somebody didn't get paid. You know it is just that simple. It is the same with a lot of things. If somebody didn't get paid, they wouldn't have them. Yogi is one of a kind, and it is too bad. Let me put it this way. I hit in 56 straight games. I think that record will be broken. He played in 75 World Series games. That record will not be broken. The 75 games and the other records are not what makes Yogi different. Yogi is what makes Yogi different. We had breakfast one time, and he looked at the menu and said, 'I only have eggs in Cincinnati.' Joe smiled with admiration. "I didn't ask him why, but you can bet he had a good reason."*

◆

The late Vic Raschi started the second game and was sharp. He remembered the game, of course, but also wondered about how important it was in what he called the "Grand Scheme." Vic was a very sharp guy. We talked about the Red Sox game not too long before he died. Even got into an argument about some of the pitches I called in that game. Yes, the 1949 game. I am not going to bore you with the details, but Vic said, "Yogi, sometimes I shook you off just to show you who was boss." I have known it for years. It was great to have him admit it. He was a great pitcher and it was good to know he still had the fire. Our conversation made me think of a movie, *The Sunshine Boys*. If you saw it, you will know. If you didn't, you should try to see it. I would have given it a Home Run if I had been in the movie review business when I saw it. If Joe D. had been in top shape, we would have won the game 5 to 0. As it was, we won 5 to 3 because of some ragged play in the ninth. I think by this time even if they had tied it up, and they might have, we would have won the game in extra innings. I am sure I felt that way at the time.

Knowing that these two games seem to be more important to some people than they were even to some of the players, I tried to think of some reasons. I hope I will name a few that are on the list. I hope there is a list. If not, somebody should make one. I am always impressed when somebody can say more than, "It's good," about the wine served at a fancy dinner. Some people can sip it, look at the ceiling, wait a few seconds and say, "It is quite good." I am not one of them. We used to have a guy in a foursome I played with who liked to tell us the three functions of motor oil: lubricate, clean, and cool. I thought it did just one thing, lubricate. I think he wished motor oil had five or six so he could tell us all of them. All of them and often. You know the kind of guy I mean. Well, I am not one of them, but I came up with a list.

The pennant in 1949 was the first for Casey Stengel. He won 10 more, but the more popular he got, the bigger that first win seemed. That first win may have seemed bigger than it was. Something like my first pinch-hit World Series home run. People made it bigger over the years, and what I remember is that we lost the game. I think Casey had a lot to do with making what he did important, and I don't mean that was bad. It wasn't bad. It was more that Casey knew how to do it.

I heard Ted Williams on Bob Costas's radio show, and Ted said that Casey was one of the most important baseball personalities of all time. I think he mentioned Judge Landis, Babe Ruth, and Casey. I thought it was interesting that Ted put Judge Landis and Casey together. Casey was always on stage, but one time he said, "Yogi, do you know what Landis said to me?" I had to say no, and Casey said, "Stengel, you are good for only one thing. Shoveling manure, horse or cow or donkey. That is the one thing you are good for." I never knew if it hurt Casey, but I think it did. I told him I thought the judge was wrong and I still do.

Ted always spoke his mind and he had a good one, so even Ted may agree that Casey had something to do with that two-game series being a big deal. Ted Williams—I admired him for a lot of reasons. Some people will say that he gave our son Larry a free ride at his baseball camp. He did, but I admired him before that. The thing I liked about him the most was that he was secure enough that he didn't care what anybody thought. The press ripped him, but he did what he thought was right. He was secure from the first day. It took me longer.

I heard an example from Bob Costas's radio show of the way Ted is and was. Ted was a guest on the show and from what Costas said, Ted didn't do it very often. I am sure that is true. Ted would rather fish than talk unless he can talk about hitting. When he does that he needs to be on TV or have a bat in his hand. Costas read from a book he called *The Fireside Book of Baseball*. I am told it is not a good idea to read something on a radio show. It bores people and they turn you off. I guess you could read if you are Orson Welles, but it is not a good idea for most people. Maybe Costas thought, Ted is my guest. He did it his way. Why not do it my way? I am going to read.

Anyway, he read. It was a story about Ted and Ty Cobb talking in Scottsdale, Arizona. The book said they had a fight about hitting—about who was the greatest and who was better. That sort of thing. Ted said it never happened, and you know you have to believe Ted. If Ted said it didn't, I will bet it didn't. You know for sure that if Ted talked with Ty Cobb anywhere, he didn't forget it. I met Ty Cobb, and if you are a baseball player, you don't forget it. You also know that Ted would have said it was a misunderstanding, or something like that. So make book it didn't happen but somebody said it did.

Since I seem to harp on the "don't believe everything you read" thing, you might think I am thin skinned. I don't think I am. I know this, the writers writing about me were good for me. At least in the long run. I just want to try to use this book to make you a little skeptical, at least a little, about what you read. Maybe it's that I didn't go to college. Whatever the reason, let me point it out every now and then. Don't believe everything you read, even in the *New York Times*.

Joe McCarthy was another reason those two games meant more than if the Yankees had been playing another team, even Cleveland or the White Sox.

McCarthy had been the Yankee manager for almost 15 seasons. He won eight American League pennants for the Yankees, and now he was managing against them. Well, he didn't win them, his team did, but that's another kettle of fish. So that made it a big deal in the same way that it would be a bigger game if the Oklahoma and Texas coaches changed jobs, and then met in the Cotton Bowl. Or any other game like that. Ohio State and Michigan, and you can think of some others.

When Leo Durocher left the Dodgers and went to the New York Giants, the Dodger–Giant games were already big. Now they were bigger. They really were big, but I think you had to live in that part of the East to know that. I am talking about the days when it was the New York Giants and the Brooklyn Dodgers.

Maybe some Yankees and some Yankee fans thought they were better than the Dodgers and Giants and even better than their fans. I wasn't one of them. I thought the rivalry was great then and I think so today. The Los Angeles Dodgers and San Francisco Giants may not be quite the same to people my age, but if you are young and that's the way it was when you grew up, that's the way it is.

The Red Sox were not only a great team, they had great fans and a lot of them hated the Yankees. A lot of people hated the Yankees then, but the Boston fans really hated them and some of them even knew why. I don't remember all the details, but Larry Ritter, the baseball writer who also has a Ph.D. and teaches finance at NYU, is writing a book about Babe Ruth and he will tell all about it. To this list of reasons, you can add that I think some Boston fans still feel New York, all of New York, should be hated because Babe Ruth left the Red Sox and came to New York.

Babe Ruth was a pitcher and outfielder for the Red Sox, and the main reason he came to New York was not so the Red Sox could get a shortstop or a guy to play first base. The deal was made because of money. Can you think of how mad you would be if your team sold Babe Ruth and he came back to haunt you? I think only a Red Sox fan can understand. They really seem to care about their team, the way some states feel about their football teams. And the way Indiana feels about their basketball team. Hate makes things important, even though I think it is important not to hate.

As long as I made that comment about hate, let me interrupt my list and stay on the soapbox for a little bit longer. I am a grandfather. It really is not good to hate. Don't do it and you will live longer. Someone told me that hate was refried anger. I never forgot that statement, but I didn't hate even before I heard it. The players I managed knew that I didn't bug them all the time about the way they played. I tried to let them ask for advice. Since I have said don't hate, I should at least offer this advice even though you didn't ask. Don't do it because it doesn't work.

The 1949 World Series was on TV, and that makes everything seem more important. Now we get so much of TV, it doesn't work that way but it did then. The next year was 1950, and that was important. The end of the 1940s is what I mean. End of the war years, too. That is also the end of my list of reasons . . .

In 1951 Bobby Thomson hit the home run that was heard around the world. That's the way it was described on the same day, and then it got even bigger. Some people say it was one of the greatest moments in baseball. It may have been. The reason I bring it up is that I am often asked what Reynolds said to me. Or what I said to him or to Whitey Ford or to the umpire. Last year a 94-year-old gentleman from Alabama wrote me and asked me what I had said to Vic Raschi in a World Series. He had very shaky handwriting, and he said that when I went back to the plate, Vic was smiling. You know, I would like to have told the man from Alabama what I really said but I couldn't remember. I get a lot of "what did you say" questions. I almost always have to fake it or at least make up what sounds good. I was trying to play the game, not keep a notebook.

I have never been asked what I said when Bobby Thomson hit the home run in the Polo Grounds off Ralph Branca. It put the Giants into the World Series with the Yankees. I had gone to the game because I wanted to see both teams. We would be playing one of them the next day. The Yankees had a workout early that morning, and most of us went to the game. The Polo Grounds, the Giants home park, was only four or five blocks from Yankee Stadium.

What I said was, "Guess I should have stayed." I said it to myself about halfway across the George

Washington Bridge on the way home to New Jersey. I also said it to Carmen when I got home. I had left the game early.

One of the biggest games of modern times, and I am the guy who said that it isn't over until it's over.

6
NORMANDY

"**H**ow can Yogi's biography have 90,000 words? He is over 60 and still has 25,000 words to go."

I have no idea who said that, and it's not true. Somebody did and it may have been Catfish Hunter. If it wasn't, it sounded like something he would say. I like Catfish. Really like him. As much as almost anyone I know in baseball. I don't want to get into a best friend thing, like who was the best baseball player you ever saw? (Joe DiMaggio is still the answer to that question.) I said Cat was a good friend to show that we knew each other well. Even though we were friendly, he didn't know that I can talk a lot sometimes. My speeches are bad and I really hate to give a speech. I can say, "Hello, I am glad to be here," and answer

questions. I like to do that if it's a good crowd and I
don't mean big, I mean *good*. Sometimes I think people
in the crowd want the speech to be bad so they can
tell other people the next day how bad I was. That's
not good. It's not good for me and if you think about
it, it's not good for them to be talking bad. It's a lot
better if they say I heard, say, the Love Doctor—Leo
Buscaglia. And then say I really feel good today and
hug somebody. That's good.

Other Voices
JIM HUNTER

*"My Goodness, she's up early," commented Catfish Hunter.
The "she" in this case was a mannequin seated at a piano
looking more lifelike than the live employees of the Phoenix
resort hotel. It was shortly before 6 AM. The maitre d'
explained that the room doubled as a night spot, and they
hadn't taken her out yet.*

*Hunter said matter-of-factly, "Yogi would never eat
in a place like this even if the team were paying, but if he
did they would try to get him to pose with that mannequin,
and he would. I used to like to have breakfast with Yogi
when we were on the Yankees together. He always knew
how to find the best place and the cheapest place. I think
an hour with him can make you feel good all day."*

*Hunter then told a story that he felt required him to
imitate Berra's low voice. The North Carolina drawl, low-
ered to a rasp, would make the most mundane tale riveting.
"Cat, you like ice cream?" asked Yogi during spring training in Ft. Lauderdale. "Sure I do, are you buying?" said
Catfish. The two Hall of Famers walked the four blocks to*

the place Berra had found and was eager to show and tell and in this case do some buying.

Showing Catfish the various flavors, Yogi was like a father with his young son going for his first haircut. Jim Hunter concludes the story, "So we went up to the cash register and the owner says, 'Oh Yogi, it's an honor to have you in my store! It's on the house. Come back anytime, please.' Then as he beamed at Yogi, he turned to me and said, 'That'll be $1.75. Would you like a napkin?'

"You would have to hold my feet in the fire before I would bad mouth him. The only thing I will say is that if he were good looking and tall, watch out."

Do you care to make any comments about George Steinbrenner? "What can I say. He gave me a lot of money. I shouldn't say anything more than that. Did Yogi ever tell you about the Red Man commercial?" Yes, but I would like to hear your version. "Okay, if Yogi will tell what he said to George." His name hasn't come up but when it does your question will be on the top of the list. "That's good," said Cat, "I know George goes into a blue funk when Yogi's name comes up."

"I had a deal with Red Man, and they were going to finish filming a commercial in Yankee Stadium. It happened to work out on a day I was going to pitch, so I told the people that I had to get it over with as fast as possible. They said okay. It was only some final shots and it would take 10 or 15 minutes. No more, just a wrap up. I knew these guys and they knew me.

"We were down near the bullpen and George was in his office and saw us. It really bugged him. He didn't think I should be making money for myself on a day I was going to pitch. I can understand that but this was not going to

take any longer than talking to a reporter. Anyway, he sent some guys from the ground crew down to sabotage the commercial. They sprayed water and did everything they could to screw it up. What should have been over before he sent the troops took an hour or so and everybody was mad. The ground crew, and I knew all of them had implied authority and we dug our heels in. They knew they were being stupid. It was stupid.

"I lost the game. George knocked me in the press. We flew to Cleveland after the game. He was not on the plane, but he was in the hotel the next morning. We both had breakfast in the hotel coffee shop. I don't know if he came to my table or I went to his. I do know this. I said I didn't like being ripped in the press. He said what my mother would call some hateful things, and I left the table. That was it, and Yogi would say Steinbrenner liked doing it. George told some writers he liked me for standing up to him. I am sorry I had to. It was something that should never have happened. The Red Man people, the ground crew, and the guy who was going to pitch all got hot over nothing. Really nothing.

"When Yogi was named the manager in 1984, he wanted me to be his pitching coach. I wanted the job. I didn't think I was going to be the world's greatest pitching coach, but I wanted to work with Yogi. I didn't even need or want a lot of money, but I had to make sure my farm was covered. You know, we couldn't get together. Yogi and I could, but it never worked out with the Yankees. It was a big disappointment. I don't know to this day why it didn't work out. It wasn't my fault. It wasn't Yogi's.

"I know this. If he ever asks me to invest in something, I will send the money. Billy Martin said that if Yogi dug *a hole next to second base, he would strike oil. I always believed Billy was right."*

I've had to give a lot of speeches, and almost every time I mess up part of it. Like the time in St. Louis when I was given a night by the fans. It was a great thing, and I thanked everyone "for making this night necessary." I meant to say "possible," but I didn't and I paid for it. Sometimes I would really kick myself. Then somebody would tell me about something he had said that was wrong and I would forget about it. It's hard at my age to say more than I did the best I could and it worked out well. I can still feel the cotton mouth and the sweaty palms when I have to give a speech, and I know it will be that way next time.

Several times friends would get me to go to someone they knew who could tell you how to speak and how to relax. One of them told me like he had just figured out how to pick horses, or when to change pitchers, or something important. He said, "Yogi, just pretend that everyone in the audience is naked. Then you will feel above all of them and not have any more trouble making an outstanding speech. You will be relaxed and great, just the way you hit, and could you leave me two tickets in your name for the Saturday doubleheader with the Tigers?" I am not kidding. He really said that, and I was told he was an expert and was well paid. At least he didn't ask for a check or bill me. I guess that's why he wanted the tickets.

The next time I gave a speech I thought about his advice, but it didn't work for me. It may have been because of all the naked guys in the dressing rooms for all the years. I never felt above any of them. I was taught not to feel you were better than anybody but to feel good about yourself. The locker room still has naked men, and the last ten years or so women sports-writers are allowed in. If you are a sports fan, you may remember all the noise about it when it first happened. I was not really in favor of women going into the clubhouse. Maybe it would be better to say I just felt more comfortable if they didn't.

Once I wanted to join a country club in New Jersey. I had lunch and played the course once or twice, and they said something like "We'll be in touch." Something like that. It was sort of the "I'll get back to you" or "I'll have my people get with your people" that you hear in movies. They never did. One of the board members asked me for World Series tickets one year and I said I was fresh out. I was told, and the friend who told me was uncom-fortable, I wasn't accepted because I was Italian. But they knew that when I had lunch and played golf, so I never understood, but I know what it means not to be welcome. Women in the locker room is not the same thing. Not the same, but not different. I think getting into country clubs and where you can buy a house, things like that, are better now. Getting into a country club is not as important as where you can buy a house. I didn't mean to say that it was.

Women in baseball locker rooms may be con-nected to the whole thing, but I don't see how. Maybe it would be better to say I don't want to see how. The last thing I will say about women in the clubhouse is this, and I can't prove it and don't even want to think about trying. I was a sailor, and most bad language doesn't shock me, even though I try to watch mine. Some players, like Bobby Richardson of the Yankees, never used more than "damn" and it had to be a bad, really awful thing for him to say even that. Bob Knepper on the Astros is the same way. I have never asked him how he feels about women in the locker room and don't think I will, but I know he seldom swears. I think that having women in the clubhouse has made the language rougher than it used to be. It is as if some guys want to show off, or as one guy on the New York Mets used to say when the issue of women in the clubhouse was talked about by players, "If we get raunchy enough, they will leave." It didn't work. They didn't leave, but he did. Was returned to Tidewater. Not for what he said. Nobody minded that. What they minded was that he had two weak points in his game. Casey Stengel used to love to say this and I do, too. "He is weak in only two portions of the game of baseball. Thrown balls and batted balls."

To get back to talking or using 90,000 words. Carmen gave me what we call what-for after I talked too much, according to her, at a dinner party. I didn't think I talked too much, and I thought the people at the table were interested. Here's how it happened.

None of the men at the table had been in World War II. Some were too old. Some were too young and had not been in the service, at least not during that war. They got me going about the Navy and D-

Day. Carmen said I brought it up. She was wrong. I didn't bring it up. I may have gone on a little bit but, as I said, they seemed interested.

I played baseball for the Norfolk (Va.) Tars, a Yankee farm team. I turned 18 that May, and they said I would have to go into the service at the end of the season. This may sound strange, but I didn't know who they were. I knew they were the draft board and all that, but I didn't know any of them. Some guys in small towns did. I do know this. I wasn't trying to get out of going or anything like that. It was only that the military man I talked with said to come back at the end of the season. I did, and while I was talking with the Army sergeant, he told me I was in the Navy. He was an Army sergeant but also a kind of clubhouse man for the rest of the services. I wanted to join the Navy because the Tars had played the Norfolk Air Base team. They had some big-league players: Phil Rizzuto, Dom DiMaggio, Hugh Casey, guys that good, and the manager, warrant officer Gary Brodie said, "How old are you, kid?" And later, "Let me know if you join the Navy."

When I said I wanted to join the Navy, the Army guy was writing on a paper. I asked him how long could I go home if I joined the Navy, and he said, "A week." I asked about the Army and he said, "A month." I forgot about playing with the big leaguers and thought about that month in St. Louis. I had been away for over three months. So I said, "Make it the Army." He said, "You're in the Navy." And I was. I was mad, mostly at myself. I complained, but not too much—I mean I didn't say "You can't do this," or anything like that. When he spoke he meant it. I did not know it at the time, but this was a big thing in my life. The three extra weeks in St. Louis were not as important as I thought they were. The Navy sent me to Little Creek, Virginia for training. I think it was for six weeks. It was called boot camp. After the six weeks (it may have been longer—it seemed longer), we didn't do anything.

I was given an emergency leave during the training to go to St. Louis to see my mom. She was in the hospital, and they let me stay until she got out. The Red Cross helped me and the Navy was good. It was really hard on me to know my mom was sick and not to be able to do anything about it, but the doctors told me it was good for her just to see me. I now know how that feels, although I didn't have to go into the hospital to find out. When I got back and finished the training, we were sent to Little Creek. It is right next to Norfolk, and we didn't do anything. We just sat around. I know sitting around will come as no surprise to anybody who spent time in the service, but it drove me batty. Some of the dinner guests said the Army and Navy must be better managed than that now. Maybe. We won the war. I am not complaining about any of this, just trying to explain. Doing nothing was hard for me then, not so much now.

One day they asked for volunteers for rocket boats. I did. When I told this to the dinner guests, none of them said what a lot of World War II, Korean War, and Vietnam vets will say: "Didn't anybody ever tell you, never volunteer?" It gives you some idea of the dinner party, but they were interested. And I was more interested in telling the war story than I was in telling for the thousandth time that Jackie Robinson was out when he tried to steal home in the World Series (I know the umpire called him safe, but he was out and he knew it) and a whole lot more interested in the war story than rehashing the third game of the 1952 World Series, also with the Dodgers. I had a passed ball error in the ninth and cost the Yankees the game. I still think about it. It's too bad the good times don't block those days out, but they don't. Not all the way, and when you write a book, they come back. That's not all bad because it makes you count, and I had a lot more good times than bad. Mickey Mantle hit a home run in the ninth to get us back in the game. I forgot who made the last out, but the guy who made it hasn't. Nobody forgot the passed ball but no one mentioned it in the clubhouse. That was the way the Yankees were in those days.

The rocket boat training was not too long, and it was exciting. Not too long after we finished we went overseas. We were on the sea so it seemed funny to say we went overseas but that is what they said. Not the Navy guys; I think they said "Ship out." We did, from Lido Beach, Long Island, after a two- or three-week stay. They gave us jobs while we waited. I was a soda jerk and it was a good job and to this day makes me understand that job, although I don't think any-body does it any more.

We went to Glasgow, Scotland, by way of Bay-onne, New Jersey, and Boston. We went on an LST —Landing Ship, Tank. I couldn't guess how many sailors were on it, but most of them were sick. It was

awful. My dad had told me how rough his trip was
from the old country, as they all called Italy. Our cross-
ing was enough to make you want to forget it. Four
bunks from the floor to the ceiling, loud speakers
going all the time. You would lie in your bunk and
think what would happen if you hit a mine or were
hit by a torpedo. The bulkhead, as they called the walls,
would cave in, and you knew you couldn't swim. It
was not a good time. We were cannon fodder or whatever the Navy term is, and at age 63, I can now understand why old men send young men to war. I didn't
say that at the dinner table, but I wish I had.

The guys on the rocket boat stayed together. The
five enlisted men did, anyway. The only one on the
boat I remember was Ensign Holmes. He was the
captain, and I tried to find out about him for this book.
He said he had gone to the University of Texas, but
we tried to find out where he lives now and struck
out. The Alumni office didn't have anything on him.
Maybe I had the wrong college. Or maybe he just told
me he had gone to college, like some people tell you
they had a tryout with the Dodgers or Twins or someone. I know I am right about one thing. We didn't
get along.

We didn't get along on D-Day and not before
and not after. As I said, all of us knew that this was a
big thing. Even while we were in training in Little
Creek we had been told not to talk about what we
were doing. Not to tell our folks in letters or anything
like that. Made me feel important. Some of the other
guys said they tell that to everybody, even the cooks,
but I didn't believe him. Our rocket boat was in the

water for about 15 days. We would lay down smoke screens. Since a lot of them didn't count, it seemed to us we were practicing, or maybe they called off the invasion. Our base ship was the *USS Hayfield*, and General Eisenhower was on it. I never saw him then, but he saw me play in some World Series, and I met him. I never talked about D-Day. It didn't seem right, but now I wish I had.

The 15 or so days were not bad except that I got sick of K rations and all the oranges they gave us. When the landing did start, June 6, 1944, it looked like the Fourth of July and I stood up in the boat. I was a machine gunner. We were too far away to shoot, so I stood up and it was like the Statue of Liberty fireworks except not in color. Ensign Holmes told me to get my head down, only he didn't say it that way, and I did. Later on we got close enough to shoot and I did, but like most guys I have talked with, I don't know if I hit anyone. I also don't remember seeing colors. Color is not big in my life. It is in some people's, and not only women. They want a certain color in a suit or tie or dress or couch. Couch for sure. I know that the facade in Yankee Stadium was a nice shade of green. It was copper and it changed in color. When they tore down the old stadium they sold that part to a team in Japan, so I'm not color blind even though I am not like Carmen and some, all of my daughters-in-law. They know robin's egg blue from other blues. As for D-Day, I couldn't tell you the colors if my life depended on it. The Germans wore blue. But I think I say that from seeing them in the movies, not from seeing them in June of 1944.

I don't know the day because the three or four days were one long day, but we were told by Ensign Holmes to shoot at anything that moved and we shot down one of our own planes. I am not sure if he said "moved" or "any plane below the clouds," but we all shot at the first plane below the clouds. If I knew that I had shot our plane down I would say so, but it was one or all of us. The rocket boat was 36 feet long and had six machine guns, and I think all of them were shooting. But come to think of it, we only had six on the boat so I don't know. I only know I don't feel guilty about what happened. The pilot was mad as hell, and you could hear him swearing as he floated down in his parachute. Another rocket boat picked him up.

The reason they picked him up is they got to him first, but we wanted to because we thought he was a German. He wasn't, as I said, and was he mad; I remember him shaking his fist and yelling, "If you bastards would shoot down as many of them as us the goddamn war would be over." It wasn't funny then and it is not funny today. I don't think anyone said that he was sorry, at least not on our boat, and I don't recall Ensign Holmes getting upset. When you think back on a day or several days like D-Day, it is amazing what stands out. Like thinking, over forty years later, that no one said he was sorry. Nobody on our rocket boat was killed, and that should be what stands out.

After D-Day our company was sent to the Port of Bizerte in Africa. They let us have a new LCR and some shore time. The sailors, and others for all I know, used to sing a song, "Dirty Gertie from Bizerte," but,

like a lot of other tourist attractions, I never saw her.
Don't think I ever sang the song, for that matter.

After about a month—it could have been
longer—we were sent to be in another D-Day. It
wasn't really D-Day but when they shoot at you it is
D-Day, the Battle of the Bulge, and Gettysburg all
rolled into one. This was on the southern coast of
France and we were going to do the same thing we
did at Omaha Beach. I think I was more scared this
time than I was the first, but that may be just because
I think I should say so. As I said about D-Day, it is
funny what stands out. Yellow beach, the one we
shelled, had a large hotel. I can't picture too well the
boat or sailors, but when the beach was secured, when
we had taken the beach from the Germans, it was like
magic. Hundreds of French people (it seemed like that
many) came out of nowhere. They ran out on the
banks and shouted and waved. Old people, kids, even
some dogs. They carried flowers and bottles of wine.
I never could understand where they had been hiding,
and if you saw it in a movie, you would say it was
overdone. On that day, it wasn't, and I can still see
them. It may have been the numbers and the view of
them and the sky behind them that made it stick.

In 1950 or 1951 some Yankees went to Japan for
a baseball barnstorming trip. In Tokyo, and only in
Tokyo, they put each player in an open car and drove
us through downtown. I never saw so many people.
It was like a sea of people. It was not only another
example of a clear memory of a crowd, but it made
me wonder why 72,000 people in a baseball park is

not the same. It is not and I guess it has to do with a ballpark, a huge crowd in Japan, and the coast of France when you are 18 years old.

I spent a little more time in Africa and was then sent back. And before going on, I did not tell the dinner party all this. If I had, Carmen would have said she was sick and had to go home. Even if the party had been at our house, and come to think of it, it was.

Back to Norfolk, they put us through a bunch of medical tests. The doctors could ask you some dandy questions like "Were you scared over there?" I said, "No, not at the time, but I am now." I thought I was going to be sent to the Pacific. After several days, maybe a week, I was told I was going to New London. I knew what that meant, and I said "I didn't volunteer for submarines." I may have made one error when I volunteered for the rocket boats, although I don't regret the time spent, not one day, but I had been shot at twice and I didn't want to go under water, so I complained. I didn't even want to go on water again, and thinking back on that so-called troop ship makes me, well, not shudder but shake my head. About like I did when Marv Albert asked me how I felt about colorization. I think it was on national TV. If you happened to see it, you will understand, and if you didn't, it is just as well. It was one of the most embarrassing things that ever happened to me.

My complaint? It didn't do any good. I went and I never understood how this happened. I was sent to New London to help build the baseball field (it's still there) and to play baseball. Not just those things—I took tickets in a base movie theater and was the equipment manager for the football team. We played Cornell, Dartmouth, Harvard—schools like that. It was great to see the colleges and the college girls. I did play a lot of baseball and with some major-league talent. It was that year, hitting against all kinds of good pitchers, that made me know I could play in the big leagues. I really knew it then. I don't think I told anybody, but I knew it.

I am making the year in New London sound good and it was, but when I first was assigned to the sub base, they wanted me to box. Jimmy Gleeson was a lieutenant and the manager of the base team. He had been an outfielder for the Cubs and Reds and the Cleveland Indians. I don't think he believed that I was the property of the New York Yankees, and he really did try to get me to box. I didn't want to and after a while he let me play. I hit well and after that I played a lot. When I managed the New York Yankees I brought him back as a coach. By then he knew I belonged to the Yankees, and then he did, too.

I went down to Yankee Stadium several times, so it was not true that the first time I saw Yankee Stadium was the first time I played there. I was in the Navy but my heart belonged to baseball and the Yankees. When I went to New York, I would go to the front office and then go into the dressing room. One time I told Big Pete Sheehy, the equipment manager (the clubhouse is now named in his honor), that I would play for the Yankees some day. I said that on D-Day. Ensign Holmes told me to keep my head down, but he used stronger words. Big Pete said this and just this, and he said it like he was bored, "Not a chance kid, not a chance." Later when I did come back in my sailor uniform, and I never again said that I would play here, someone said so he could hear, "This kid is playing well in New London and he is the property of the Yankees, but he sure don't look like no Yankee." Pete said, "He don't look like no sailor either."

I have seen those words in the papers, I've heard them in person, and now I am seeing them in my book. My boys know about them and a lot more, too. My grandchildren are going to see them. I guess I'd better tell you how I felt: bad, but not too bad. I was used to kidding with teammates but not with club-house men, at least not until I got to know them. I couldn't say something like, "At least I don't pick up dirty socks for a living." I didn't say anything. I was hurt but not enough to show it. All I did was say to myself that I am going to come back here and show them I can play baseball in the big leagues. I did come back at the end of the next year and hit the first pinch-hit home run in World Series history. It didn't win the game so it was not a good time to remind Big Pete, so I didn't. I am not sure I ever reminded him, but he used to tell me about it and anybody else who would listen. He was a great friend for many years. I cried the day he died.

I didn't tell all this at the dinner party or I would have deserved the what-for I got from Carmen, but I told a little of it to Tim McCarver and Jim Palmer on the fortieth anniversary of D-Day. They were broadcasting the L.A. Dodgers–Houston Astros game from Dodger Stadium. A writer from a California paper was listening. He said as the bull session broke up, "Yogi survived D-Day and George Steinbrenner, and all in 40 years." I thought it was funny. They thought it should be in this book and so it is.

7

CHILDHOOD

et me give you our family tree. My mother was Paulina and my dad was Pietro. They were born in Italy in Malvaglio. Malvaglio is in northern Italy. Some people think that if you were from there you were better because it was closer to Germany. I didn't think so for sure, but some people did. Maybe they still do. My mom and dad dated in Malvaglio, but I am sure they didn't call it that. I don't think it was called courting. I don't know what they called it. My dad came to this country and after he worked in Colorado and California, he got a job in St. Louis. Then he went back for her and they were married in Italy. After settling down in St. Louis, they had five children: Tony, Mike, John, Lawrence, and Josie—four boys and then one girl. We were close but not a TV family. Growing up in that family is so different than most today it doesn't make much sense to describe it. If you are my age you know, and if you're not, you wouldn't believe it and probably don't care. Let me say this much. Our dad was the center of the family. We loved and respected him for what he was doing for us, and we tried to please him and to get along with each other. I have said before and will again. Without my brothers' support, I would not have been a baseball player—Single A, Double A, Triple A, or any other A's. All of them knew how I felt.

None of them became what you would think of as successful. They didn't own a Ford agency or a bank or go to an Ivy League college. They were good people, and as I did well in baseball they made sure I knew they were proud of me. Every now and then a reporter who thinks he is Freud asks me if being the youngest boy is why I made it to the Hall of Fame. I almost always say yes. I don't think it had anything to do with it. I was spanked, only we didn't call it that. I can't think of what we called it, but it hurt like hell. Maybe that's why it didn't bother me too much when Red Smith said watching Berra play third base was like " . . . watching a guy put a pup tent up in a high wind." It didn't hurt when he wrote it, and after I got to know Red Smith, he couldn't hurt me no matter what he said. I mean he had too much good in him to be nasty to someone like me. When I got fired by the Mets, he wrote a nice column about it and ended it this way, "The next day Yogi played golf in New Jersey. I hope he hit them straight and putted like an angel." I didn't, but it made me feel good that he hoped I did.

Carmen Berra nee Short (they used to say it that way) and I were married in January of 1949. I know the day, the 26th. We had three boys. I don't mind my age, I really don't. As I have said, I wouldn't change a thing I have done, but I am not crazy about having our youngest son, Dale, be over 30 years old. I can remember when I thought 30 was old, so you can see my problem.

Our oldest son, Larry, played baseball in high school and signed with the New York Mets. Larry tried hard for several years but stayed in the minors, hurt his leg, and had to give it up. I think he thinks he had a good chance, and I know he is glad he quit. He went to college and now has his own commercial flooring business in New Jersey. He is married and has three children.

Timmy, our second son, went to the University of Massachusetts. He was a wide receiver good enough to get drafted by the Baltimore Colts. He played for them and the New York Giants. He is a co-owner and manager of Yogi Berra's Hall of Fame Racquetball Club in Fairfield, New Jersey. He is married and has two daughters. I hope he buys his floor from his brother, Larry.

Dale, our youngest son, played for almost ten years in the major leagues. Most of them with the Pittsburgh Pirates, but the last few with the New York Yankees. I was his manager. Connie Mack, the owner-manager and legend in Philadelphia for 53 years, was at that time the only other dad to manage his own son. I had the job for 16 games until I got fired. Cal Ripkin managed two of his sons for Baltimore, but that didn't last long. I think it was 6 games. Connie Mack managed his son Earle for 5 games. Only 5 games, and it took Earle three years on the team to get into those 5 games. Maybe Connie didn't want to be accused of playing favorites. At least I didn't have that problem.

The year I managed for 16 games was 1985, give or take a few, depending on when it was decided to set me free. I had to play Dale. Dave Winfield, Rickey Henderson, and Don Mattingly were all hurt. When you have three guys like that hurt, you are glad you have someone on the team who can play three positions. Dale could. Once he even pitched but not in the big leagues. It was to fill in when he was in the minors. I was told he did not have a good move to first base, and I understand he had a lot of practice in the few innings he pitched. Dale is married and has a daughter.

I want to say one more thing about Connie Mack. Old baseball fans may remember that he said some tough things about my catching. After the 1947 World Series he said, "I have never seen worse catching." He also said that he didn't know how bad we were, and that he was going to run us to death the next year. It did not make for a restful winter.

On the other hand, for a rookie catcher to be knocked by the great Connie Mack made me work at little bit harder. It also made me a little bit more important. You don't talk about the guy who can't hurt you. The bench jockeys never yelled at the .220 hitters.

It may not be a great idea to give a 22-year-old catcher with a lot of incentive any more desire by saying we are going to run you off the field next year. I don't know if it made a lot of difference, but I do know that this is the first time I have thought about it since the winter of 1947. Another good reason for me to work on this book, and I hope a little something for you as well.

I was never sure whether Casey Stengel had a childhood, but I do know he said what I am about to tell you because I was standing right next to him. We played the New York Giants in the World Series. We beat them 4 games to 2. I made an error, hit .261, and didn't have an RBI during the six games. The third game was in the Polo Grounds, the Giants home park. It's been torn down, and replaced by some huge, high-rise apartments. Casey was holding court. He always did, no matter what park or the time of day. He was telling several of us about the time he hit an inside-the-park home run in the Polo Grounds. Rat-tat-ta he went on, and threw his arms out toward the outfield. "The guy in left ran after the ball and rat-tat-ta." He had a face like silly putty and all of a sudden he stopped talking, looked at Mickey Mantle, who had been watching as all of us had, and after a moment, during which he let his jaw drop, "You know, this kid—" and he looked right at Mickey, not in a mean way but like an actor, and he was one, "This kid thinks

I was born at age 60 and began managing in the big leagues."

I read in *USA Today* that when a kid first learns he can lie to his parents and get away with it, everything changes. The kid can be very young, but now he knows that life is not all centered on mom and dad. The professors who did the study said lying had a lot to do with learning independence. I don't know about all of that. I only read the story because someone told me, "Yogi, you wouldn't know how to lie if you had lessons," and the word "lie" caught my eye. After he told me, he told a lot of other people, and it still gets back to me. No need to give you the guy's name because he was wrong.

While I am not sure about what place learning how to lie has in growing up, I do know two things about my growing up. One was that I never lied to my folks until I got into baseball, and the far more important part, that pleasing your parents is a good way to grow up. Now, I know that my three boys are going to clap their hands together and say something when they see this, but I am only telling you what worked for me. I would like to think it works for everybody, unless your father and mother are bad like Bonnie and Clyde.

Wanting to make my folks happy and proud was important to me, and it was important until the day they died. One day when they were filming a *Yogi at the Movies* (I think it was in Los Angeles), we had some time to talk after the three-hour session. One of the guys asked me about my folks. During the conversation, I was asked when they died, and I opened my wallet to get out the picture of each of them. One of the technical people got tears in his eyes, and said, "How many 63-year-old men do you know who carry pictures of his mother and father in his wallet?" I don't want to embarrass the guy by putting his name in this book, and I don't want to say he was some sort of an Ann Landers, and I don't want to say he just fell off the turnip truck. I do want to tell the story and let you judge for yourself.

I wanted to please my folks and it worked for me. My dad did not think playing baseball or playing anything was good. Work was good. Work was why he came here from Italy, and as soon as he could, he sent for my mother and my two older brothers. I worked and I worked hard, but I had a dream of playing baseball in the big leagues. The big leagues, not any particular team in the big leagues, just the big leagues. It would have been nice to play for the Browns or the Cards, but that was not part of my dream. Playing good in the big leagues was not part of my dream, and I really mean that. I just wanted to get to the big leagues and then see if I could get good at it. I don't want someone to think I was so *naive* as to think I was going to get a tryout if I played the way some people thought I looked. I am just saying that I have always been one to take one step at a time. George Weiss used to work on me to get me to sign a two-year contract when I was playing for the Yankees. "Yogi, you did a good job this year and we want to reward you with a two-year contract for, say, thirty thousand. Sign right here." I never did and I think I was right. I wanted to take it one year at a time. That way if I had a good year, I could ask for more the next year. If I got to the big leagues, I could see how good I could get.

So I had a happy childhood, and most of the time my folks were happy with me. A lot has been said about my skipping work to play baseball, but it was not an everyday thing. I did a few times, but never enough to make my folks stay awake at night. I know I leave myself open for a reader to say that I just knew how far I could push it. You might say that, but you would be wrong. Pleasing my folks was like staying in shape when I played for the Yankees. Important. If Mickey and Whitey Ford wanted to have a second drink after a big game, I went along. But I knew when to go home, too. The way I knew when to go home was by looking up at the lights in the bar. If they were a little bit blurred, I went home. I would do it quick, saying something like "Time for me to go."

I took my job home with me from the ball game. Some people who know me are going to laugh and say that they never saw me do that. What I mean is that I took my job everywhere. It was important to get in shape and take care of yourself. All the time. Nobody else was going to do it for you. I was able to do what I did without being kidded, or maybe I was being kidded so much it didn't matter. I didn't need to fit in with anybody who stayed out too late and maybe had a few, but I did. And I don't know how, and I can't tell you how, but you can ask the other guys on the team and they will say I did. I know it.

I don't know when my mom and dad first saw my name in the paper. It may have been when I signed with the Yankees, and it may have been before. Whenever it was, it was a big thing for them. Hemingway told me that the secret of writing is, "to tell the reader what the world was like." Well, if you work in a factory in a small section of St. Louis called Dago Hill, and your kid signs a contract to play baseball or gets a hit or does something good so his name is in the paper, then it is a big thing. They never saw me play in a World Series in person, but they did see me on TV. My dad never told me, but I think he was happier to see me on TV in his home with some of his friends than watching in person in New York.

Let me get to that lie. I got paid 90 dollars a month for playing for the Norfolk Tars. The newspapers in St. Louis that I sold on the corner—the *Post*, the *Globe*, and the *Times*—each of them cost 3 cents. That's 3 cents each or 9 cents for all three, but nobody, not even Joe Medwick who used to give me a nickel and tell me to keep the change, bought all three. I don't know what a paper cost in Norfolk in the early forties, but I know that I used to go to bed hungry because I had to pay for my room, I had to pay for part of my uniform, I had to tip the clubhouse guy, but I didn't have to eat, at least not like I used to at home. I didn't tell Larry, Tim, and Dale this story very often, but when I did it always got the same reaction. One, two, or all three of them would start pretending they were playing a violin. The Dodgers had an outfielder named Ferrara, Al "The Bull" Ferrara. He played the violin in the off-season, and I used to wish he would come over when they did that and bang them together.

That violin story may have been just to put off writing down a painful memory. My mom knew that I was not eating and she knew why. I don't know if I told her, or if she just knew without anyone telling her, that $90 would not cover my expenses—just like she could tell if you were sick even before you knew. She was not as smart about money as many women are today, not only because she didn't have much but because she didn't think she should know about money. That was what men did. All of us worked and we all gave Mom our paychecks, even my dad I would guess, and then she gave back what she wanted us to have. So it was kind of a shell game—now you see it, now you don't—but it worked. I hope you can understand that. If you can't, ask someone over 60 with an Italian mother. Moms aren't supposed to know all they know, but they do.

I am reminded, telling this story, of one time when we had a rookie pitcher who had to face Ted Williams. He kept fooling around, walking behind the mound. I called time and went out and he asked some dumb questions. I went back and he did pretty much the same thing. It dawned on me, and I went out and said, "Kid, you're going to have to throw it sometime or Casey will take you out."

My mother sent me money, and we lied to my dad when he asked.

8

MANAGER

"**H**ow would you like to manage?" said Ralph Houk. "Manage who?" asked Yogi Berra. (Spring training, 1963)

"A manager manages people, and one of them is the manager."

I don't know who said that, but I know he was smart. It might have been Peter Drucker. When Drucker lived in Montclair, New Jersey, we went to some of the same parties and I liked talking to him. We never went into a corner to talk, and now that I am writing about management I wish I had, or maybe listened better. He had a little accent, but he was not hard to understand and he never used big words. He told me once that he did some research for one of the big car companies. I don't remember which one, but I know he said it was true of all of them. What he found out was that way back, say in 1947, you had to have a high school education to hold a job as foreman. Now, and this was late in the 1950s or even in the early 1960s, the same job required a two-year college degree. He said his study showed that the job of foreman was the same. Then he said, "Soon they will require a four-year degree," and he laughed. Lots of times people tell me something about going to college to make me feel better about not having gone. At least I think they do. Peter Drucker's story was just a cocktail party story, but it stuck with me.

The first time I managed in the major leagues was in 1964. I took a cut in pay to get the job. I would do it again. I was 39 and the team was the New York Yankees. We won the American League pennant and lost to the St. Louis Cardinals in the seventh game of the World Series.

After we lost, at least 30 reporters were in the Yankee manager's office, and several of them asked me if it was tough to lose to St. Louis. What they really meant was is it tough to lose to your home town. I remember thinking I should say, "No, it made it easy," but I didn't. I probably said, "It's tough to lose, but we played well and some guys got hurt, and somebody's got to lose."

I don't think the guys getting hurt had anything to do with what happened to me, but it did hurt when I got fired 72 hours after the last game. When I say that the injuries to Yankee players were not the reason I got fired, I mean just that. I think the Yankee brass had decided to fire me no matter what happened. I think they didn't think I could manage. I thought I could. I also feel this, and it is the first time I have said it because it sounds like sour grapes. Whitey Ford hurt his arm in the first game and was out for the Series. If he had been sound, we would have won the last game. He came back in 1965 and won 16 games. It was the first time I was fired.

I got fired two more times, and I want to talk about all three because I learned a little something. And I will talk about them in a chapter on sacking, a term I picked up from reading a Groucho Marx book about his TV show. I was asked to be on the show, but I said no. Groucho could make people laugh, but he could be tough. I wasn't sure I wanted to be a fall guy. I was a fall guy almost every day in the papers. Fred Haney, who at the time was the manager of the Milwaukee Brewers, was a contestant. Groucho said, "This is the man who made Milwaukee famous, you know. He also made Milwaukee come in second." I read the whole book. Very funny.

It hurt some more when the Yankees, 48 hours later, hired Johnny Keane. He had been the manager of the St. Louis Cardinals, the same team we played in the World Series. His team won the seventh game, and he got fired. He was having a fight with the front office and he got fired or quit. Maybe it was a little of both. I should add I was not fired in the office after the game. It was season long. Some people think I got fired after the first game of the season, some halfway through, and a lot of others have different dates. All I know is that they told me 72 hours after the last out.

Other Voices
AL DOWNING

Al Downing pitched in the big leagues for 17 years. He now fields questions about the Dodgers on a radio call-in show for a Los Angeles station. He is the host of Dodger Talk. *Downing pitched for the Yankees, Oakland, and Milwaukee in the American League and for the Dodgers in the National League.*

"When I first joined the Yankees, I was only 20 years old. Yogi was 36 but I thought of him as at least 50. The first time I pitched to him he said, "Let me take anything in front of the plate." He meant bunts or topped swings and that I should stay back.

"I found Elston Howard. He may have been the only other black on the team and I felt comfortable talking with him. I told him what Yogi said, and he laughed and said, 'Let Yogi do whatever he wants. He may look slow but he is quick as a cat.' And he was. I did not have a chance to pitch to him often, but when I did, I was amazed at how he would pounce on anything in front of the plate. Later on I pitched for him when he was the manager. When he came out to the mound during the game, his mind was as quick as his body.

"A lot of managers overmanage, I think they do for several reasons. They want to show who is the boss, and they think it makes the fans happy if they talk to you a lot. Not Yogi. He came rolling out and would be practical and realistic, although if you told him that he would say, 'I am what?' But he was, and he would run back to the dugout. What would stick in your mind is that he knew exactly what was going on and it was your job to give him that strike out or ground ball. You didn't always do it of course, and if you didn't, he would come out to get the ball and say 'nice try, kid,' or something. You would bust your butt for him.

"That first year it must have been tough. The papers were saying he was too dumb to manage, that he was too close to the players to manage them, and you name it. The media was all over him and it must have been tough, but you would never have known it to play for him. I still think him getting fired was unfair, and to this day I don't know if Ralph Houk supported him because you know 1964 was Houk's first year as general manager and he was learning his job. Or if the players let him down. But if they did, they only let him down for one game because we did go to the seventh game of the World Series, and here is the ring to prove it.

"I think that some of the players took advantage of Yogi. They didn't feel they had to work hard for him, so in that sense the press was right." When asked to name names, Downing showed his mettle as a radio call-in show host by controlling the interview. "I think it is enough to say 'I think.' I don't want to go into who did what because I really don't know. I may be just thinking that the press was right, if you know what I mean. I know this much, he was a pleasure to play for and he must be tough to write about. He never said much but it made sense, and now it seems everybody tells Yogi stories. Everyone that is but Yogi."

◆

You might have noticed I have mentioned the seventh game twice. Some people don't think I have an ego, so now you know they are wrong. I am proud of what I did in 1964. The Cardinals pitcher Bob Gibson struck out nine that last game, and we lost 7 to 5. Bobby Richardson, our second baseman, set a World Series record of 13 hits and had 3 RBIs. Joe Pepitone had 4 hits and 5 RBIs. Bobby's average for the seven-game Series was .406, and Joe's was .154. You figure it out.

The other thing about 1964 that sticks in my mind is something I said that was reported like I was some sort of Socrates. It was just this: "When you think you know baseball, you don't." Or it may have been: "Just when you think you know baseball, you don't." It was true when it was first said (and I doubt that I was the first who said it), and it is true now. From what I am told, it is true of a lot of other ways to make a living. From the stock market to a supermarket, nobody knows for sure. We used to just say, "Whadya know for sure?" I never said, "Not much," but if I had been smarter, I would have. Come to think of it, I don't know what anybody said when someone said, "Whadya know for sure?"

I knew Johnny Keane, but we never talked about how he got my job or if I wanted his old job in my home town. The papers talked about it, and a lot about what they said was wrong. I don't remember that it was all wrong, but a lot of it was. A lot of what you read and hear is wrong, and it's up to you to figure it out. I don't mean you ought to be a clubhouse lawyer and say, "Prove it," when somebody says, "It's going to rain." But have what people in Missouri like to call a "show me" attitude. I grew up in Missouri and I never remember anyone talking about "show me." I sat next to a gentleman from Amsterdam, at a dinner once. He didn't know anything about baseball but a lot about the Netherlands. I didn't do well in school and didn't like it all that much, but I liked reading about how they made Holland larger and about the little Dutch boy with his finger in the dike. He told me he had never heard anything about it. Makes you wonder. About that Paul guy from Minnesota and his big Blue Ox.

———— Other Voices ————
AL JACKSON

Al Jackson spent ten years pitching in the big leagues. Little Al was five feet ten, and after Bob Murphy the Met's announcer called Jackson "Little Al," he seemed to invariably add, "the last of a family of thirteen children . . . Waco, Texas." When Little Al pitches in the next Old-Timers' game for the Mets, the announcers can add, "and the last one to pitch to Hall of Famer, Yogi Berra."

Jackson expressed surprise. "I was not aware it was the last game Yogi played. I remember the game very well. I shut the Phillies out. I had the feeling before the game that I was being showcased, you know, put on display. The team they thought might be interested in me was Philadelphia and so if I showed them some stuff, it would help the Mets get a better price or trade. I did my part. I think it may have been one of the best games I ever pitched. I am sure it was the most strikeouts in one game.

"Yogi was famous. I knew all about his Series records, but to tell the truth, it didn't mean much. He was the

catcher. At the end of the first inning, it was clear to me he was remarkable. Let me put our relationship before the first inning this way. I was thrilled to be pitching in the big leagues, and if I was thrilled to pitch to him it was overshadowed by pitching in Shea Stadium. This was the big leagues in the Big Apple.

"Yogi was an asset, a huge asset to me. He didn't know the National League hitters, but he knew hitters. He worked with me and got me to throw change ups. I threw off speed, but he had me throwing a real change. I went along with him. You had to. You had to listen to him. When he called for a change, you looked in for the sign and the guy went back to the bench. You looked in for the sign like he had some magic. He did.

"In the sixth inning he got a hit, moved to second, and scored from second on a single. I watched him come back to the dugout. He stepped into the dugout. He didn't hop in. He looked tired. After he sat down for just moments, he got up and went over to talk to Casey. I was sure he wanted out. I didn't have the nerve to go down and say anything when they were talking. I can't think of anybody on that team walking up when Yogi Berra and Casey Stengel were talking business. Maybe in the clubhouse but not the dugout.

"I was right, Yogi wanted to be taken out. After he moved away from Casey, I went over and told Casey that I would just as soon not have to establish rapport with a new catcher this late in the game. I said something like that and I cannot recall a thing he said or that Yogi said. To be honest I can't recall what I said, but rapport was one word I used, and we are going good. I will not forget the look. The first from Casey. He didn't say anything,

*but he looked at me like he could see through me. Not mad
but a strange look. He said something to Yogi, and Yogi
looked at me. Again not mad. As I said, Yogi didn't say
anything, but he strapped on the catching gear and went
out for the seventh inning. After the game I went on Ralph
Kiner's Show, and later on I learned that Yogi had called
it quits. We have never talked about it because our paths
just don't cross. I hope they do."*

◆

The only jobs I was ever offered in St. Louis were in
a clay mine and in a shoe factory, but that was before
I played baseball. Two winters I worked in St. Louis
during the off-season. You had to work in the off-
season in those days. One year Joe Garagiola and I
worked in Sears and Roebucks. I used to add the "es"
to Roebuck, so the book did. Sears took away the "es"
and the Roebuck, too. Joe was in hardware and I was
in sporting goods, or it may have been the other way
around. It doesn't matter. I think what mattered to
the store was that we were major league baseball players, so that's why I say it doesn't matter.

One year I was the headwaiter in a nice restaurant.
The kind where the headwaiter doesn't have to bring
food to the tables. It was Rugerio's. Several years later
somebody asked me about going to eat at Rugerio's,
and I said, "Nobody goes there any more, it is too
crowded." It made the papers, and I was sorry that I
said it. Tony Rugerio was a friend of mine and had
given me a job that winter, and I didn't want him to
lose customers. But they had asked me if they should
go there to eat, and I had told them the truth. Tony

not only was not mad, his place got even more crowded. Tony taught me the most important business or management lesson I ever learned. "If you are going into a business and you are afraid, don't."

Johnny Keane managed the Yankees in 1965. They finished sixth. The next year he was the manager for 20 games and got fired. He died not too long after that. Not because he got fired, but I don't think he liked being a manager in New York. Some people don't like the added pressure of New York or L.A. One thing management should do is to find out if the individual they want to manage their team does want the pressure. Or if they think he does and can handle it. I think it might have been easier for the manager of the Yankees to go to St. Louis or another town like it than the other way around. On the other hand, it could backfire and you might miss all the attention and think you were back in the minors. When I say "you" I don't mean *you*, I mean somebody. I don't think the Yankees thought about how Johnny would handle the pressure. I think they should have because it is different. They should have at least talked to him about it. I doubt that they did. I think Ralph Houk knew Keane from the minors and that was enough. I am sure he didn't think it was fair to fire him after 20 games.

I did not think about fairness when I got fired, but it was in all the papers for my kids to see and my friends, too. But life goes on, and the guys who told me I should have asked for a two-year contract said, "I told you so." They always do.

It is hard to keep on track when you are writing

a book. Thinking about getting fired even back in 1964 is painful, and getting my mind and heart back to that time in my life caused some wandering and wondering. A manager might well do a little wandering and wondering, but not while driving. Thinking about it is a good thing and maybe I can put it best by saying that a manager ought to spend as much time thinking about what he or she is doing as doing it. But then getting fired is part of being a manager, so maybe I am not off the track.

It is still hard to be told: "We don't want you to do this anymore." They may say it like: "We want to make some changes." But it hurts, the same way it hurts to ask a girl to dance and have her tell you no, only worse. The hurt can last longer. You have to get over it, and that is like a lot of things, easy to say and hard to do. The main thing you have to do is not let the hurt make you bitter. Bitter is bad. You can't let that happen to you. Lee Trevino has a good swing and all that, but most of all he has a great attitude. "How can you feel sorry for yourself when you can go a mile from where you live and find somebody in worse trouble than you."

Getting people who play for the manager to have a good attitude is like winning. It makes up for a lot of things that don't go right and can help things go right and help you win, too. I don't have any rules, except that attitude isn't given like a shot from the doctor and it isn't given in a speech by the manager. It might be in Pat O'Brien's "Win one for the Gipper." But that's not 164 games, and it's not college kids playing a contact sport, and it's not the movies. I like that movie. If I were reviewing it, I would give it a Home Run, even though I can't think of its name.

The guy who said a manager must also manage himself was smart. I think a manager should have a sign on his desk reminding him. Or on her desk if a woman is the manager. I don't think that a woman is going to manage in the big leagues, but I have grand-daughters and daughters-in-law and hope that some of what I have to say is of interest to them. I don't think a woman will manage a baseball team and I don't think one should, but I'll get heat for that. Just like IBM has that "THINK" sign or President Harry Truman had that "THE BUCK STOPS HERE" sign on his desk. It's a good idea to move those signs to different places on your desk, so you are reminded. Del Webb was one of the Yankee co-owners, along with Dan Topping. Most of the time I was there he had a big sign on his desk. It was a "NO SMOKING" sign. It never moved and nobody ever smoked, at least that I saw, but that was different. You need to remind yourself of what you are trying to do. Just like the IBM "THINK" sign.

I did say to some writer that you can't think and hit at the same time. I meant it just that way, but hitting and managing are two different things. You have to think to manage.

You also have to think about what you are thinking. Casey Stengel used to say "You could look it up," but he never said where. I never asked him, but I did listen to him talk about what he thought about. Since I was on the team, I knew what he said was true, and I know it better now, if you know what I mean. With some guys on a baseball team, you have to think about guys who are not thinking. I am not trying to be cute. I am trying to tell you a little about what managers of a major league baseball team do or try to do. Something about their problems. Not so anyone will feel sorry for them because it's a good job and they can quit (and do you notice that few of them ever do), but just to show what happens.

─────── **Other Voices** ───────
DON ZIMMER

"I managed the Red Sox for five years," said Don Zimmer, "and I can get in a cab in Boston and not be recognized. But if I am with Yogi, and I am every chance I get, everytime, and I mean everytime the cab driver, the hotel clerk, or the cop on the beat will say, Yogi, Yogi! How ya doing. Yogi will say, 'Fine,' and he is. If you don't like Yogi, you don't like your wife. When I got fired in Boston, I coached for a short while with the Yankees. I said it then and I say it again: If you can be on a team with Yogi, and that means bat boy, bat girl, clubhouse man, player, manager, or coach, jump at the chance.

"Let me tell you this. Pick your day, any day, after all 26 major league teams played the previous day. By 9:30 the next morning Yogi Berra will know more about the games, who did what, and the next games than anybody in the world. Baseball has been paying me for over 30 years, and I have never seen anyone like him. Forget that he was a great player, that he took teams he managed to the seventh game of the World Series two different times in two different leagues, forget all that, and the fact that

women for some strange reason think he is cute, and forget that he has yet to pay for a meal. Just try if you are a baseball fan, tomorrow at breakfast, read about the 26 teams that played yesterday and see if you can write down the line score after lunch. One time we were going on a short road trip and Yogi said he was going to take his navy brown and navy blue sport coat. If I had a memory like his I would wear a navy green coat. The green would be for envy.

"I am sorry to stop. I could talk about Yogi for hours, but the game is about to start and I need to let the reporters have a crack at me. Stay if you like. One more thing. Make sure he tells you about the dog track."

◆

A player who did not think, and I had to think about his not doing it, was Joe Pepitone. Joe could play first base as well as the best and he could hit as well as the great hitters, but he didn't think about what you have to do every day for 164 games. The main thing you have to do as a player is take care of yourself. He was a hotshot and let himself get caught up with the wrong kinds of people. It is easy to do.

He would come in late but not too late, look at the line-up and see that the other team was starting a pitcher who gave him trouble. "Hey, Yogi," he would growl, and he did it before Rocky did it in the movie *Rocky*. I mean the "Hey." He would tell me he was sick or something. I would walk away and say, "You're playing." He did play, and he told me and a lot of other people that he played better for me than for any other manager. But I know that I failed to make him think, and I tried. I don't know what I would do if I had the same problem again. High talent, high living was the problem.

When a baseball team goes on the road the traveling secretary gives meal money to each player, to the manager, and the coaches. It is in cash and might be $300. On the road trip I want to tell you about, I asked the traveling secretary to put Joe and Phil Linz near me in the hotel. Phil did not have Joe's natural ability as a baseball player, but he was as good as Joe at finding ways to raise hell. I knew that they knew they were next to me in the hotel. I also knew they might not think, but that did not mean they did not think they were important. It was a big series.

The very first morning I saw Pepi in the hall. He said, "Hey, Yogi," and I started to say, "You're playing," when he said, "I need ten dollars for breakfast." He tells the story this way: "Yogi had zippers on his pants pocket and he takes out this huge roll. He flips through the roll and says, 'I don't have a ten,' and walks away." He is right. I did not have a ten and I walked away, but I never had a zipper on my pants pocket, not even as a kid.

Thinking for someone else is not a good thing. Most of the time you can't. Reaching Joe was a full-time job, and I had 24 or 25 other guys. At least in 1964 Joe was not making four or five times as much as I was making. That would have made it even harder. Although when players get real big money, you also get agents and sometimes the agent can get through. I am not saying agents are good or bad. I am saying some agents dress like ballplayers. They have long hair

and use hair dryers like ballplayers. They might talk
to the players better than someone older who comes
from what they might think of as the wrong side of
the tracks.

Today a team can be almost 50 people. The players and coaches are about 30 of that 50, and they report
to the manager. The other part of the team is mostly
men, and they think and write and think and talk. Most
teams have several of what are called beat writers who
travel with the team and a broadcast team that goes
on the road. Sometimes some front-office people go
on trips, so that's how you get to the number 50. It
might be 45 at times, and when you are in a pennant
race it might be 100. So the sportswriters are the thinking and writing, and the broadcasting people are the
thinking and talking.

The late Bob Scheffing, one of my close friends
in baseball, was a player, coach, manager, and a general
manager of a team that went to the World Series (seven
games) and a TV and radio announcer. He told me a
lot of times that the radio/TV job was the best job in
baseball. The other people don't report to the field
manager. They do report on him. Not all the time,
and it's not the big part of their job, but you know
what I mean. They can say something like the right
fielder was playing shallow, and it gets back to the
owner and a lot of things can happen. And shallow to
you may not be shallow to the manager.

The one guy who gets reported on the most is
the traveling secretary. I want to tell you that even the
bad ones, and I have never known a bad one but have
heard about some, do a great job of shepherding 45

or 50 people around. Most of what they hear is bitch-ing. The Astros' traveling secretary is Barry Waters. He is one of the few with that job who came up from being a bat boy. (The Braves may have one, too.) Most people seem to take his hard work for granted. I don't.

When the team went to St. Louis last season, I asked him to get a room for my mother-in-law. The team gets a discount. He said he would. He tells it this way. "I said, 'Sure, Yogi.' I am always solicitous of Yogi [whatever that means]." Then Barry asks me my mother-in-law's name. I said, "My mother-in-law," and he says, "But, I need her *name*." I thought a little and told him that we always call her "Momo," and we do. He tells the story like he thinks I don't know her name, but I do. Her name is Mrs. Short.

Getting back to the team. The people who say "we" when the team wins but "they" when the team loses report to a newspaper, our front office, or a TV or radio station. Because they see so many games they can get to know a lot of baseball, and sometimes that can be a problem. Second-guessing is part of baseball. The fans get that right when they buy a ticket, or even if they don't, but some managers and players get mad when someone on the 50-man team does. The writers have the right to second-guess, and those in Boston are the best at that. The announcers are different in different towns. All I am trying to point out is that it is not one big happy family.

I am very proud that Columbia University in New York has a scholarship in my name. I go up every year when they give it, and I have been in the School of Business. When they built the Columbia Graduate

School of Business, they put the restrooms in the corners. I was told they did it that way to keep the professors from fighting about who got a corner office. If that group had some political problems, you know a baseball team does, too. Milton Friedman said that professors fight about things that are unimportant. "That is why their fights are so nasty" was, I think, the way he put it. I am not sure I buy that. If it makes you fight, you must think it is important. A third strike may not seem important unless you haven't had a hit for a week.

The guys doing the most thinking about what the manager is thinking are the seven or eight guys not playing. The coaches sometimes wonder why they are not coaching third, because people think that is the next best job to being the manager, but most of them are older and would talk about it if they were bothered. They might not talk to the manager about it, but they would talk and that could make them feel better.

I managed three different times—the Yankees, the Mets, and the Yankees again—and I don't think I learned a lot about how to handle the thinking problem. I am sure that winning helps, but it can make the next year tough. You can win and everything seems to work, like when you do well in golf, but the next time you play you are lousy. In baseball you can win and the next year you have more press following you and one thing leads to another.

I guess the best thing a manager can do is talk to the guys not playing so they know why. But I know managers who don't do this and still do well, at least for several years. Dick Williams didn't talk to his players, and I thought he was a good manager. So you have to do it your way. I do know that it is not a contest to see if you can get everyone to love you, because you can't.

I know a lot of people who say that if you can describe a problem, you can figure out how to solve it. I don't argue with them, but I think it is only true about simple problems. Like if you are fat or don't have enough money. Then it is simple to say stop eating so much and get a job. But if the problem is that you're not a good father or husband, that is a real problem and it needs work. I guess you can see that I think the family is important. That may be why it seems harder to manage a baseball team today because it is harder to raise a family, too. On the old Yankees we felt like we were a family. I know that sounds cornball, but you can ask any of the guys I played with and they will tell you it was just that way. It makes me happy to have my three boys know how it used to be, but sad that it is not that way anymore. I started out working on this book saying I was not going to play the "good old days" song, but I was wrong.

A lot of baseball people told Tom Horton, the guy working on this book with me, that I knew a lot about baseball. Gene Mauch, for example. I am not putting this down so I can feel good, because I do already. I am putting it down to make a point. Gene Mauch—and if you don't know about him, most baseball people think he was one of the smartest managers around—said, "Yogi knows more baseball than anybody in the world." Thanks Gene, but you're nuts. If I knew as much as some people think I know, I would

win every game. I have been managed by some of the
best. I have managed in both leagues and have been
in two World Series, one in both leagues.

Baseball is not supposed to be solved. It is supposed to be played by the best players you can get at
each position. Even then, you are going to lose a third
of your games and your best hitter will get on base
only three out of ten times. Nobody has all the answers, and only a fool would say he does. The main
thing a baseball manager can do for his team is know
how the other team is going. Know who is hot and
who is in a slump, and not let the hitter on a streak
beat you. Just as soon as you know that and walk him,
the next guy, a punch and judy hitter, will hit one out.
At least if he does most of the guys on the team, even
the 50-person team, will know you played by the book.

Other Voices
MIKE SCOTT

"*I used to hear Joe Garagiola go on about Yogi Berra. I
don't mean in person, I mean on the NBC Game of the
Week. I would think, give it a rest Joe. I was a student
at Pepperdine and some of the guys watching would yell
at the set the same way they did at Howard Cosell. When
Yogi joined Houston in 1986, I didn't know what to expect.
He is a quiet man. He knows what he is about. Yogi is
not trying to impress anyone, but he does that just by what
he sees and what he can tell you.*

"*Sitting next to him during a game is an eye-opener.
He sees things most of us don't see and sometime when he
tells you, you don't understand until a day or two later.*

I know that may sound like I am trying to make him sound like he can't communicate, but I am not. He can communicate more sometimes than I can understand. He knows more baseball than anyone I ever knew. He tries to downplay what he knows by saying that 'when I played, we only had 8 teams and we saw the other teams 24 times so we got to know them better,' but he knows more about the game right now. Forget the 8 teams. We could have 50 and I would bet on him knowing more than most of the rest of us.

"He may say something about 'Ducactus' is going to have a rough time beating Bush. Or he may tell us to pair up in threes to run wind sprints, but you know what he means. What he means to me is a chance to learn. What was it the league president said, talking with Yogi about baseball is like talking to Homer about the gods? Something like that. It was a great line.

"I think the best thing about Yogi is that you feel good when you see him. I don't want to sound like I am on the Carson show and saying he is a great human being, but that is what he is. I would pay to play golf with him, and if he knew, he would charge me.

"We played in a baseball tournament last fall. I got to the hotel after dark and learned right away that he had gotten in early. He is always early. After a game we think he hides in the shower and then goes back to his locker so he can be the first in the next day.

"I ran into Yogi in the lobby and he was still in his golf outfit, so I asked him how he was playing. He grunted, "I was awful. Couldn't putt, Scotty." I don't know how he was when he was a player but he doesn't like excuses, so I was not only surprised he gave me one, but the excuse *was vintage Berra. I think they just got through marinating the greens.'*

"I know a guy who went to Harvard and we like to kid him by asking him to say something smart. Yogi can't come up with his lines and the guy from Harvard can't pop out wisdom. So it is hard for me to explain in a sentence what he knows, but after seeing him for three years I can tell you he knows what has happened, what is happening, and what could happen in the next two or three innings. I don't know anyone on the team who doesn't feel that way. If you don't love the little guy, something is wrong with you. I will bet that someone, maybe a nun or his dad or mother, took him aside and said, 'Lawrence if you can't say something good about someone, don't say anything at all.' A lot of us may have been told that. With him it worked."

◆

If this book didn't have something about my being too nice a guy to be a manager, somebody would say I was not only a nice guy but a chicken. I know I am not a chicken, at least not a physical chicken. I mean by that I am not afraid of the ball. Don't smile about what it feels like to have a hard ball thrown right in front of you at 85 or 90 miles an hour. Or let someone like Jim Lemon of the White Sox slide into home plate when you are blocking it. Better yet, make that Jackie Robinson, who was a UCLA football star, and you better not be a chicken.

I didn't mean to get so carried away, but since I have maybe I made my point. Getting back to being a nice guy, the press and several books said I couldn't manage because I was one. That bothers me. Larry, my oldest son, suggested that I should pretend I am Richard Widmark and push people in wheelchairs down staircases. But it would be just that—pretending. I don't think you should try to be something you are not because most of the time you can't. I did some hard things when I was a manager, like sending a kid down who I knew wasn't going to come back. I know baseball can be a cruel game, but I don't have to be. I also don't think having meetings all the time is good. I played hard for the managers I played for and I expected the same when I managed. I think I got it most of the time, even though I know that a lot of people said that I was too close to the Yankees in 1964 because I had played with a lot of the guys I managed. I always try to do well by my friends, so I never understood that.

The way I feel about managing is simple. If someone has confidence in you and gives you a job managing his or her baseball team, you should have an understanding—an understanding that if the owner's confidence changes, he or she should let you know. What I am saying is this. When I told Don Mattingly I had confidence that he could play first base, I had to give him a chance. Then if he does do well, part of my job is to keep him happy. If he doesn't, my job is to try to help him. If I have to bench him, I need to let him know why and work with him, extra hitting or whatever is needed.

The same should be true of the manager. If you hire him, you can't bench him but you should treat him the same way you would want him to treat your first basemen. I am not talking about the times confidence has nothing to do with a manager getting fired. He is fired to get a headline, but that is not something I know about. That's a public relations move. Nothing wrong with that because dealing with the press is part of the job. In fact when Peter Gammons wrote a story in *Sports Illustrated* last year, "Rating Major League Managers," he put Dealing With the Media in his list of things you had to do well to be a manager. The others he listed were People Management, Judging Talent, Teaching and Preparing, and Handling Pitchers. It was a good piece, but I would argue that your pitching coach is the one to handle the pitchers. You treat him the same way you want your boss to treat you, but he is the boss of the pitchers.

I like to read that sort of story, like the one Gammons wrote, because you get to second-guess writers like they do you. He said that the managers who were the best at dealing with the media were Sparky Anderson as number one, and then Whitey Herzog, Roger Craig, Bobby Valentine, Davy Johnson, and Tony LaRussa. Tommy Lasorda was number seven. I know all of them, and as far as I know they are good at dealing with the media and all the rest. But Don Zimmer, who spent five years in Boston and now manages the Cubs, would get my vote as the best. He was good and he is getting better, is what I understand.

Another thing I would like to say about managers, and I believe this goes for baseball and every other kind of management: Beware of the ones who try too hard to look like one. Oh, it's okay to look like one when you are changing the pitchers or arguing with an umpire, but I mean all the time. A manager should take the job seriously but not himself.

--------------------- **Other Voices** ---------------------
BILLY MARTIN

"A brilliant baseball mind? No, I wouldn't say Yogi has a brilliant baseball mind. I might say he has a natural baseball mind, but I don't think I would ever say brilliant.

"You know about the Peter Principle? The one that says people rise to their level of incompetence? Well, that's Yogi. I love the guy, but he was not meant to be a manager. He is a good coach but too nice to be a manager. I really do love him.

"He will always be my friend but that doesn't mean I think he was a good manager. I don't think he can be. He is a great coach, he knows more baseball than almost anybody, but he is not mean enough. You have to be mean to manage these guys, they make 20 million every two weeks and you, well, you just have to be mean. He is not. Never will be. I am sorry he didn't stick around when George fired him. He had the chance, you know. I know George would love to have him back. So would I." Billy Martin looks tan and fit. He gazes out on Tinker Field in Orlando, Fla., in March of 1988. "You know, I almost got fired here one year. It was in spring training and I was coaching for the Minnesota Twins. I don't think anybody is interested in that anymore."

Billy Martin smiles, takes a puff on his pipe and brushes some ash off his corduroy pants. "Yogi has always been underrated. People think it's a gag that he is a movie critic. They don't know. The Yankees were more interested in Yogi's reviews than what they saw in the papers. I mean Mickey, Whitey, and Bobby Brown and even Joe D. would ask Yogi what to see. If Yogi says it's a good movie, it's a good movie."

Billy the Kid explains it is time to dress for the game and goes down the tunnel to the clubhouse. When he returns in uniform he moves on to the field and is quickly surrounded by reporters. Harvey Greene, the Yankee PR man, hovers in the group with a checklist. A writer asks a question about Billy and George. "That's the eighteenth time this week that question has been asked," says Greene with glee. Martin tells the group he is harder on the coaches and himself than he is on the players. He says he loved Casey Stengel and that he spends time with the guys who are not playing. "I learned that from Casey," says Billy with admiration. Martin is fired before the season is half over. It was the fifth time. This time he is replaced by Lou Pinella.

Several days after Billy's last sacking, he returns to Yankee Stadium one more time. The Old-Timers' game is the occasion. He dresses quickly, as far from the manager's office in the clubhouse as Nick the clubhouse man can set him up. As soon as he was spotted, he was surrounded by writers and TV cameras. Catfish, Sparky Lyle, Bobby Murcer, and Whitey Ford were free during the time Billy was questioned, but the reporters wanted to talk to him. Martin looked trim and relaxed. He talked about Stengel and was asked his thoughts about Casey's comment, "Whatever you say about Martin, remember he could have been much worse outside of baseball." Billy took some time and said, "Guess we can find out now, can't we?"

It is hard not to like Martin. Harvey Greene had

issued 250 press passes for this game. Martin spoke to one writer directly, not in response to a question. Looking over the mob scene, he said, "Work hard on Yogi's book. He deserves your best."

◆

Almost every day a reporter will ask me if I want to manage again. I should say not every day but every *series*. So when Atlanta comes to Houston or we go to Pittsburgh, one will ask me. I say, "No, I am too old," or "Nobody wants me," or "What's a manager?" or something like that. I would like to if I were younger, but I think you should try to find out what makes you happy and then do it if you can. I managed three times, and I am just as happy now as I was then. If I hadn't managed, I would not be as happy.

I had a chance lots of guys don't get. I also think that just like my bat slowed down and I couldn't hit a fast ball and had to quit playing, you have to keep up with the game if you want to manage. When I say the game, I don't mean what goes on during the game. What I mean is the game played by agents. Each year that game gets harder to follow. Players now have contracts saying that if he stays under 188 lbs., he gets so much; or if he goes to bat 400 times and makes the All-Star team, he gets so much. Or a pitcher's contract will say that if he pitches in 150 innings, he gets $10,000, and just suppose he has pitched 149 by the last week of the season. You see what I mean. If someone wanted to manage in the big leagues, he should keep up on all that, and I don't. I did but I don't. You might say that it is getting harder and harder to manage in the major leagues, and I think you would be right. Business people I meet are always telling me how tough it is to run their business, and "how hard it is to get good help." I guess that is a song a lot of people like to sing. Sometimes we not only don't have the right people doing jobs, we can have too many of them.

Baseball has an office in New York City. The American League, the National League, and the Commissioner of Baseball all share an office on Park Avenue. I hate to think of the rent and the payroll. Over 100 people are in the baseball office. That seems like a lot to me. I am not picking on the baseball office. Next time you watch a college basketball game on TV, count the coaches. Seems like some teams have one for every player. I think even some baseball teams can have too many people telling players what to do. Having been a manager, I know that can be a problem, and I make sure I don't confuse any of the players. I give advice when I am asked and say, "Try it this way for a while and see if it works." That's the way Bill Dickey handled me and I believe it is the only way. Most of the players want to do well. It is hard to overcoach if you let the player ask first. If a manager tries to make everyone hit a certain way, he is going to be in big trouble. To give you some idea, try to think what would happen if a big league manager said, "All our outfielders are going to catch the ball with two hands."

I haven't seen a Little League game for years. I wonder if they still use two hands? I am not a big fan of Little League. I think too much organization too soon is bad for kids. Too much competition, some of it from the parents, is bad. We used to play work up and sometimes we would get up to bat 80 or 90 times, maybe 100 times. Now they get to bat three times and they go home. I knows that is an old-fashioned thing to say and that in some towns if you don't have an organized league, nobody plays. I just don't like to push kids too soon. I don't like to and it doesn't work.

9
FIRED

Dick Buskirk runs the Entrepreneur Program at the University of Southern California. He told me that most entrepreneurs have been fired. Maybe not most but a lot of them. He said they "march to a different drummer." Then he added, "They don't hit the ball the way most people do." I understood right away.

I have been fired three times, but Buskirk said that in baseball it doesn't count. That's good. If getting fired counted, Billy Martin could go into the real estate business and become the next Donald Trump.

The first time I got fired I had some inkling. It was in the papers. Writers can get one player to tell them something, and then they build on it. Some people said I had lost control of the team. I didn't think Casey Stengel controlled me. He did in the sense that he made out the line-up, but once he did that and I was catching, it was up to me. I felt that way about managing the Yankees—the first time, anyway. They were Yankees and should want to control themselves. It was up to me to put the best players on the field, and that meant the best pitcher, too. I think saying who is going to pitch and how often he is going to pitch is the most important thing a manager has to do. Casey used Whitey Ford every four days. Walter Alston used Don Drysdale more like every three days. Don will tell you he might have pitched more years if he had had more time between starts. I know that's hindsight. I am just trying to point out how important that part of the manager's job is and to give Ford and Drysdale something to talk about when they get together at a Hall of Fame affair.

I did not know it was as hard on me as Jerry Coleman said it was. You know, when it happens, even when you think it might be going to happen, it knocks you down. I didn't know it showed as much as it did to Jerry. Maybe later on that day I shook it off, like a foul tip. To tell the truth, I had forgotten that I had run into Jerry Coleman until I saw what he said about me for this book. Guess that makes what he said about my looking bad add up. Anyway, here is how I felt— or at least how I *think* I felt. It happened way back in 1964.

I didn't ask for the job. They offered it to me, and the only regret I have is that I should have taken the two-year deal they offered. But I didn't feel that way until after I got fired. I believed in one-year deals and I always had. When George Weiss tried to sign me for two years, and he did that more than once, I always turned him down. Let me prove my value and then I can get even more next year. I was thinking like a player, and could you blame me? I had been one for 18 years. Roy Hamey, Jr., who had been around the Yankees for a long time, told me to take the two-year deal. When I got fired after one, he said, "I told you so." He said it just that way, like you might on the way home from school.

They wanted to make a change. I don't know who "they" are, but it was Del Webb, Dan Topping, and Ralph Houk, at least. One or all wanted me to step down and I had no choice. Houk and Topping looked me in the eye and said that they would like me to stay on the team. I said I would think about it. I did think about it for a few days. I guess I was hurt, and so I took a job with Casey Stengel and the Mets. As for the first job with the Yankees, I would take the same job the same way, but I would take the two years. That way the Yankees would have been paying me for playing golf all during 1965. Well, maybe not, but it was the only thing I would change. When I say "maybe not," I mean that in those days if they had you signed for two years they might have kept you on. I don't know that, but maybe. The Yankees at that time seemed to stay with a manager longer than some teams.

Sometimes you feel the best about what you did, but not the same day or even the next day. A friend told me that the hole-in-one he got was that way. He felt better the next day and it got better for a long time. Now he wants another. I still haven't come close—in forty years.

It is a good bet that Del Webb, one of the co-owners of the Yankees, was in on my getting fired. It may even have been his idea. I didn't try to find out at the time, but I did for this book. Since Del Webb and Dan Topping are both dead, I struck out. I do know that when Webb died, he told the doctor who was with him that when he saw me, he should tell me he had made an error. He said something about being proud and not wanting to say he had made a mistake, but that he thought he should tell the doctor, who was a friend of ours. Red Smith wrote a column about it 10 years after I was fired. That made it 1974, a long time ago. I still remember one line, and if Casey were alive he would say, "You could look it up." Red Smith put it this way: "Webb said to his physician, 'How often do you see Yogi?' He said, 'Every chance I get.'"

What Webb said will keep you warm on a cold night in Candlestick Park. I am glad he told the doctor and that the doctor told me. He was a good doctor. He said I should take an aspirin a day. He told me that in 1952. Some of them are just saying it now.

─────── **Other Voices** ───────
JAMES PARKES, M.D.

James C. Parkes, II, M.D.'s face lights up. It does not seem a face that does so on a regular basis. "Yogi Berra! What a wonderful man to break in with. My first year as the team doctor was his first year as the manager, and that's what I mean by break in. You want to, even as a physician, feel part of the team, and he set the tone from the first day. I don't know where he got it, but he knows how to use it. I am speaking of the wonderful way he has of not letting things get in the way of what he wants to accomplish. I have learned more about the dynamics of a major league clubhouse that I knew than I could possibly know that first year. So, the way he made everyone feel comfortable seems even more impressive in retrospect. He took over at a tough time because Hodges had done such a good job and Gil's death shocked the team—everybody on the team. He was great to be around and I never recall seeing him waste a word. If one would do, he would never use two."

◆

When Gil Hodges died, the Mets asked me to manage. I had been with the Mets since 1965, and every time they changed managers the papers said I was passed over. Maybe or maybe not. I know I was very happy to be back with Stengel. When he left, they put Wes Westrum in the job. I thought he was a good choice. He had the job one full year and most of the next year. Then Gil came in 1968. As I have said, I think he got the most out of the team that year. We lost a lot of one-run games. In other words, we were in every game. If I had to name the best manager I ever saw, I guess I would have to say Gil Hodges. Stengel was good but probably not as good as he thought. He had a great team. The catcher was really outstanding.

All I am trying to say—except for that attempt at humor—is I was happy working for the Mets. Maybe it made me happy to be a manager who managed once and won. The winning-and-then-getting-fired list was not a long one. At least the papers said that not many people were on it. That may have helped me feel better. I did get some other offers. Atlanta, Baltimore, and Boston were interested in me, but I didn't think it was worth it to leave New York. You have to get an apartment in the new town and I wanted to stay in New York. I wanted to work in New York and live in New Jersey is a better way to say it. So when Gil Hodges died and they offered me the job with the Mets, I took it. We came to terms in less than an hour. I didn't feel right about asking for a two-year contract. Gil's death was hard on me and I just wanted to help out. The next year I was given a three-year contract. I don't remember if I asked for it or they gave it. I really don't.

My first year as the Mets manager was 1972 and we finished third. Pittsburgh and the Cubs were 1 and 2. Leo Durocher and Whitey Lockman managed in Chicago and Bill Virdon in Pittsburgh. Somebody asked me if when I managed and went around the league I was ever worried about the other manager—like Leo or Gene Mauch. What I said was that the only people who worried me were the players on the other team.

The next year we won. That was 1973. Maybe it seemed too easy, although it sure wasn't. What I mean by too easy is this. I had managed three seasons and had won twice. On top of that, a lot of people thought everything I touched turned to gold. See what I mean? We lost the Series in seven games, and the next year the Mets finished in fifth place. Pittsburgh with the late Danny Murtaugh won, and the Cards with Red Schoendienst were second.

———— Other Voices ————
BUDDY HARRELSON

Buddy Harrelson's bust in the New York Mets Diamond Club sits next to George Weiss and Johnny Murphy. Murphy and Weiss are both Yankees. They are in the circle along with Joan Payson, Ralph Kiner, Lindsey Nelson, and Tom Seaver. The Yankee circle of honor features more players than broadcasters and executives.

Harrelson said, "I never understood why Yogi called me Shorty, but he did. I was at least two inches taller, but I was never earlier. I don't think I ever beat him to the ballpark.

"One year in spring training I took my wife and a friend out in a boat. We were going to play a night game with the Dodgers and when the boat first broke down I was not worried. I thought I could get the engine started. I couldn't and had to swim to shore. I was late and Yogi went by my locker several times, maybe three or four. He was mad and I knew it. The last time he came by he caught my eye and said, 'Next time get a boat that works.' I thought about saying I got one that didn't on purpose, but I didn't.

"The reason I remember it so well is that it was just like him. He never complicated anything, and that is why some of the players didn't understand him. Some of them didn't want to understand him. I think he may have been too nice, but that was in the papers so much that it is hard to think what was true. I mean what was really true at

the time. I know this, he was fair and he knew the game as well as anyone. I don't think he was the best manager I ever played for. Gil Hodges was. I am not saying Gil knew more baseball because he didn't. Nobody knows more baseball than Yogi, but sometimes he thought that everyone wanted to win as much as he did. They didn't. Gil put fear in you. Yogi didn't."

———— Other Voices ————
MEL STOTTLEMYRE

Mel Stottlemyre, now the pitching coach for the New York Mets, was brought up to the New York Yankees from Richmond in August of 1964. Stottlemyre was placed on the roster in time to play in a World Series. Pedro Ramos, the relief pitcher so useful to the Yankee effort during the months of August and September, joined the team too late to be eligible.

The trim sinker ball pitcher smiles when Berra's name is mentioned. "I think one of the most important things a manager can do is to make a new player feel welcome. Not so much welcome as comfortable. When I came up Yogi took me into his office like he was a country doctor. He knew what I had—'I know you can throw a good sinker' —and he told me what he wanted me to take. What he wanted me to take was some time. In a few days he told me I was going to pitch, and later he told the press that I threw ground balls. He told me the same thing, but what he told the press made me feel good. He was a big name in New York and the manager, but he knew what it was like to be new. I won my first game and nine more that year. I lost three and did well in the World Series. I still

*think if Whitey Ford had been sound we would have won
the thing. He pitched the first game and was hurt and
didn't pitch again. I pitched the seventh game with two
days' rest and lost. A day or two later they fired Yogi and
I still don't understand why. I used to think about it. If
Ramos had been on the team in time to pitch in the Series
or if Ford had been healthy, but I don't think about it
much anymore unless it comes up like this. It doesn't seem
possible they would have fired him if he won, but no one
thought he would get the ax after coming that close."*

◆

The next year, 1975, the Mets finished third, but I
wasn't there at the end. I was 56 and 53 when I got
fired and replaced by Roy McMillan. He won 26 and
lost 27, so I didn't have to squirm like John McNamara
when he was fired in 1988 and saw Joe Morgan run
off all those victories. Or Larry Bowa when Jack
McKeon replaced him in San Diego, even though that
was not such a big turnaround.

The Mets didn't look me in the eye because the
guy I reported to called me on the phone. All they
said was that they wanted to make a change. We had
not been winning and had some guys hurt, but I am
not saying that is the reason. The guys being hurt, I
mean, wasn't the reason. Not winning always seems
to be the reason. I wasn't given a reason, but I think
that when Cleon Jones, a gifted outfielder, thought he
was bigger than the team and I told him he wasn't,
the team's support of him didn't do me any good. To
tell the truth the team really didn't support him, but
it seemed that way. It was a bad situation. I don't

mind going into what happened but I really don't know. I think it probably is that way on most teams and in business, too. Things get started. Some people thought it was racial. It was not.

Another reason I can't go into it too much is that some of the people are dead. M. Donald Grant for one, and since he was chairman of the board, he had to okay the sacking. I think it is fair of me to say this. Baseball is a great second-guessing game. If some of the players didn't like the way I was running the team, they knew I was willing to listen. I told them that and I think some of them who went upstairs either didn't have the guts to talk with me or thought they were too good to talk. Some of them wanted to feel they had something to do with getting a manager fired, and the Mets management went along. I did the best I could and was sorry to get canned but was not bitter. It is hard to be bitter when the fans in New York were so much on my side. I really believe the fans knew how much I wanted to win. I got booed sometimes when I put a new pitcher in and he got shelled, but I never felt bad about getting booed. I already felt so bad about the guy getting shelled.

As I said, I never got booed as a player in New York and I think some of that rubs off. Getting booed is not fun. I never understood why the New York fans booed Mickey Mantle, but I am sure the press played a part. I don't know if anyone from the press saw Mickey cry when we lost to Pittsburgh in 1960. He wanted to win so much he cried. You shouldn't boo a guy who cares that much.

It was strange in 1961 to hear fans boo Roger

Maris and cheer Mickey. They didn't mind if Mickey broke Babe Ruth's record of 60 home runs in one year, but they didn't want Roger to do it. At least it seemed that way. I said that just when you think you know baseball, you don't. With fans you could say that you never know them. The only thing I know is that I was glad they felt like they understood me. Roger did break the record but Commissioner Ford C. Frick, who had been a sportswriter, ruled that the record should have an asterisk. Ford said that Ruth hit his 60 home runs in a 154-game season and Roger did it in 162. I didn't think it was a good thing at the time and I still don't. Maris hit his 61 in a season and so did Ruth. Don't get me wrong, I am not saying Maris was as good as Ruth. He wasn't. He is remembered for one thing and so is Ford Frick. It is too bad, but that is the way it is.

Phil Linz is remembered for playing "Mary Had a Little Lamb" on a bus in Chicago. We had lost three one-run games to the White Sox, and he shouldn't have been playing a mouth organ. When I was a player, no one would have done that. I really don't think it could have happened but if a new player did, Joe D. would look at him and he would stop. When Phil played that song, I told him to quit. When he didn't, I knocked it out of his hand. It was a big deal. Some people said that we won that year because I got mad and slapped a harmonica out of Phil Linz's hand. I wish it was that easy and so does Phil. We could go to Las Vegas as a team, and I could pretend I was General Patton. Phil got a contract from a harmonica company and I forgot about it until now. I think if some fool had booked Berra and Linz in Las Vegas, I would have heard some good booing.

In 1975 the Yankees were playing in Shea Stadium. The same park with the Mets. Yankee Stadium was over 50 years old and was being rebuilt. It cost a bundle. Bill Virdon started as the Yankee manager. He is the answer to the trivia question: Which manager of the Yankees never managed in Yankee Stadium? He got fired, and so both New York teams had new managers. As I said, Roy McMillan replaced me and Billy Martin replaced Bill Virdon. This was the first time Billy had managed the Yankees. He asked me to coach for him, and I was happy he wanted me. I said "Yes" right away. I was happy to be able to stay in baseball and in New York. As for the Mets, I was sorry they fired me but not sorry I worked for them.

Billy Martin wanted the Yankee job. I think if he could have fixed it so that nobody knew, he would have paid them to let him have the job. That is how much he wanted to manage the Yankees. His pride would never let him pay to get the job or even work for free. I am just trying to tell you how I think he felt. He may tell me my mind is gone when he reads this. He was a Yankee the same way Lasorda is a Dodger, the same way Jackie Robinson was a Dodger. Jackie felt so strongly about it that when the Dodgers traded him to the New York Giants, he retired. You could say that he was old and ready to retire and the Dodgers would have been better off to ask him to step down. You can say whatever you like. He didn't say anything. He did something. He quit. He could have gone to the Giants and the Giants and Dodgers games might have had bigger gates, and he could have gotten a few more paychecks, but he walked away. Came in with class and went out the same way.

Other Voices
WHITEY HERZOG

"He is a better manager than coach. I don't mean teaching baseball. That's a different thing altogether. I mean coaching at first or third. He knew what to do when he was running things. And I mean he knew. He knew who could hit what kind of pitch, and he was quick to make his move. That gives the team confidence. What I mean by coaching is this. When he was coaching first and I was on third, it was my job to give the sign to him after I got it from Hodges. One day Ron Swoboda missed the sign or Yogi did on a hit and run. I asked him if he got it. When he said yes, I said, 'When did you give it to Swoboda,' and he said, 'When the pitch was on the way.' I told him, 'That's too late, man.' I am not saying this was a huge problem and it may be that he did everything else so well that I picked on that one time. He was a hell of a guy to be around."

Jack Buck, long-time Cardinal announcer, tells about the conversation with Berra during a World Series. "'What time did you guys get in?' asked Yogi. 'About 12:30.' 'Was that local time?' asked Berra." Red Schoendienst interjects, "He knew what he was saying and to prove it, here we are talking about him and it happened 25 years ago. I would rather talk about that than what he hit in the seventh inning on."

Herzog goes on, "He was the best hitter I ever saw when it counted. He thought the world of those boys and Larry played for me in the minors. Never saw a kid work harder, but he had a bad knee and just couldn't overcome it. They operated and it was a big operation in those days. It didn't help. I think Gil Hodges's kid had the same problem. Timmy was a good football player, but I think he could have been better at baseball. I always thought Dale should have been a switch hitter, but if you knew Yogi, you knew one thing about him. He was not going to push his kids. So many fathers do. He didn't but I think he should have taken Dale aside and told him. You know one year Dale Berra was rated the second best player in the minor leagues. Clint Hurdle was number one and Dale was number two. I never understood why Dale didn't switch hit in the big leagues."

In 1976 the Yankees went back to Yankee Stadium and I went back as a coach. I coached first base part of the time, but most of the time I was on the bench with Billy. Billy was on the bench all the 1976 season. The Yankees won. As I said, Billy was a Yankee. He may have been sold to Detroit as punishment for the fight they said he had at the Copa, but now he was back and bigger than he ever was as a player. I think the Yankees did sell him because of the problem at the Copa, not because he couldn't play second base. He really wasn't sold. He was traded to Kansas City. It was Billy, Ralph Terry, Woodie Held, and Bob Martyn for Ryne Duren, Jim Pisoni, Milt Graff, and an outfielder with a great nickname, Harry "Suitcase" Simpson. Sold or traded—it didn't really matter. They thought he was the reason for the fight.

The Copacabana, in case you have forgotten or never knew, was a New York nightclub. Some Yankees had a birthday party and a fight there one night. I was one of them. It was early in 1957. One more thing on the Copa. If it had been a bowling team from Far Rockaway, it would have been over in 10 minutes. Because it was the New York Yankees, it was front page. I am not complaining, and I hope by now it is clear that I am not a complainer. An old clubhouse man, a guy about my age now, used to say, "If you dance, you pay the fiddler." Joe Garagiola said a lot of things about me. Some of what he said was true. The thing I liked the best was that I was a Christmas Eve kind of a guy. I really try to see the best in what happens. I like that and I don't mind paying the fiddler.

The Yankees won the American League East in 1976. We beat Kansas City and got to the World Series. It had been 12 years since the Yankees had played in the Series. Baltimore and Earl Weaver were second. The Yanks won 97 and lost 62, Weaver was 88 and 74. New York had a fine team. The late Thurman Munson, a great Yankee catcher, hit over .300. Graig Nettles was one of the best third basemen I have ever seen. He had 32 home runs and 93 RBIs. Catfish won some big games and Sparky Lyle saved 23 games. Good teams can go bad. We didn't do well in the World Series. We never got out of the gate, and the Reds beat us four straight in the Series. You could say a good team shouldn't get beat four straight. I am sure the owner did, too. Sometimes it happens. If it didn't happen sometimes, somebody ought to see that it does. It is good for baseball. Don't get me wrong, I am not saying fix it. I am just making a point.

Billy was on the bench all of 1977 and we won again. We beat the Dodgers in the World Series and Reggie Jackson hit three home runs in one game. The Yanks won four, the Dodgers two. Reggie's three home runs in one game seemed even more important to some people than winning the series. I am not going to say Reggie felt that way, but some people did. I know this. A friend went to the game. Because he was having some heart trouble, he was wearing a 24-hour monitor. The thing strapped to him told the doctor what the line score was on his heart. He took the monitor in the next day, and later on the doctor called him and said, "What in the hell were you doing last night?"

During 1978 the Yankees had three managers and one owner. Billy was fired and the late Dick Howser took over for one game. Then Bob Lemon finished the season and we won again. We also beat the Dodgers again, four games to two. If you saw the Series you saw Graig Nettles play third base like he was the offspring of Brooks Robinson and Tinkerbell. Tommy Lasorda still doesn't believe it. He doesn't even want to talk about it and can you blame him? Nettles' play at third made him as important as, say, a Bob Gibson. Most times third basemen as third basemen are not as important as pitchers like Gibson. Nettles in that Series was. But I don't think anybody said that Nettles was bigger than the Yankee victory.

I also think the owner got the feeling that if he fired somebody, things got better. He got his name in the paper for sure, and that may have been as important as winning. At least some of the papers that printed his name said that right in the story. I don't even try to understand the news business. I talk to reporters because I think it is part of my job. Part of their job is to write about the ballclub. But when I was playing, the owner didn't want to see his name in the paper; if he wanted to, the reporters would write about something else.

The next year, 1979, Bob Lemon managed 64 games. He won 34 and lost 30, and he was replaced by Billy Martin who won 55 and lost 41. The team ended up in fourth place behind Baltimore, Milwaukee, and Boston, which were managed by Earl Weaver, George Bamberger, and Don Zimmer, just in case you have forgotten. Even though I was there, I had to look it up. I mean I was there on the bench for the first return of Billy Martin. I want to say this. When Billy came back, or for that matter when Lemon took over, I always went to see the manager and said something like, "I just want you to know that I don't want to be here unless you want me to be here." I used words like that. Each time, the manager, in this case Billy, said he wanted me to stay. My deal was made with the manager, and the team then sent me a check as long as he wanted me to stay. Some big league clubs let the manager name one coach and the general manager picks the rest. Some let him pick two or all. It is not the same with every club, except that the owners always sign the checks.

In 1980 Dick Howser won in his first year as Yankee manager. The funny thing, not to us but to others, was that we had gotten used to beating Kansas' City in the playoffs. This year they took us three straight. In 1980 the play-offs were the best of five. Now they are best of seven, and I think it is better. If you win your division, you should have a chance to play seven games. At least I think so.

In 1981 we ended up in third place behind Milwaukee and Buck Rodgers and Baltimore and Earl Weaver. We had two managers, Gene Michael and Bob Lemon again. I don't know what happened to Dick Howser but I know this, he was a fine manager and made me think a lot about Gil Hodges. Well, I shouldn't really say I don't know what happened to him. He was fired because he lost to Kansas City. I just don't know if they had other reasons. I liked Dick, but we never talked about what happened. I didn't ask him and he didn't tell me. Some guys tell you all about it. They do a "He said" and "I said" thing on you. Dick wasn't that kind of guy.

The Yankees ended up 16 games out in fifth place in 1982, and we had three managers that year: Bob Lemon, Gene Michael, and Clyde King, the old Dodger pitcher. He liked to say *former* Dodger pitcher.

Billy was back in 1983 for a third place finish, behind Baltimore and Joe Altobelli and Sparky Anderson and Detroit. In 1984 I came back and we finished in third place, 17 games out. Toronto was in second, 15 games back. The Tigers won by 15 games and the rest of the American League East was out of it. It was over early. Some people said the

Tigers won all those games early in the season and then coasted. Winning early helped, but you can't coast. Just ask Gene Mauch about 1964. Ask him how far out in front he was with the Phillies. I think at one time it was 15 games, and they lost. You can't run out the clock in baseball, which is another reason I like it.

If you haven't asked the question, I will ask it for you. You had been with the Yankees during the Bronx Zoo years. At least that was what the papers called them, and Sparky Lyle even called his book *The Bronx Zoo*. Why would you take the job in the first place? Put a different way, you had been a coach and knew the owner so why would you want to work for him?

I can give four reasons: it was offered, it was home, and I thought I could win, and (even some of my good friends didn't catch on to the fourth reason) I was already working for him. I just didn't report to him. I guess "reporting to" is more of a business way to put it. When I think about it, even when I was the manager, I shouldn't have been reporting to him. The field manager on most teams reports to the general manager. Not in New York. You and I know I was reporting to him, and that's the way he wants it. The general manager knew it, too, and that was not a good thing. If you are the general manager, you should have some authority. Now you might ask me if I were offered the gas chamber, would I walk into that? I suppose I have to say no, so no one misunderstands.

Now I hope you will try to understand that I believe in the good people have in them. I don't expect you to think Carmen is objective, but she is tough and fair minded. She says, "Yogi trusts people until they prove otherwise. A lot of people are the other way around." I like that she feels that way, and I think she is right. I had seen the way Steinbrenner had treated people. It was not the way to make your mother proud, but I also knew he was a new owner. He was not a self-made man, and that can give some people problems. Remember that the Yankees signed me for $90 a month, and the $500 didn't come until I had played all year. Don't forget that George Weiss used to call the dugout and say, "Have Berra change his shirt," or "Tell McDougald to stay off the grass." What I am trying to say is that I was a different kind of individual. So was George. I thought he would be able to change and mature and that I was going to win, and most of the time that solves problems. As I said, a team I managed had been in two World Series, although both times we lost. What I really wanted was to have one more crack at being the best in the world.

The Tigers crushed the dream, but in 1985 I was on cloud nine. We had traded for Dale Berra and our youngest son would be a Yankee. That spring I was asked at least five hundred times how he would be treated. I said that if he plays good he plays; if he doesn't, he sits. He had a pretty good spring.

He started the season at third base and he had to. We came North with Winfield, Mattingly, and Henderson all on the disabled list. Sixteen games later, George put me on the DL. Sixteen games and he wasn't man enough to tell me face-to-face.

————— **Other Voices** —————
DON MATTINGLY, DAVE WINFIELD, AND RON GUIDRY

Big league baseball players look at the boss much the same way the rest of the world does. A boss is supposed to take care of them, and how well it's done is the index for rating a boss. Not how smart, not how good looking. How am I treated? That is the nub of it. Basketball players call it "playing time." Baseball players have different names for it, but it comes down to being given a chance to show what you can do. What can you, the boss, do for me so I can show you and the general manager and the owner what I can do?

The last time Yogi managed it was different. Not all different, but something does not have to be all different to be very different. Berra managed the 1984 Yankees, the year the Tigers left the other teams in the dust by winning what seemed to be April, May, and June. He also managed what was thought to be 16 games in 1985. Included in the 16 was the "crucial" third game of the season. The third game was labeled crucial by the owner. Perhaps all Yankee games in Cleveland are crucial since the owner calls the often maligned city on Lake Erie home.

When Yogi first managed the Yankees in 1964, most of the players had been his teammates: Ford, Mantle, Ellie Howard, and Skowron to name four. The mix of the 1964 25-man roster had teammates and friends. None of the New York Mets had been a Berra teammate. His tenure with them, 1973 through 1975, could be labeled traditional. Traditional in the sense that he was not a storied player for the franchise, brought back to lead the team.

Not a Pete Rose as in the Big Red Machine. More a Harvey Kuenn, a player who had been a star but not in the same park. Yogi had been a long-time coach under Stengel, Hodges, and Wes Westrum, but his fans thought of him as a Yankee. One of them you could love even if you hated all the rest. The Mets managed by Berra finished third, won the East, and beat the Reds. Then in 1974 they placed fifth and third the next year when he was dismissed.

The leader of the Mets, Tom Seaver, was never comfortable with Berra. Tom Terrific was 21 and 12 in Berra's first year, 19 and 10 the second when the Mets won, and 11 and 11 the next year when they ended up in fifth. The twenty-year pitching star won 22 and lost only nine in 1975, the year Berra was sent packing. Seaver had been happy with Hodges and might have been happy with Sinclair Lewis or Ashley Montagu, but not with Yogi.

In 1984 it was different and so was Yogi. Don Mattingly, one of the two or three best players in baseball, is clearly one of the Yankee leaders. Mattingly speaks of Berra in the same tone he uses when he talks about hitting. "You really wanted to do your best for him. He was and is a legend. If you went to sleep and screwed up, he would never get on you in front of anybody, but the next day you could expect a phone call in your room. 'Stop by after lunch would you, Donnie?' Yogi would say. You did of course.

"When you went to see him, and he was almost always in his underwear, he would make sure you knew two things. The first was that he knew you didn't have your head in the game in the seventh or whatever inning. Second, he didn't want to talk about it again because he didn't want to see it happen again. He never got on you for what you couldn't do, only for what you didn't do. He never tried to make himself feel better by making you feel bad. He never showed you or anyone up in front of the team. He was secure enough not to have to. As a result, you played harder for him than for someone who was insecure and tried to make you the same. That can happen, too, you know.

"He had a way with pitchers. When he took them out, sometimes they were mad as hell, most of the time mad at themselves. But Yogi would put his arm around them and say, 'You ain't mad at me are you?' Even if they were, they had to say no. He was flat out the best. He doesn't know how happy it makes me that he won't come back to Yankee Stadium. He said he wouldn't as long as George is here. He doesn't cave in. I wonder what he might have said if he had been the manager when I said the owner was not smart enough to know that you can't buy respect, that he had taken the life out of the team."

After being made aware that Berra knew about his outburst aimed at the owner and had responded with a meaningful grunt, Mattingly laughs warmly. He takes a moment to savor the picture of Berra and says, "I read the part in Joe Garagiola's book about Yogi. He said something like if you could say something in a paragraph, Yogi could do it in a sentence and so on down to a word. You know you could use one word. Joe said, 'Well, if you can say it in one word, then Yogi could grunt it.' It was a great line and is really true." Mattingly goes on, pleased with himself and with the information that Berra understood his comments.

"I can't tell you how happy it makes me that he won't come back. I would need to take acting lessons. Maybe someone like Dustin Hoffman could get it over. All I can *say is it is a deep profound joy that Yogi won't sell out. The man has character. He has pride. It was an honor to say I played for Yogi Berra. I hope some day I will be able to call him a close friend. When he first saw me play in Nashville and said, 'Nice hitting kid, keep it up,' it felt like he was kind of a baseball ET. He could make his finger light up, and you, too."*

People pay to see Ron Guidry pitch. Thus far he doesn't make a living talking, but with the soft Cajun cadence he can be very good listening. Of Berra he sings songs: "Yogi was different than the others. He was New York, and he still is. We could be in any town in the American League and people would be yelling at us. Berating us, saying the most vile things, and Yogi would come out of the dugout [Guidry had really said the words in Cajun—'out the dugout'], and the same people saying awful things would say, 'Oh, look! Yogi, Yogi! How ya doing Yogi?'

"It always amazed us. Even though it happened a lot, it made you realize that he was New York. At the same time he transcended the part of New York people didn't like. They still don't like it, but nobody doesn't like Yogi. Remarkable, but he is a remarkable guy."

It is suggested to Guidry that berate and transcend are not words found in a Yogi-ism. Even one made up by a writer for a Sports Illustrated *piece. "Very true. His vocabulary is limited. His understanding of baseball and people is not. When I first came up he was a coach and I lockered right near him. You know he doesn't talk a lot, but if you go up and ask him about things, he will tell you more than you can understand. There was something about him, you looked at him and you liked him. Then you respected him, and then you grew to love him. The only* people I ever heard bad-mouth him were guys that were envious of him. He knew that about them. Maybe he knew it in a way even they didn't. I don't know, but I do know he didn't hold it against them. He was like a kid. His mother or some uncle told him, 'If you can't say something good about someone, keep your mouth shut.' He was told that and it took. A lot of us were told that, but with most of us it didn't take. I will bet they only told him once, and it is still working at age sixty.

"It also took a lot to make him mad. You couldn't make him mad in the usual way. Petty didn't make him mad. Matters of integrity did. Hell of a guy, and baseball needs him. Every team should have a Yogi Berra. Makes you feel good about going to work. When you are pitching for him, you want to make him happy because he makes you happy just by being Yogi. If he didn't exist, he should be invented. I sure hope I got all this down the way he wrote it for me."

Guidry's laughter is as infectious as his voice. Pleased he has gotten the dig in that Berra wrote his comments, Guidry turns back to his locker and is thanked for his time. "For Yogi, I always have time," says Guidry. A writer listening to the conversation (no secrets in a locker room) comments, "Must be fun to write about Yogi. How much does he make you pay him?" Guidry squeals, "Lots, buddy, lots!"

Dave Winfield, Yankee outfield star and best-selling author, says, "Yogi brought a stability to the clubhouse. Not for long, but he brought stability and class as long as he was here. When he managed, it was a comfortable place to be. I know that word can be worked on by people who want to say it was complacent, but they are missing the *point of what he is about. He knew what the clubhouse felt like when you play on 14 winners in 18 years, and that is what he was about. They didn't let him do what he knows how to do. Win. He knew what to do with the players, but they didn't know what to do with him.*

"I don't know this, but I feel it. I don't know it because a clubhouse is a complex organization. You have 24 players, coaches, clubhouse people, writers, trainers, broadcasters, and the manager. You can get mixed signals so I could be wrong, but I think this. George thought he could push Yogi around. He couldn't, and he fired him. He thought Yogi would crawl back. Then the next time he gave him the job that he would dance the George Jig. I am not saying he would have given the job to him again, but George would have the carrot. It's a job everybody wants until they get it. Anyway, it makes him crazy that Yogi won't play his game. The rest do, how come this funny little man everyone used to make fun of won't do what I want? That is the sort of whine you would hear if you could hear it. We don't hear much from him anymore. He speaks to us through the press and they let him.

"When you fire somebody 16 games into the season, you do something to a team. If Henderson, Mattingly, and Winfield are hurt those 16 games and you fire the manager, somebody looks stupid and it isn't the manager. I don't care how much you think it doesn't hurt the chemistry on a team, it does. What did George possibly learn between opening day and his sacking of Berra, except that he would be out of town and he didn't have to do it face-to-face? I understand they still haven't talked, although I know George would like to get him on the leash again."

It wasn't really 16 games that Berra got; it was 15.

Billy Martin replaced Berra and was flown into Chicago on Friday night. Berra was through, but the message was on hold. Is it possible that the NBC Game of the Week coverage with Vin Scully and Joe Garagiola was not a good time to dispatch Berra? The Executive House was booked and the man told to reserve a room for Billy couldn't do it, nor could he locate Martin in Comiskey Park. Had he looked harder, Martin would have been discovered. Billy was in the White Sox's owner's box and in a large corner suite at the Executive House. Perhaps the Yankee employee instructed to reserve a room for Martin got the "No Vacancy" sign, but Martin missed the sign. We are out of rooms but not out of $300-a-day suites. The dark side of the owner's box is the place to watch the game if you don't want to be watched. "Now managing for Berra, number one, Martin, number one." That's the way Bob Sheppard, the Yankee public address announcer, would put it. But not quite yet and not in Yankee Stadium. Berra would be relieved of his duties in Comiskey Park, the oldest park in the major leagues. The man who had taken a team in each league to seven games in a World Series and who took the job, "Because I thought I could win," was fired before he had a chance.

Clyde King, the general manager, went into the manager's office after the game with the White Sox. It was game 16 of the 162-game season. He closed the door, and when he came out Berra had been hung out to dry for another day. To be recalled like the rest. Only thing was, Berra didn't see it that way. Then or now.

News moves fast in any clubhouse. The oldest park has an old and, by today's standards, a small clubhouse. Players kicked over ash cans and cursed the owner. All of the players had seen managers fired, a lot of them had seen a lot of Yankee managers fired. This seemed different. Several cried. Jeff Torborg, a Yankee coach and onetime Cleveland manager and current manager of the White Sox, went into Berra's office and hugged Yogi. "He is not the huggable type, but I think he understood," said Torborg years later. "I didn't know what else to do," said Torborg, who had been fired at Cleveland several years before and who had turned down a job as the baseball coach at Princeton to join the Yankees. A thoughtful, sensitive man, Torborg was as proud of being a Yankee as he was of catching no hitters. He had a few, courtesy of Sandy Koufax and Nolan Ryan.

"They say that catchers make good managers," said Torborg. "That may be true, but I think Yogi understands the game from all nine spots on the field. His instinct is hard to explain even to someone who has played the game for years. One example I like to relate is when he managed Dave Righetti, he knew exactly when to give the sign to the catcher for a change up. Dave threw over 90 miles an hour, and every so often Yogi would signal for the change. In the year or so he did it, I don't ever recall it was not the optimal time for the pitch. Yogi knew. It was like magic."

The Yankees' next game was with the Texas Rangers. Billy Martin had gone down to Texas after the last out, maybe before. He was flying commercial. The two-bus caravan headed for O'Hare Airport. Berra was in the front seat, the seat always reserved for the manager. On a normal night, the bus would drive out on the tarmac and park next to the chartered jet. This was not a normal night.

The bus driver was told to drop off one passenger at

the passenger gate. The huge buses lumbered up the ramp and stopped. Berra stood up, picked up his carry bag, turned and said something, then started off the bus. Nobody remembers what he said, but nobody on the first or second bus will ever forget what happened when he did. The bus came alive with clapping hands. The first bus, the Berra bus, could hear the second bus. They were cheering and shouting. Some on the buses were yelling because they knew how bad Yogi must feel. Some were shouting because they knew how bad they felt. It was electric, an indelible memory to all who saw it. "I wanted so badly to clap to let him know how I felt," said a writer who had covered the team for years. "But I knew it was not my place. It was not the thing a writer did. A writer covers the team. That means you don't feel good when they win or bad when they lose, you write about how they feel and how the fans feel. Most of all it was not my place to take part. It would have been unwise, but I wish I had. I could never write about it and I get paid to do that. It would be like writing about your own funeral."

The bus pulled back out to make the long circle back around the terminal to the charter and both sides of the bus could see the solitary figure walking alone for a flight back to New York. Seeing their manager through the looking glass of the airport, with the artificial light overhead, created an image. It was different for everyone but memorable. "I will never forget it," is the phrase one hears over and over. Followed by, "but don't say I said that, George will read the Berra book. You can bet on that. I don't want to get caught in that crossfire. He has a thing about Yogi and maybe I would, too. Every time he tries to get him to come back, Yogi says no. He wouldn't even *come back when they put up a plaque for him in center field. That really hurt George. He really hurt Yogi. A lot of people think he meant to all along. Something happened in 1984 that made George feel he had to make Yogi heel. Sort of like, he may be Mr. Yankee, but I am Mr. Owner.*

"Sure they broke the all-time home attendance record in 1988. Sure they are the biggest name in the sports business. George knows all that. He also knows and likes to boast that the Yankees have the best won and lost record in baseball since 1976. What he doesn't like is they don't play in October. The World Series, getting into it, and then winning it is all he wants. I really think if he could win one and lose money, he would do it. He would not want anybody to know he lost money, but the money is not important. Winning the World Series is."

From 1921 to 1964 and from 1971 to 1981, a total of 50 years, the owners watched the Yankees play in October 34 times. From 1972 until 1988, the owners watched the Yankees play in October four times: 1976, 77, 78, and then the last time in 1981. In the past it was "owners." Now the principal owner plays only one game in October. The game he plays best. The one with the press. He changes managers and pitching coaches so often to give the illusion of progress. And because the team he frets over and fiddles with is the New York Yankees, the press goes along. Even the Commissioner has asked the owner to refrain from stealing the ink of the World Series, but since 1981 George has lost the chance to see his team play in October so he does. It doesn't play well, but it is the only game in town for the guy Mike Lupica of the New York Daily News called, "The bouncer in a blazer."

Yogi, do you remember what you said on the bus after

*you got fired in Chicago? You know, the last time? "No,
I don't think I took the bus, the team was going to Texas.
I think I took a cab," said Berra. No, at least 15 people
said you were on the bus and you said something and the
bus broke into applause. "That many guys said I was on
the bus? Well, I must have been. I've been on a lot of
buses. I probably said, 'Good luck and go get 'em.' Something like that. Maybe a few guys clapped," said Berra
matter-of-factly.*

The Yankees were the first team to retire numbers.
They were also one of the first teams to put up plaques
on the center-field wall. Ruth, Gehrig, Joe D., Miller
Huggins, Joe McCarthy, Casey Stengel. They put one
up for me in 1988. I am proud to be on that wall with
Ford, Mantle, and Phil Rizzuto. I also have enough
pride not to go back to see it as long as George runs
the team. Another George has a plaque on that wall
in center field in Yankee Stadium, George Weiss. He
was a tough, hard man. I sometimes wonder how the
two Georges would have gotten along.

I don't get mad easy and even when I do I don't
stay mad. I got mad in 1984. We had a meeting in
the owner's office. We had too many meetings, I
thought. When Webb and Topping owned the team,
they didn't have a lot of meetings with Casey Stengel
and we played nine innings then just like now. Some
things like players' contracts are much tougher now,
but in 1984 we didn't have meetings in the owners'
office about that sort of thing. Instead we had meetings

about who should play right field. Or left field. Or some other field. Or pitch or catch.

One time we had a meeting and the owner wanted to see the list of the 24 players and so, of course, he did. I don't want to tell the names for two reasons. One is that some of the guys are still playing. The second reason is that they are all still alive. I thought Jim Bouton's book was bad because he told things that went on in the clubhouse and things that didn't go on in the clubhouse. I guess I feel this way about it. Every at-bat I ever had in the big leagues is in the *Baseball Encyclopedia*. They have everything I did for 18 years. I was having lunch with a big-name businessman and he said if everything he had ever done was down in a book like that, he would be behind bars. He was not just kidding, so I don't think it would be right for me to put down his name.

But I do think it is right for me to put this down. The 24 guys I wanted to be on the team were not the same guys who the owner wanted on the team. It was not just one guy like Willie Mays when he came to the Mets in 1973. It was four or five guys who the owner wanted and the coaches and I didn't.

We talked a lot and I said something like, "If you want that team, can I say that it is *your* team if we lose?" You see, I feel that if you ask a guy to play first base, you have to think he is the best you have and that your job is to make him better. One way you do that is to not run out on the field and tell him he threw to the wrong base. You may tell him that but not on the field. I feel the same way about a manager. If you say he is the manager, he should have some say about the guys on the team. Not all the say, that's the job of the general manager. In a sentence, the general manager gives the manager the tools, and the manager uses the tools to win games.

Anyway, to get back to the meeting. I knew that the coaches and I knew more about judging baseball ability than anyone else in the room. We wanted the 24 guys on the list. We went around and around. When I was a coach I had seen this sort of thing go on before the Mayor's Trophy game, a charity game played between the Mets and the Yankees. It was a big deal for the owner. He wanted to win it and so did we. One year a manager (and I really can't remember which one), after the owner had spent more time talking about who should play the Mayor's Trophy game than it would have taken to actually play the game, joked, "Tell me who to play and I will if I can say that your team lost if we do." The owner said, "Oh, no, we can't have that." That happened during a meeting in 1984.

I have had guys yell from the stands, "Who scouted you? Frank Buck?" I have been called awful things, but I have never been told I didn't know baseball, or who can play baseball.

This meeting got so bad that I called the owner some bad names and threw a pack of cigarettes at him. One of the coaches said I threw the pack down on his desk and it bounced up and hit him. I don't know. I know I threw them, and I know I was hot.

He said, "Nobody ever talks to me that way," or maybe it was "Nobody can ever talk to me that way."

I have forgotten because when you get mad you do forget. But I remember this. He was mad, I was mad, and nobody said a word. I mean nobody said a word after the bad names I used and "You can't talk to me that way." It was like a movie. After we left several of the coaches said, "Atta boy, Yogi, stand up to the bastard," but it was quiet in the meeting. Not a surprise to me. I wondered if the thrown pack of cigarettes came back my way the next year.

What I mean is the next year, 1985, I managed sixteen days and it was over. No one ever wrote about that meeting because only a few knew about it.

The *New York Daily News* writer Phil Pepe wrote just about the time I got fired that the owner would not have the guts to fire me because I was so popular. I don't think that was a favor but Phil may have thought it was. I was never told why I was fired, so I don't know.

I do know this. I don't think it is smart to change a manager before you get to the stream. It makes you look like you didn't do the right thing in the first place. If you want to settle a grudge, that is a different game. But it isn't baseball. Dick Buskirk, the professor at the University of Southern California I mentioned earlier, likes to say, "Never let ego enter into a business decision." I would say it a different way, but it makes sense as long as you know what an ego is.

10
MILTON FRIEDMAN

Casey Stengel was quick as a cat, but when he finished talking, people scratched their heads. He wanted it that way. Milton Friedman, the Nobel Prize-winner in economics, is quick as a cat, but when he finishes talking, everything is clear. He wants it that way. He asks questions that you have to answer. So when he says it's over, he has a good idea of who's on first. We had a three-hour breakfast in San Francisco. I'd like to tell you about it.

He is even shorter than I am, and he thinks that is one reason he and I both did well. We were "out to prove something" is the way he puts it. I don't know about me, but I know he feels strongly about it and most everything else as well.

He is not a baseball fan, and I am not as much a money fan as most people think I am. I say this because I was not trying to tell him about baseball and he wasn't trying to tell me about economics, although Carmen had given me a list of questions to ask. For her—not for me.

I thought Friedman would fall out of his chair when he heard I had asked what paper Ernest Hemingway worked for. He tried to make me feel better by saying that he didn't know the names of all the major league teams. He said we are all dumb about different things. I think he is probably smarter than most of us. I was interested in how he brings economics into everything. Even things he doesn't know much about, like baseball. He said one reason he is not a baseball fan is he doesn't understand the game. He said that in order to really enjoy a game, you have to understand it like he understands tennis.

Up until 1946 or 1947, players in the major leagues left their gloves on the field between innings. The second baseman would throw his glove into short right field. The rest would do the same. The catcher would take his mitt into the dugout. I think he did because there was not much grass behind the plate. When the infielders tossed their gloves, they landed on grass. Nobody minded a dirty catcher's mitt, but nobody wanted dirt inside the mitt. At least I think that's why the catchers kept their mitts. I don't know why it started or why it stopped. Friedman had what he called a "speculation": We left them for the other team to use. At one time gloves were harder to come by, so we tried to "extend their use"—his words, not mine. I do know that we didn't use baseball shoes when I was a kid. Our folks would not buy any shoes you couldn't wear to church.

Friedman thought the practice of throwing the gloves stopped because TV did not want to see the gloves on the field and the cost of gloves came down. I don't know if what he said was true, but I was interested in how he thinks that most everything has what he calls an economic factor. I'm also not sure I have done a good job of telling you what he told me. I never talked with anyone quite like him, and a lot of what he said was new to me.

Carmen loves Georgia O'Keeffe, the artist. One of the things Georgia O'Keeffe says is, "Seeing takes time." Carmen does her best to tell me, and anybody else she loves, the same thing. She can take an hour looking at a painting. I don't get it half the time, but I think I got more from Friedman than from some of the paintings Carmen made me study.

I don't want to get into who is right and who is wrong. About the baseball gloves on the field, I mean. I don't think that is as important as telling you about what the *Houston Post* called the "Odd Couples Breakfast." I will say one thing: At least in the big leagues, one team did not use the other team's gloves. We didn't at Newark, and I don't think we did in Norfolk. One more thing: I don't remember ever seeing a ball hit a glove on the field, or one getting stepped on. They didn't cause a problem, and thinking about it now it is hard to understand why those things didn't happen.

It is important to me that I make this clear. Wise guys are always jumping up with an answer. Milton

Friedman is a very wise guy, but he tries to make *you* come up with the answer.

We talked about George Weiss calling the dugout with orders for Berra to change his pants or shirt. Friedman said that when he first taught at the University of Chicago, the men who worked for Prentice-Hall Publishing Company had to wear hats. He said it was the same thing—the owner wanted the workers to look professional. I said I thought that maybe some of the fans would like to see their catcher dirty so they knew he was a professional. I also said that having to change could break your concentration, although I didn't really believe that. He said that the owner is always adjusting. I said, so is the catcher, and as would happen in any good conversation, we moved on.

I am not quite sure how we got into this, but he was interested in the way Gil Hodges managed the Mets. As I have said, I thought the world of Gil, and I learned a lot of baseball from him. I also liked the way he figured things out. When the Mets went to Philadelphia, some of the players would try to get permission to drive their own cars. He would always say no and make them go on the team bus. One time I asked him why he let his coaches drive if they wanted to, and he said, "I can replace you, but I can't the players." He didn't say it in a nasty way, and I didn't ask it in a way to make him mad. I just wanted to know why he did certain things. I thought he was a fine person and a fine manager. His answer made it clear, and I probably should have figured it out myself. Just like I figured out that hockey players are better golfers than football linemen.

One thing I don't want to forget. Friedman was talking about Hemingway and said the two best books he had written were, *The Sun Also Rises* and *The Fisherman and the Sea*. He meant *The Old Man and the Sea*. Do you suppose anyone called him on it? No. Suppose I had done the same thing?

What I am going to say next really interests me, and I hope it will be the same for you. Some of it may sound like it was written by my press agent, but I have never had one and am not going to start now. What I am trying to do is to explain.

Someone at the San Francisco breakfast said, "It is frustrating to hear baseball people say so many things about Yogi's ability to see what is going on during a baseball game, but then those people will be unable to tell me what Yogi sees that they don't." Professor Friedman said, "I don't understand." The person continued, "Just last night an advance scout, a guy who had been a manager for two teams, told me how Yogi knew this and that, and really put him on a pedestal." I asked him, and I have asked this question a lot, "What would he see that you don't?"

Friedman came up in his chair. "That is true in baseball, in business, in every walk of life. People often complain that somebody makes a million dollars as CEO of a large firm. They say nobody can be worth that." Friedman lets that sink in and then says, "And of course they are wrong. One man can take over a corporation and turn it around, yet he looks the same to you and to most everybody else. If he can do that, he is worth a hell of a lot of money. The other guy, and you can't tell the difference between the two of them, can come in and fail. The same thing is true with Yogi. He has a second sense. You can teach some things, but some things you can only learn. Yogi has learned things that he couldn't teach anybody else."

As I said, Friedman expects you to say what you want, so I said, "Well, you can try to, but they gotta do it." Friedman said, "You can't, you can't, they gotta do it, nobody ever learned anything from anybody else. You can only learn from yourself. People only learn from themselves. They have to learn on their own. I have always said that the teacher doesn't teach anything. All he does is give the student topics to think about. The only person who can teach you is you. Yogi, in the course of his life and his experience, has had the quality to enable him to learn things, but if he tried to teach you to do these things, he couldn't do it." I looked at the third party whom Milton was talking to and said, "Naw, I couldn't teach him—he is bad."

Friedman said we needed a better subject to work with, and a good laugh brought some glances to our table. Nolan Ryan walked by. I know he wondered what I was doing, spending so much time at breakfast.

As I said before, I don't know how much of all that Friedman said is true, but I will say this for it. It is a different way of looking at me than I have heard before.

I don't really understand what you do to get a Nobel Prize, but I do know that the books Friedman reads and writes are full of math, and I am not talking

ERAs. I think that if he ever got interested in baseball, he would try to run Elias Sports Bureau—you know, the people interested in all the stats.

Here is one reason I say that. Friedman was told that Jerry Coleman and some other people said that I never threw to the wrong base. He said this was "improbable," which he explained by saying that it was not even a long-shot bet. It wasn't even a bet. He said that nobody's perfect. He did all this by asking me the number of games, outs in each inning, and all that sort of thing.

I didn't want to argue. I usually don't, and I wasn't sure who was going to spring for breakfast. I knew it would go for $50 plus tip. I did say this much. I don't know whether I did or not. I threw late because I couldn't get the ball out of my mitt, or high, or low, but I don't think I ever did throw to the wrong base. It was interesting. I didn't say all this right away, but when I did, he didn't argue. I think he thought I was right that I didn't ever throw to the wrong base. I think I am right, too.

For at least 30 years, maybe longer, I have been saying that at least two of my brothers were better players than I was: Mike and John. I don't ever remember anybody second-guessing my saying that. In fact, it has even been written in the papers. As I mentioned, I told my dad that if he had let us all play, he could have been a millionaire. He said, "Blame your mother." Well, Friedman, in a very nice way, says, "That is a nice thing to say, but that is as far as it goes. Your brothers were not put to the test, and you were.

There is a big difference between being good on the Hill in St. Louis and doing what you did."

He was interested in what I did, and when I told him about doing piecework in the shoe factory for $60 a week, I got a speech on Adam Smith. He was a Scottish economist who did some of the same sorts of labor-savings thing in a pin factory that we did in the shoe factory. I also told him that I made the $60 a week because my brother and I were fast, and he said, "Of course." Then I told him that I gave my mother the $60 a week, and she gave me back $2, and he said, "Of course, you were a good son." My brother used to make almost $75 a week, and he gave it all to Mom also. I think my dad gave her his check, too. Friedman said, "Wasn't it all nice?" I had to agree.

I was happy that he had read some things I had said about Little Leagues in *USA Today*—too much competition and organization. When I was a kid, you chose up sides and played. Sometimes I would get to bat 100 times a day. In the Little League, you bat maybe twice and go home. Friedman not only agrees with some of what I said but thinks that a lot of our life is too organized.

The story in *USA Today* had a picture of me in an Astro uniform, and he was interested in how I felt in it. I guess he had seen me in the pinstripes of the Yankees. I don't know what I have on, but I do like a uniform that doesn't fit so tight. That is not just because I used to play at 195 pounds and am now 212. It is also that I like a more comfortable fit. I think some of the uniforms are so tight that the base runners can see the pitcher's buttocks tighten when he is going to try to pick them off. You could not tell when Whitey Ford was going to go to first by watching his butt.

"Television dresses golfers, tennis players, and all the rest of the players, don't they, Yogi?" When Friedman asked me that, I had to say yes.

As I said, he is not a baseball fan, and one way you knew that was his asking me if I still hit. I said that I didn't and that even if I wanted to and could, they wouldn't let me in the cage. "These guys are hitting all the time," is what I said. "Are they any better because of it?" he asked me. I said no, and I am going to hear about it, I know. It is true that when I played we were lucky to get eight swings a day, so I think you can take too much batting practice. You can't hit in a game too much, but you can have a guy lay them in so you can hit them too much. At least I think so. In spring training some guys get fifty or sixty swings. That's why they need batting gloves. Speaking of batting gloves, one of these days you are going to see tennis players wearing gloves. Somebody is going to invent one.

You may think I invented some of what you are going to see now, but I didn't. I said that I think hitting is the hardest thing in baseball. Nothing new about that. I said either you get it or you don't. If you don't, take a hike. Ted Williams said that it was the hardest thing in sports, because if you did it three times out of ten, you were very good.

Professor Friedman said, "You may not believe this, but economics is like that. Either you have it or you don't. Some of the greatest people in the history of the world have been terrible in economics. Winston Churchill, for example. Every time he touched an economic issue, he got the wrong answer. But he was a great man. I am sure the same is true in your business, Yogi. If you are a .250 hitter, that is the way it is going to be." You know, I had to agree again, and no amount of batting practice is going to help.

I don't know if he was trying to make me feel better because I didn't finish high school, but the last thing he said to me was, "Don't confuse education with schooling. They are not always the same." He has a Ph.D. and a Nobel Prize, and he said that some of the most educated men and women in the world are not smart. He said that if I had been in his class, I would have gotten a good grade.

11
SUMMING UP

I don't use the word "nifty" much any more. Maybe I never used it. It doesn't sound like me, but it's a good word—better than saying "interesting." You know, when somebody says something that is interesting to you, you should say, "That's nifty." I don't mean interesting in a serious way but in a nifty way. The best advice I ever got, and it was serious or it wouldn't have been the best advice, was something Frank Crosetti told me. Frank played for the Yankees for seventeen years. He played shortstop, and then he coached third base for what seemed like forever. He became a fixture and should have been kept in that job. People like to come to a ballpark and find that some things haven't changed. It makes good business sense to do that, unless Frank or the guy you want to become a fixture is hard to get along with, makes too many demands, stuff like that. I am sure Frank didn't do that, but I could be wrong. I know he told me he got out just in time, whatever that meant. What he said to me in 1948 was, "Get married young and grow up with your kids." It was truly the best advice I ever got, but I was not a kid when he told me. I had done some growing up in the rocket boat off the coast of France.

The nifty or interesting comment I am trying to bring into this was something one of the coaches on the Astros said to me on a road trip. I don't want to mention his name. He gets enough flak now. I don't want to mention my source. That's what the writers say in the papers. Or at least that's what they say when somebody tries to find out who told them something. They say that their source will dry up. This guy is not dried up, but he is close.

What he said, after asking me if I had changed a lot over the years (what I said to that question was, "Yaah, I got older."), was this. "You are less interested in yourself than anyone I have ever known." This guy knows me pretty good, so I will take his word for it. I told him I didn't know whether to say thank you or try to think of a smart answer, so I just said, "That's a nifty comment." He said what they always say when I use a word they don't think should be a word I use. I mean they say it enough so I could live without hearing it again. They say, "Is that a word Carmen told you to use?"

Sometimes I will use a wrong word. Like I will say "Don't get me right," when most people say "Don't get me wrong." Nobody says anything about that, at least that I can hear. But let me say "tranquil" and all hell breaks loose. I don't get a chance to use "tranquil" very much because the places I am are not, but I read somewhere that it was the most beautiful word in the English language. I don't think it is true—nobody knows what the most beautiful word is—but it is a good one.

When I retire and start feeding pigeons in the park, I can say I am tranquil if anybody is interested. I doubt they will be. Since I don't like to fish, I don't think I would like to feed pigeons or play shuffleboard, or anything like that. I have been active with my body all my life, and I suppose I should think about what I would do if I did retire. To tell you the truth, I don't like to think about quitting.

What the Astros coach said was nifty. I asked some people about it, and I am smart enough to know that if you ask someone, "Do you think I am interested in myself," you may get a smart answer. Lots of times people will say they are not asking for themselves, they are asking for a friend. They do this when the question is embarrassing, like I have a friend who has the hair of the dog, you know, a drink in the morning. Do you think it's bad if he only does it once a month or so? You can't really say "I have this friend who wonders if he is less interested in himself." You see the point?

While we are on the subject of your or our friend who drinks in the morning—he or she has a problem. Baseball sends people around to talk to the teams about drinking, and that is one of the things they tell us. They do a good job. More and more businesses try to tell their people about drinking and what it can do to you. One of the things the people who have talked to us have said is how much more a drink will do to you after you are 50, or even 49 for some guys. Since most of the team is way under that age, they mean the coaches and the other older people. The guy talking never looks at us, but the players do. Sometimes when we have these meetings, and we have them every so often, people kid around. I think it depends on the mood and on the way the guy from the baseball office brings the thing off. If he is a former ballplayer, and Ryne Duren the former Yankee pitcher has talked, it can be better, but that is not the key to solving the drinking problem in baseball. I am not sure what the key is, but I know that people should be careful of drinking. It can sneak up on you.

Baseball players have a lot of free time. Today they have a lot of money, and they have always had a lot of failure to think about. Not a good parlay, so ballplayers have to be careful. Even more careful, I am told, when they are out of baseball and the cheering stops.

I talked about the "interested in myself" comment with some people I respect, and they used words like "introspective," "inner directed," and "other directed." One even said "full of himself." I said you are all full of something. I think if there were a scale of "How interested are you in you," I would be batting about .120. Some days maybe less than that. The day a good friend dies, or I got fired, I might be .200. Here is an example.

I worked in a coal yard when I was a kid. I hated

it. I didn't mind the work, but I hated being dirty all the time. In one of the books written about me, the writer said, "I hated being dirty and I got fired." I don't think I was fired. I think I quit, but I would not say for sure. Most people would remember being fired is what I am saying. I don't remember about the coal yard, but I do about the Yankees both times and the Mets, too. It was in the papers, as I said. Milton Friedman, the Nobel Prize-winner in economics, asked in a very nice way that I can't explain. I mean that his question was not like one a reporter or even a friend would ask. He asked me if I had ever been fired as a player. I told him, and he is not a baseball fan, that players don't get fired, they get sold. Maybe I can explain the way he asked his question. It was like a doctor would ask in the room where they examine you—a Marcus Welby kind of doctor.

Reggie Jackson would bat 1.000 in the "You" league and I am not saying that is bad. I am just saying it. Bobby Thomson would be a .120, and some guys want you to think they are .120 but are .999. Bobby Thomson is the New York Giant outfielder who hit the home run I mentioned that put them in the 1951 World Series. I am not trying to play that game they play on the *Today Show*. You know, the host says, "I will mention a name and you tell me the first thing that comes into your mind." I am just trying to give you some examples so you will know what I mean and then get to a question that you may already be asking yourself. Bobby Doerr was .150; Ted Williams was .800; Casey Stengel was .990.

Let me tell one story on myself that even I thought

was funny. At least I laughed when it happened. Not right at the time I said it, but I saw why people were laughing right away and I laughed, too. I don't always do that. I have forgotten just where this happened, but the interviewer said we are going to play the *Today Show* game, although he didn't call it that. I think he called it "Association" or something like that. He said, "You tell me, Yogi, the first thing you think of," and so on. I knew what he was trying to do and maybe I got a little bored. Sometimes people talk down to me. They don't need to if they will use plain words I can understand. Somebody told me that when you say things like I just said, you should say, "I don't want to sound defensive, I am just trying to be informational," so I am. After a long set of directions about the *Today Show* game, the guy said, "Yogi, are you ready?" I said, "Yes." He said, "Mickey Mantle," and I said, "What about him?"

What's a .120 doing writing a book about himself? The best answer? If you had a good life, it is good for you. If you had a bad life, and it isn't over, doing something like this could, maybe, make the last part better. (I'll get back to that.) When I say it's good for you, I mean it can pay well, but part of the reason I have a good life is that I don't worry as much about money as a lot of people think I do. Saying this in a book will not make it true or even make you believe it, but I am going to say it anyway. The biggest reason for doing this book is not money. I mean, I am happy with what I have, so it is not just what you get paid to do it. The most important thing is how it makes you think. To add up all the good and to look at the bad, too. So it's a good thing to do if you have the time and someone wants to work with you. Another reason is that some people in the publishing business said that since I was elected to the Hall of Fame and have been around so long, someone else will do it if you don't. That's another good reason.

To get back to help for the unhappy life. I am not saying you are going to get a big advance for *My Forty Years of Misery*. From what little I know about the book business, you will be lucky if you get a publishing company to look at it. It could still be good for you. Just sitting down or going for a walk, like Carmen does every day, and thinking about your book can be good. I mean *really* thinking about it. Maybe only ten minutes. Like ten minutes of batting practice, or BP as the players today call it. How do you want to start? When you got out of the Army? Your first real job? What do you want on your gravestone? That's a good thing to think about. Don't say you don't care, like I do, because you are only kidding yourself. You don't have to start with where you want to start, but it is a good idea to at least write out the batting order. Maybe save the best for the fourth chapter. In the cleanup chapter, you can get even—you can write all about the people that were mean to you in grade school. I am only kidding about that. Trying to get even in life is not wise. Play for a tie.

Back to the book. Suppose you say I am going to start with my childhood in Minnesota, or Maine, or North Carolina, or the Hill in St. Louis. You decide that the first chapter will go into things like: my dad never liked me as much as Bobby and Gretchen. Or you can say that your mom never told you bedtime stories or never said that the paintings you brought home from school were good, and in fact, she never said anything at all about them. Or you can come up with your own, more serious complaints (so you don't think I am trying to make fun of this). Do as much of this as you want. Do it for several days. The book is going to take a lot longer than that. After you have taken all the batting practice you think you need, say this to yourself. I am 40 years old—and don't get hung up on 40, I just picked that number—and when I was a kid these things happened and they really don't matter anymore. If your pipedream book does that for you, it has done a lot. Sometimes I will say to Carmen and I don't know why I haven't learned not to do it, "Carm, tomorrow I am going to go to that fishmarket in Montclair and get some shrimp, or I want to have a steak tomorrow with some kind of sauce." Something like that, and "tomorrow" is the word that sets her off: "Tomorrow! Tomorrow! Yogi, whatever possessed you to think about tomorrow. Today is the important day. Live today, don't wish away today."

I am not doing a good job of writing it like she says it except that I did use the word "possessed." That's one she likes. She also doesn't have the same reaction if I say I am going to take the car in tomorrow. I know the difference, but I thought I would needle her a little in this book so she will read all of it to see if I said anything else about her.

We do have a good time together even when we are not having a good time, and that's important in a marriage. One thing she likes to accuse me of doing —and if I do, I don't know it—is following her around trying to catch her doing something wrong. Like she will say I made the toast too dark in the morning. I will watch her all day so I can find fault even if I have to wait until she goes to bed so I can, as she puts it, point and scream, "You left the toothpaste cap off." I never did that even when she did leave the toothpaste cap off.

To get back to that book. If you see that what happened when you were young is over and done and it is time to get on with what you want to do, then thinking about a book is a good idea. Live today and don't waste time thinking about old things that shouldn't matter. You can't change them anyway. Some things you have to plan, like taking the car in or going to the dentist. A baseball manager has to plan the pitching rotation. Don't plan to be happy later because you won't. I guess that's what I am trying to say. Almost all my life I would have been happy to freeze things just like they were at the time. That is just the way I am. If Iacocca can have a list of Managerial Rules, I can have a sentence or two on how to manage yourself for happiness.

What I am trying to do in this chapter, and maybe I should have said that right off the bat, is to let you know what makes me tick, by ticking. Somebody asked me if I felt sorry for a friend because he was down in the dumps. I said no, that people feel the way they want to feel. I really mean that. I am not saying you feel good all the time. I am not some sap, but by now you know that. Let's hope.

──────── **Other Voices** ────────
DON DRYSDALE

Don Drysdale is six feet five and, it seems, still growing. He might not attract a glance in a truckstop, but in a baseball press box the Big "D" turns heads. And this is before he speaks. Jimmy Cannon, a New York sportswriter who is only a memory to anyone under 40, used to say, "The winner is not always the big, fast guy but it is the way to bet."

You would have to bet that if Berra and Drysdale were on the same playground, Don would be the first chosen and Yogi would be one of the last.

Listen to Don Drysdale: "I am thankful for a great many things. Being selected to the Hall of Fame, of course, was my greatest thrill. I am not suggesting that not having to pitch to Yogi, except in several World Series, is way up on my list of blessings, but the man drove me crazy. In the first place, I loved the little guy. When I first met him we were assigned the same room at a Florida hotel. It was a charity golf tournament. It was 1957, and I had gone 5 and 5 the year before, my first. I was really knocked out when I checked in and they told me Yogi was my roomie. Sure enough, when I got to the room his stuff was all there, his name on the bag and all. I made some phone calls and said, 'Guess who my roommate is?'

"Pretty soon Yogi came back and was the same then as he is right now. The only thing I recall is that his eyes lit up when I said he could use my brand new 1957 Ford

Fairlane station wagon, and later on he locked the keys in the car.

"So I was not only very fond of Yogi, I was also impressed how he could keep his feet on the ground and his head screwed on, getting all the attention he got. When we played the Yankees in spring training and I was not pitching, I would sit in the stands. Two couples would be at the game. When Yogi would run out or be seen, the two women would say, 'Oh, look, look at Yogi. Isn't he darling?' Darling, cute, something like that. I never understood it and none of the others with me did. We were not envious, and I know that may sound hard to believe, but I at least was not. Say it were Robert Redford, well, that's different. Sure I would like to look at him, and wouldn't you? But Yogi? 'Envious' was not the word, 'perplexed' is. But let me get back to pitching to him. The whole country knows that the little Dago has his own brand of charisma, and it is a shame he can't put it in a bottle like Yoo Hoo and sell it.

Right down the middle, that's the only way to pitch him. I really mean it. Every time I tried to waste a pitch, he reached up or down and creamed the ball. When I come back, if I pitch to him again, I will know how."

Another Don, Don Newcombe, happened by just as the interview concluded. Dressed like an executive on his way to an important meeting, both of which seemed to be true, Newcombe said, "Call the Dodger office and make an appointment. I just can't talk now." "Sure," was the response, "I just want to ask you a few questions about Yogi. Mr. Drysdale was very generous with his time and told me he finally figured out how to pitch to Berra." Newcombe turned, and while striding down the ramp, throws back the line, "I am glad somebody did. I never did get him out, never."

◆

My best friends seldom ask hard questions. I don't mean hard, like how many angels can dance on the head of a pin? Or hard, like why did you change pitchers in the ninth inning, Yogi? The pin question isn't a hard question, it is an impossible one. You always have a reason for changing pitchers. It might sound like a good reason when you try to explain it to George Vecsey of the *New York Times* 20 minutes after the Red Sox scored three runs off the guy you brought in. But it is not a hard question. As I have said, you know you are going to get that question when you go out to change pitchers, and you know you are going to get questions if you don't change. The tolltaker on the George Washington Bridge wants to know the same thing, "Why did you take him out, Yogi?" The guy in the car behind him might even start to honk (at least the sportswriters don't do that, not in the office anyway). Some tolltakers might even let you skip the toll if they feel good and you won. Sometimes the tolltaker could have won even if you lost. I don't know if tolltakers bet more baseball than the general population, but I know some of them did and not always for my team. They were always nice. Sometimes, as I said, they said, "pass on," like I didn't have the quarter, but they knew I did.

The hard questions were questions like, "Do you like George?" Depending on a lot of things, I might answer, "George who?" or "So far, so good" or whatever came to mind. I read once that President Roosevelt got so tired at the White House receptions that he would say things like, "You look simply dreadful" or "My good dog Fala died this morning." People would smile and move on.

I thought it might be fun to try something like that but I never did. People in the public eye get some strange comments. I have to stop here a minute and say something about being in the public eye. I don't feel like I am, but I know that I am wrong. I guess the number of World Series I have been in, the way I look, the TV commercials and now the movie critic thing. I have to face it, I am. Carmen says I am, and every time she sees me on TV I am spitting. I do spit, but I swear I don't know when the camera is on me. Sometimes I know it has to be off because it's between innings, but when I get home Carm will say, "Spitting again." She really doesn't like it. I got into the habit of chewing snuff and if you get into that habit, spitting is what you have to do. Just like if you have the smoking habit, you blow smoke around. Sorry I got into that, but I am explaining. What I am trying to say is I don't feel different now than when I first played for the Norfolk Tars. My friends know it and even some guys who don't like me know it.

Years ago a friend's sister drove me to Shea Stadium in her station wagon. She had it full of her kids. I rode in the very back seat. It faced the rear of the car. By the time she backed the car in, a gang of kids that hung around the ballpark looking for autographs came all around the car. She had to come to the back to let me out because the car had some kid locks. When she opened the door and helped me out, she said, "Oh it must be wonderful to be famous." I said, "Not all the time."

A lot of times I will be with someone and be asked for an autograph. After I sign, the person asking for the autograph will say to the man I am with, "Are you somebody?" Most of my friends say no. I wish one time somebody would come up with a good answer.

If you don't want to sign autographs, one of the best ways is to keep your head down and keep moving. I am talking about being in a hotel lobby or someplace like that. Gary Moore told me a great story about that. He was coming out of the CBS or NBC building in New York City after a TV show and started down the street. This guy said something to him and he just kept going and said something like, "Gotta go, gotta go." When he got to the corner, it hit him that the guy had been trying to stick him up. He told the story well, but he was paid to talk on TV.

I thought the best story like that was the one about Kirk Douglas. Not the one about him getting held up, the one about him picking up a hitchhiker. He was driving from Los Angeles to Palm Springs, and he picked up a sailor. After the sailor got in the car and Kirk Douglas started driving again, the sailor looked over at him and said, "Do you know who you are?" I wish it had been a soldier, but I think it is a wonderful story.

I can remember very well seeing Joe Medwick or

George McQuinn and getting back to the Hill and saying, "Guess who I saw?" I was real pleased to be able to do that, so I know how that is. I got to meet a lot of famous people when I played for the Yankees. I am going to tell you two stories, and what happened later is better than what happened. Maybe better. I guess you will be the judge of that.

I played golf with Bing Crosby in Los Angeles on a very fancy course. Two things happened. He beat me on every hole, and I hit a ball out of bounds and it broke one of Howard Hughes's windows. Now here is the funny part, and I don't know if this happened because I didn't want to seem high hat or if it just happened. When I got back from the road trip, I was with some friends playing cards and I wanted to tell them about the window. Howard Hughes was a hermit sort, and people were interested in what he was up to. Even with good friends you don't want to say, "Oh yes, Bing and I. . . ." Anyway I was telling the story and after getting about halfway through it, somebody said, "Who is Ben Crosby?" You see, I had not wanted to say the Bing real loud and it came out Ben. From then on they told their friends that I didn't know Bing from Ben, or even Bob Crosby, for that matter.

So you can see how stories start. I really do think part of the reason was I didn't want to be Hollywood, and then I get tagged with the dunce hat. I am not sure that Howard Hughes was at home or if he was starting to be a hermit. He was rich and famous and if he had been a baseball player, he would have been called a flake. That's a word I don't use but a lot of players do.

──────── **Other Voices** ────────
DALE, LARRY, AND TIM

Dale Berra looks more like a 25-year-old Harvard MBA than a 31-year-old ten-year major league infielder. When he analyzes his years in the big leagues he can sound like an MBA as well.

"I knew that I could never be as good as my dad. I could just be as I could be. I never had a chance to talk with George Sisler's sons. I think they were the only other sons of Hall of Famers to play in the big leagues. I hope they felt the same way I did. Just do the best you can. You sure didn't want your dad to be lousy so you could look good.

"The Baseball Encyclopedia has me down for 11 years. I hit 49 home runs in 853 games during the 11 years. My dad hit 30 in one season twice during the 19 years he played. He hit 12 in the World Series games.

"I had some huge shoes to fill. When I played for the Pirates the organist used to play the Beatles song, "Here Comes the Sun," when I came up to bat. If I hadn't been Yogi Berra's son, I would have been a better than average big league infielder. Would I have it that way? The answer of course is no. The more important question for this book is would I if I could? The answer to that is if you can have a father like Yogi Berra, count it as a blessing. Even if you stay in the minors and then get a job in a bank. I had 11 good years, and if I had been able to play part time I think I would still be on a big league roster. Chris Speier can sit on the bench for weeks and come in and play well. I just couldn't do that. Chris is 39 and plays for the San Francisco Giants. He has a gift. He can play an inning *or two a week. I had a gift. You call him Yogi. I call him dad."*

Larry Berra spent several summers living in the Grand Concourse Hotel. It is two long blocks from Yankee Stadium. He has no memory of life in the Grand Concourse. No memory of his mother paying the bellhops 25 cents a day to retrieve the shoes and toys he pushed out of the window of their room. The room looked into Yankee Stadium. As luck would have it, the items baby Larry pushed out of the crack in the window fell on the roof of the grand ballroom. The bellhop had only to slip out a window on the second floor to retrieve the items and earn the 25 cents. It was bedtime for baby Berra and 25 cents for the bellhop at about 7:30—just about the time night games are played today. In 1950 only a few games were played at night.

Larry Berra's memory of going to Yankee Stadium with his dad are vivid. Most of the players called him Carmen. He looked that much like his mother.

"I think the time I remember the most was when I was under ten, and so Timmy was, say, eight. Mickey Mantle struck out three, maybe four times. His locker was right next to our dad's and when Mickey came back from the shower, Tim said, 'You stunk.' Maybe he said, 'You stink.' I really don't remember, but I will never forget the look on my dad's face. It was a look I had never seen and never saw again. I don't know what Mickey did at the time. We have a good laugh about it now, but I know that my dad belted Timmy. He told him in chilling terms, 'Tell Mickey you are sorry, sit down, shut up, and we will talk about this when we get home.' We didn't stay long like we did most of the time.

"I suppose when you are in school the worst thing you can hear is your name over the loudspeaker. If you hear you got a D, you can handle that, but your name over the Intercom. *LARRY AND TIM BERRA, REPORT TO THE PRINCIPAL'S OFFICE AT ONCE!* Even a red light on a police car is not as bad as the Intercom summons. I was in eighth grade and Tim was in sixth. The principal took what seemed like forever to sit us down, close the door, and clear his throat. He tapped his fingers, looked at the ceiling and out the window, and then began. 'You are both young. But you are growing. Soon, very soon, sooner than you can even imagine, you will be older. Life moves everyday.' I forget what else he said, but I can't forget looking at Timmy and thinking: our folks were killed in a car wreck. While the sermonette went on, I thought about what we would do. My dad's brothers were close, and we would have to go to St. Louis. I remember thinking how good it was that my folks had bought the house in Montclair. We had moved a lot and it was tough being Yogi Berra's son. We had been in Montclair long enough so no one cared.

"Just about the time I wondered what I would call Uncle Mike if we lived with him, the principal said, 'The New York Yankees dismissed your father about 20 minutes ago.' I know it was tough on dad, but I can tell you I walked out of that office trying to hide a smile.

"They were great parents. The only problem I had was that I wanted to sign a contract right out of high school. I was going good and think if I had moved right into the minors, I might have had a better chance. They, mom really, insisted on college. So I spent two years, got hurt in college, and then signed with the Mets. I never got close to the big leagues, but I loved playing. Then I went back and finished college. I am glad I got my degree.

"The Civil War, or the War Between the States as it is called in much of the South, is a major hobby of mine. Playing minor league baseball means you have a good chance of playing in the South. I did and remember one night in a small town in Virginia. Small town, small crowd. I was catching, and a huge guy right behind home plate was on me for nine innings. In that park, home plate was 30 feet from the backstop, meaning I was fewer than 40 feet from my tormentor: 'On your best day, you were not as good as your dad.' Then he would wait and yell 'On his worst!' I got that and worse for over two hours. I didn't get a hit and didn't do anything much in the game. After the game I foolishly took on the heckler. I walked back to the screen and said, 'You are right. I never will be as good as my dad. That is why I am not in the big leagues. No, I am playing in this jerk-water town in front of jerks like you.' That is the gist of what I said, and I did not use words any stronger than that. I know that. The nice thing about it is that I felt good and it made some of the fans around the guy feel good, too. In a small town like that you see the fans. It is not like the big leagues where they try to keep a shield around the players.

"I don't know how well I might have done if I had not been Yogi's son. I really don't. I know this. Aside from that year or so they made me go to college, I never gave them any trouble. I knew I was lucky to have parents who loved and supported me as they did and do today. If you ever get a chance to be a son of Yogi Berra, grab it!"

Tim Berra would win the best-looking contest and is the best golfer in the family. The middle Berra son played *football for the University of Massachusetts and was good enough to be signed by the Baltimore Colts. He played briefly for the Colts and the New York Giants. "I don't care what you say in the book about me. The book should be about my dad," joked Tim, the co-owner of Yogi Berra's Hall of Fame Racquetball Club.*

"I knew Dale and Larry would tell you I should have played baseball," said Tim and added, "and the sad thing is they are right. I should have played baseball. It was my best sport, but I just didn't want to be compared to my dad. That's all over. I don't think about it. I mean I don't think about it unless it comes up like this. You brought it up for the book. I don't dwell on it and besides who knows if I would have been as good as they say I was. Beside my dad, I guess I was the best at one time, but who knows. My dad always said that his brothers were better than he was, and that one time he told his father, 'Pop, if you had let us all play ball you could have been a millionaire.'" Tim smiles and says, "My dad said that his father said, 'Blame your mother.' I don't blame anybody. I didn't try baseball and it is over. My job now is to be a good father and husband. My father taught us that way before he had us mowing the lawn."

Larry, Tim, and Dale each tell of golfing with their father and the other two brothers. The joy of the family during the frequent outings on the golf course is confirmed by numerous friends.

Yogi, how many times a year do you and Tim and Dale and Larry play golf? "As many times as we can, and Tim always wins."

*　　　*　　　*

The other story happened at Toots Shor's, and let me say again how much I miss that place and the man. Toots had gotten us tickets to see Phil Silvers. He was starring on Broadway in *Top Banana*. We went and it was great. I think it was the funniest show I ever saw on Broadway, and we saw almost all the shows. We went back to Toots Shor's and later Phil Silvers came in and Toots brought him over to our table. I stood up and Phil asked me how I liked the show. I leaned over and whispered in his ear, "It was great Phil. I wet my pants," only I didn't say it like that. I also didn't want to say it the other way at the table. Well, Phil went nuts. He said it was the highest accolade he had ever gotten. He just couldn't stop laughing. It was nice to see him so happy after he had made so many people happy.

Several years ago I told that story to a man and he asked me right in the middle of the story, "Did you?" I was surprised and said, "Did I what?" He said, "Wet your pants?" I said, "No, it's an expression." The guy went to college. As he liked to put it, "I am not a college graduate, I am a *university* graduate." Stuffed shirt.

I am sure of this. My best friends do not ask me hard questions about George or anything like that. I don't ask them if they are still working or if they get along with their boss, or if their wife is going to come back to them. The reporters have a job to do and your friends do, too. To be friends and not reporters. Friends don't ask about a problem, even one they read about in the paper. It is like hitting—if you're not, you don't want to talk about it. At least until you are ready. If you wait until the player comes to you to ask for help, you can be that much better at helping. Maybe I can say you are ready to talk when you bring it up. That's a good rule. Sometimes you have to step in, but it is better if you can wait.

I am not crazy about answering questions I don't think should be asked. I think in some ways it is an American trait. People will ask a young couple, "When are you going to have children?" They just met them and they are asking questions like that. I wouldn't ask that kind of question if I knew both of them for years.

One baseball rule is that almost everything you do in the major leagues is written down. That will come as no surprise to a baseball fan, but maybe even some of them don't think about what it *means*. It is all right there, warts and all. I am saying "means" like the kind of college you went to, or didn't go to. To some people it means the kind of car they drive, or the kind of house they live in. I think they call it "making a statement." This statement is in black and white.

Let me make the point this way. I played four games for the Mets in 1965. I was too old. During the year that I managed the Yankees, the skills faded. At that age you have to work at staying sharp. I am not saying the skills I had would have stayed with me if I had played that year and Houk managed. They go no matter what you do. They just go faster on the bench. I was playing as a favor to Casey and George Weiss. Would I do it again? No. My point about warts and all is this. When I think back on that time, it would be nice to write a letter, Dear Mr. Baseball, would you please leave the games I played for the New York Mets out of my record when you bring out a new edition of *The Baseball Encyclopedia*? I didn't play too well and I would like to forget about it. I wonder how many players would like to write that kind of a letter? The late Walter Alston for one.

The only thing they don't put in that fat book is errors, and even Carmen was surprised they didn't. They have all the trades listed, not the number of dollars, but every trade. If you got up once in the big leagues, like Walter Alston did, and made out, they put it down. I think it is great that enough people want to see all that information to buy the book, and it is not cheap. It tells me that baseball is in good shape, but if you batted, you might like to forget about it. On the other hand, you may be very proud that you played in the big leagues at all. A lot of guys didn't.

Think about this. Wouldn't it be nice if everybody who made a living doing whatever—growing corn, making corn plasters, fixing TVs, cars, and feet, and even the shrinks who are supposed to fix your head—were listed in a book like *The Baseball Encyclopedia*. If they did, they should tell how much water they used to grow so much corn. Did you use fertilizer and how much did it cost? I think you see what I am saying. If they ever do a book like that I hope they have a column for errors. My best year for errors was 1958. I didn't have any.

Baseball has been good to me, but I have seen it hurt a lot of people. Players who were great in junior high, high school, and even college and didn't make it when they tried to earn a living playing. Maybe they didn't get any better, maybe they didn't have the mental outlook in the first place. Maybe a lot of things, but at one time they were great. At one time they were the first guy chosen and they think it is going to come back. They hang on and hang on when they could be starting to set themselves up in the real world. They lie to themselves and sometimes teams lie to them. It's sad. I try to tell young prospects to tell themselves and a few others they really trust just how long they are going to try to make it to the big leagues and then stick to that timetable. I wanted to say this because I don't want anyone to feel that I am making light of the guys in *The Baseball Encyclopedia* who have only one line. One line is more than a lot of guys ever got.

I don't make fun of anyone unless I like them and know they are good. I had as many people making fun of me as anyone in modern baseball, at least I'm told that. Some of the people doing it liked me but got caught up in the game of "let's get on Yogi." Some didn't like me but I showed all of them I could make it to the big leagues and then get good. I said that in some other place in this book, and so let me say it again. I didn't think I was going to ever make it to the Hall of Fame. I loved baseball, worked hard, and first I wanted to get to the big leagues and then see if I was any good. I would feel the same way if I were looking for a job. First, get the offer, then see if you want it, then see if you are any good.

Matt Galante, the Astros' third-base coach, thinks I would have been sent back to the minors if I had looked like Paul Newman. I like Matt and we have breakfast almost every day on the road. You can see we are close, but that doesn't mean he is right. What I used to say when I was playing and people said I was bad looking and worse than that was, "You don't hit with your face." You don't hit with a college degree, but it would be nice to have one.

I hope this comes out right. I know I was not the best-looking young man in St. Louis. I really know that. Some writers said that the reason I married Carmen was so I could show people that even though I was a Neanderthal, I could attract a beautiful woman. Makes me mad to think about it. Carmen was a knockout and she still is, but that she looked good was not why I asked her to marry me. She even tells people that she asked me to marry her. And for all I know she is right. She is right about so many other things. I liked her because of what she said and did. She was working three jobs and taking dancing lessons when she wasn't working. I never met anyone like her, and a lot of other people say that, too. Tommy John does, and he is smart enough to have been pitching in the big leagues longer than anyone else ever has.

As you can see, I get a little hot when writing about this. Got on my high horse a little, didn't I? I was tired of the low donkey. I rode it in 1949, the year we got married, and for a long time after that. So I got a little hot bringing it up to write about in this book. I guess it shows that you can say what you want about me, but don't say anything that brings my wife and kids into it.

As I have said in several different ways, I am contented with what I have done with my life so far.

It may be that the job I have makes me look at things different than other people. Let me explain. Newspapers come out every day even if nothing happens. Something always does, and in the sports section they make it happen. They have white space to fill and they fill it. They make it happen on what they call a slow newsday by asking questions of someone they think will give them interesting answers. Someone like Phil Garner, who played with our son Dale at Pittsburgh. He played with the Giants and is now the first-base coach for the Astros. I think he started with the A's. He is what writers call a good interview. Other players like Lefty Carlton are no interviews. He would not talk to the press.

If reporters can't find an interesting interview, they try me. It starts with: "A few questions, please?" "Sure," I say. Then the tape recorder is in your face and you will get a question like this: "Would you have hit more home runs if you had not been a catcher?" "Probably" is what I say. "Then would you rather have been an outfielder?" "No," I say, "I was happy with what I did." I am not going to go on because you may have read or seen one of those interviews and I don't want you to think you are reading the newspaper.

Every now and then I think about what might have happened if I had played the outfield. When I do, I also think back to when the Yankees brought Bill Dickey back to "learn me all his experience," and he told me that catching was my ticket. Good catchers are hard to find, he said, and you can hang around a lot longer as a catcher. He told me that and he should have known. He had been in the big leagues 17 years. I had been alive just a little longer. I don't think I have ever said this, but maybe I should in this book. I was always proud that I played a few more years than Bill Dickey and caught a few more games. I am not saying I was as good or better than Bill Dickey. I am just saying what I said.

Some people feel that catching is the hardest everyday position. I didn't think so. I would rather catch than play left or third base. I liked being part of the game on every pitch and I knew I couldn't be a pitcher because my arm was not that strong. People who think catching is the hardest position may be right. It just wasn't for me.

The Boston Globe did a survey about catchers and said that Mickey Cochrane, Gabby Hartnett, Bill Dickey, me, Roy Campanella and John Bench were the best catchers of all time and in that order. How they knew that Bench was six and Roy was five is beyond me. They also said that I had done a lot to fortify the image that catchers are dumb and short. They also said a catcher had to be smart, so how much can you believe of what they said? I don't know if I should be on list of the best catchers of all time, but if I am I would rather not see my name the only one with short and dumb after it.

Men my age often tell me, "I was a pretty good catcher as long as the hitter hit the ball or didn't swing. I could catch the ball but when they swung and missed, I was out of business." I never said it to them, but they weren't very good catchers. If you couldn't catch the ball when the batter missed, your name would be missing from the line up.

Forgetting about the bending and stooping for nine innings (and that could be a good idea), the hardest part of catching was calling the game and blocking the plate when you had to. Well, I forgot, pop-ups could be bad. The pop fly right over your head. Some of the big swingers like Ted Williams or Al Kaline could set the ball into orbit. With the wind blowing, it could be tough to catch the ball. Everybody expected the catcher to catch every one, and that didn't help matters. Just because the batter popped the ball up in the air didn't mean that the catcher was going to catch it, but it was hell to pay if you didn't. Same way when you miss a six-inch putt, but if you watch the pros, they do. I had forgotten how tough that could be sometimes. When Bill Dickey was working with me he told someone I needed work on pop-ups. Someone asked him if they gave him trouble, and he said no. Then they asked him if he had ever missed one and he said after thinking, "I don't ever remember dropping one."

Let me get to blocking the plate. You don't always have to, but some guys think they do so they can show how tough they are. Sometimes if you can you should catch the ball and tag the runner like a bull fighter. The bang bang play is different, and you have to stand your ground and take your lumps. A bang bang play (and the players use that name) is when the ball and the runner arrive at the same time. That play could be a bear cat. I am not that big, and some of those guys could make you see stars. So you can see you have to be able to catch the ball when the batter swings and misses or you will not have a chance to be in a bang bang play.

As long as I am thinking about catching and what I had to learn, I might as well say something else I feel. Most kids today put too much pressure on themselves. Maybe their parents do. They see Joe Montana play a super game in the Super Bowl and tell their kid, "You got to try harder. Just try harder." I think it is bad. You don't see people having a good time playing baseball. You can't give 110%. Sometimes it is better to give 85% and play up to your level. I am talking about pressure that makes you not able to produce. It is different for all of us. I just think too many kids are pushed so hard they can't produce.

One of the reasons I think you see so many guys getting called out on a third strike is they are under too much pressure. The pressure starts too soon, and then when players are making millions of dollars like they do in the big leagues, you will just have to imagine what it must be like. They would rather get called out and then at least they can blame someone else, the umpire. I can't prove it but I think more people are what we call "caught looking" today than in my day. I don't think it ever happened to me. Well, maybe a few times.

George Weiss told me that if the Yankees had to win one game, he would want Whitey Ford to start that game. Three things about what George Weiss told me, and it was way after he left the Yankees. He would never have talked to me about that sort of thing during the time we were active. The first is it would never enter his mind, and he had a good one, to say that to Casey Stengel or any other manager. The second is think about the number of great pitchers on his teams: Allie Reynolds, Spec Shea, Spud Chandler, Vic Raschi, Ed Lopat, Tommy Byrne, Joe Page, Johnny Sain, Don Larsen, Jim Konstanty, Bob Grim, Art Ditmar, Bobby Shantz, and Ryne Duren. The third thing is that George Weiss didn't have to catch Whitey or any of the others.

Since I brought this up, I need to say that if I had to win one game I would want the guy on a hot streak to pitch. I caught some great ones and even the best were lousy some days. To get back to Weiss not catching, I was not trying to be smart. I knew he had his job and I had mine. I am just trying to point out that the catcher may want one guy to pitch to win the game and another one to pitch to have an easy game. On that score, Eddie Lopat would be the guy I would have pitch every day. I could have caught Lopat with Kleenex. Used to make him mad when I told him that, but he was called the Junk Man because he threw so many garbage pitches. To tell you the truth, I didn't worry if he crossed me up and threw a fastball instead of a slider. I couldn't tell the difference. Maybe the hitters had the same problem, because he was a winner. He won four games and only lost one in the World Series. Unless he makes a comeback, and he is older than I am, that is the way it is going to stay. His winning percentage in the Series is .800, and for his 12 years in the big leagues, .597. Not bad. Better than a lot of other pitchers. I am not going to name some but you can look it up. *The Baseball Encyclopedia* has 616 pages of them from Don Aase to George Zuverink.

I like to laugh. Over the years I have been lucky enough to see and meet some of the best comics in the world. Well, at least in this country. I don't want to mention all of them because I may miss some and also be called a comedian name dropper. When you meet a president or mayor or movie actor, most of the time you don't learn anything. You just meet them and can tell your friends. I met Benny Goodman for example, and I loved his music but I didn't learn anything. Maybe that he was a nice guy or something like that. I guess I mean learn in the way I learned from Gil Hodges. The thing I learned from comics was this. The hardest thing is to get started but the really hardest thing is to finish. Their job is to get laughs, and they want to end with one and a good one. Maybe not the biggest but a good one. I know that I have spent more time trying to figure out how to end this than anything I can think of. The people at McGraw-Hill said I should say it isn't over but it is completed. What I decided to do is two things. To thank all my Astro teammates and all the Astro people from John McMullen to people I only know to say hello. I have been made to feel welcome by the whole organization and the city of Houston as well.

I said somewhere way back in this book when I was asked if it bothered me that when I meet people they talk about what I used to do. I think the question was, "Does it bother you that people say 1951 or 1958

or 1964 when they tell you what they saw you do?"
I said no, that it was nice to be remembered.

It is also nice to remember that some things that
happened to me over forty years ago that were hard
on me at the time had a happy ending. I told you
about some of the things said about me when I first
joined the Yankees so I don't need to go into that. I
used to get a lot of kidding and I used to go to a lot
of movies. I don't know when it started, but after a
year or two a lot of the team used to ask me what I
liked. At first I thought it was just to hear me mess
up Oliva De Havilland's name or some other name
like that. Turns out they were really interested. So was
the Yankee batboy. A kid named Tommy Villante. The
Yankees paid his way though Lafayette College, and
he went on to do well in business. A year or so ago
he came out to see us and asked me to become a movie
critic. Carmen almost died laughing. She said it was
preposterous and also cockamamy. Maybe some other
words. She has words she hasn't used yet.

I did what they called a pilot and have been doing
movie reviews for over a year. That I like to do them
is not important. Sure it is important that somebody
likes what I am doing so they ask me back. But what
I think is that some kid picking up bats and wet towels
was also picking up something he would use forty years
later. I used to love to watch squirrels burying nuts.
I used to wonder if they knew where to find them
when the snow came. I know that I give some people
the chance to say the old Yankee batboy knew a nut
when he saw one. If you want to, that's all right with
me. Most everything is all right with me.

You have just finished reading one of the first books published by Harper Paperbacks!

Please continue to look for the sign of the 'H', below.

It will appear on many fiction and non-fiction books, from literary classics to dazzling international bestsellers.

And it will always stand for a great reading experience and a well-made book.

Harper Paperbacks
10 East 53rd St.
New York, NY 10022

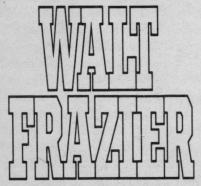